Home for the Friendless Chicago

## The Home Cook Book of Chicago

Comp. from Recipes Contributed by Ladies of Chicago and other Cities

Home for the Friendless Chicago

**The Home Cook Book of Chicago**
*Comp. from Recipes Contributed by Ladies of Chicago and other Cities*

ISBN/EAN: 9783744781916

Printed in Europe, USA, Canada, Australia, Japan

Cover: Foto ©Andreas Hilbeck / pixelio.de

More available books at **www.hansebooks.com**

# HOME COOK BOOK

## OF CHICAGO.

———•◦•———

COMPILED FROM RECIPES CONTRIBUTED BY LADIES OF CHICAGO AND
OTHER CITIES AND TOWNS: PUBLISHED FOR THE BENEFIT
OF THE HOME FOR THE FRIENDLESS.

———•••———

*——With dispatchful looks in haste*
*She turns, on hospitable thoughts intent,*
*What choice to choose for delicacy best,*
*What order, so contrived as not to mix*
*Taste not well joined, inelegant, but bring*
*Taste after taste upheld with kindliest change.*

—PARADISE LOST.

——  •◦•  ——

CHICAGO
J. FRED. WAGGONER, PUBLISHER.
1874.

# PREFACE.

Good diet, with wisdom, best comforteth man.
                              —*Thomas Tusser.*

SIR THOMAS BROWNE has quaintly observed, that at some
time or other we have all been on our own trenchers; and if
the present rendering of science be true in the relation of matter to mind, it may be a subject of no slight importance how
the psychological units that go to build up our brain and nerve
forces are set before us, and how our dinners are cooked may
be a more momentous question than who is to be the next
President.

With all supplied advice upon this subject, there are two
qualities which have been seldom attained in any treatise hitherto published upon this science, viz: the art of uniting plain,
simple and practical methods in the preparation of food, with
that finish and perfection of detail, and that delicate blending
of material, which are products of a refined and exquisite per-
ception, and a delicate and sensitive taste. In short, that
"gumption," by which the woman who possesses the genius for
housekeeping graces her table daily with viands that in her
skillful hands become a "perpetual feast of delights." It is just
as easy, for instance, to broil a beefsteak to perfection, as to

prepare those greasy and indigestible products of unskilled
hands and unsuitable gridirons, so often set before us.   It is
just as easy to make biscuits of feathery lightness, (if one only
knows just how to do it,) as to prepare those heavy and sour
compounds accepted neither of body nor spirit.

How to unite perfection and simplicity in food, is a problem
that puts many a housekeeper's soul upon the rack.   To this
end, the woman of "gumption" has come to the fore with her
experiences, and has inaugurated a new era in the literature
and science of gastronomic art in a class of Cook Books that
supply a want which no treatises hitherto published have ever
filled.   These works are made up from recipes in daily use
with experienced housekeepers, in which they have achieved
a success that makes of these methods objects of especial desire among their friends.   Although these methods have hitherto found their way into our households in the unobtrusive form
of penciled recipes, they are, like Jewish oral law and tradition,
of high—indeed, we may say, of the highest—authority and now
that they are offered to the public in the permanent, convenient
and attractive form of letter-press and binding, we feel assured
of the warm welcome that awaits them from every housekeeper
who may resort to our Book for advice and suggestion.

# SOUPS.

"No useless dish our table crowds;
Harmoniously ranged and consonantly just,
As in a concert instruments resound,
Our ordered dishes in their courses chime."

The basis of all good soups, is the broth of meat. This may be made by boiling the cracked joints of beef, veal or mutton, and is best when cooked the day before it is to be eaten. After putting the meat into the pot, cover it well with cold water and let it come to a boil, when it should be well skimmed. Set the pot where it will simmer slowly until it is thoroughly done, keeping the pot closely covered the while. The next day, when the soup is cold, remove the fat, which will harden on the top of the soup. After this, add the vegetables and the herbs you use for seasoning, cooking all well together. Before sending to the table, the soup should be strained. A good stock for soups may be made from shreds and bits of uncooked meat and bones, poultry and the remains of game. When these are all put together and stewed down in the pot, the French term it *consomme*, and use it chiefly in the preparation of brown soups.

Soups may be varied in many ways, chiefly in the kinds of vegetables and different seasoning used,—as in herbs, burned caramel, eggs or slices of bread fried to a crisp in butter, which impart a savory relish.

## BEEF SOUP.

### Mrs. Wm. H. Low.

Cut all the lean off the shank, and with a little beef suet in the bottom of the kettle, fry it to a nice brown; put in the bones and cover with water; cover the kettle closely; let it cook slowly until the meat drops from the bones; strain through a colander and leave it in the dish during the night, which is the only way to get off all the fat. The day it is wanted for the table, fry as brown as possible a carrot, an onion and a very small turnip sliced thin. Just before taking up, put in half a teaspoonful of sugar, a blade of mace, six cloves, a dozen kernels of allspice, a small teaspoonful of celery seed. With the vegetables this must cook slowly in the soup an hour; then strain again for the table. If you use vermicelli or pearl barley, soak in water.

## JULIENNE SOUP.

### M. A. T.

Shred two onions and fry brown in a half spoon of butter; add a little mace, salt and pepper; then a spoonful or so of stock; rub a tablespoonful of flour smooth with a little butter and let fry with the onions; strain through a colander, then add more stock as desired; cut turnip, carrot and celery in fillets; add a few green peas; boil tender in a little water and add both water and vegetables to the soup. If wished, the flour can be left out, and it will make a clear light colored soup. In that case, the onions should be cut in fillets and boiled with the vegetables.

## MUTTON SOUP.

### Mrs. Whitehead.

Boil a leg of mutton three hours; season to your taste with salt and pepper, and add one teaspoon of summer savory; make a batter of one egg, two tablespoons of milk, two tablespoons of flour, all well beaten together; drop this batter into the soup with a spoon and boil for three minutes.

## VEAL SOUP.

To about three pounds of a joint of veal, which must be well broken up, put four quarts of water and set it over to boil. Prepare one-fourth pound of maccaroni by boiling it in a dish by itself, with sufficient water to cover it; add a little butter to the maccaroni when it is tender; strain the soup and season to taste with salt and pepper, when add the maccaroni in the water in which it is boiled. The addition of a pint of rich milk or cream and celery flavor is relished by many.

## SWISS WHITE SOUP.

### Anonymous.

To rich broth or soup for six persons, when boiling add three eggs, two spoons of flour and one cup of milk beaten together; pour this slowly through a sieve into the boiling soup and serve.

## TURKEY SOUP.

### Anonymous.

Take the turkey bones and cook for one hour in water enough to cover them; then stir in a little dressing and a beaten egg. Take from the fire and when the water has ceased boiling, add a little butter with pepper and salt.

## OYSTER SOUP.

### M. A. T.

Take one quart of water; one teacup of butter; one pint of milk; two teaspoons of salt; four crackers rolled fine, and one teaspoon of pepper, bring to full boiling heat as soon as possible, then add one quart can of oysters; let the whole come to boiling heat quickly and remove from the fire.

## OYSTER SOUP.

### Mrs. T. V. Wadskier.

Pour one quart of boiling water into a skillet; then one quart of good rich milk; stir in one teacup of rolled cracker crumbs;

seasoned with pepper and salt to taste. When all come to a
boil, add one quart of good fresh oysters; stir well, so as to keep
from scorching; then add a piece of good sweet butter, about
the size of an egg; let it boil up once; then remove from the fire
immediately; dish up and send to table.

## LOBSTER SOUP.
### Mrs. Robert Harris.

One large lobster or two small ones; pick all the meat from
the shell and chop fine; scald one quart of milk and one pint of
water; then add the lobster, one pound of butter, a tablespoonful of flour and salt and red pepper to taste. Boil ten minutes
and serve hot.

## PLAIN CALF'S HEAD SOUP.
### Mrs. F. D. J.

Take a calf's head well cleaned, a knuckle of veal, and put
them both into a large kettle; put one onion and a large tablespoon of sweet herbs, into a cloth and into the kettle, with the
meat over which you have poured about four quarts of water.
If you wish the soup for a one o'clock dinner, put the meat over
to boil as early as eight o'clock in the morning; let it boil steadily
and slowly and season well with salt and pepper. About one
hour before serving, take off the soup and pour it through a colander, pick out all the meat carefully, chop very fine and return
to the soup, putting it again over the fire. Boil four eggs very
hard, chop them fine, and slice one lemon very thin, adding at
the very last a glass of wine.

## VERMICELLI SOUP.
### Anonymous.

A knuckle of lamb, a small piece of veal and water to cover
well; when well cooked season with salt, pepper herbs to your
taste, and a small onion, to which you may add Halford or
Worcestershire sauce, about a tablespoonful. Have ready one
quarter of a pound of vermicelli, which has been boiled tender;

strain your soup from the meat, add the vermicelli, let it boil well and serve.

## GUMBO SOUP.

### Anonymous.

Put on a half a peck of tomatoes in a porcelain kettle and let them stew; have half a peck of ochra cut in fine shreds; put them with thyme, parsley and an onion cut fine, into the tomatoes and let them cook until quite tender. Fricassee one chicken in ham gravy; then take the yolk of four eggs, a little vinegar, the juice of one lemon, and seasoning to taste, beating the eggs into the vinegar; pour this over the chicken, and put all then into the tomatoes, letting the kettle be nearly filled with water. Boil all together four or five hours.

## OCHRA GUMBO.

### Mrs. Andrews.

Two quarts of ripe tomatoes and one quart of ochra cut in small rings; put them over the fire with about three quarts of water and let the mixture come to a boil; take one chicken; cut it up and fry brown, with plenty of gravy; put it in with the ochra and tomatoes; add several small onions chopped fine; salt and pepper to taste; a little corn and Lima beans are an improvement, if you have them. Let all simmer gently together for several hours. To be served with a tablespoonful of boiled rice and green garden pepper cut fine to each soup plate.

## TOMATO SOUP.

### Mrs. Whitehead.

Boil chicken or beef four hours; then strain; add to the soup one can of tomatoes and boil one hour. This will make four quarts of soup.

## MOCK TURTLE SOUP.

### Mrs. C. H. Wheeler.

One soup-bone, one quart of turtle beans, one large spoonful of powdered cloves, salt and pepper. Soak the beans over night, put them on with the soup-bone in nearly a pail full of water and cook five or six hours. When half done, add the cloves, salt and pepper; when done strain through a colander, pressing the pulp of the beans through to make the soup the desired thickness, and serve with a few slices of hard-boiled egg and lemon sliced very thin. The turtle beans are black and can only be obtained from large grocers.

## TOMATO SOUP.

### Mrs. B. J. Seward.

To one pint tomatoes canned, or four large raw ones, cut up fine, add one quart boiling water and let them boil. Then add one teaspoonful of soda, when it will foam; immediately add one pint of sweet milk, with salt, pepper and plenty of butter. When this boils add eight small crackers rolled fine, and serve. Equal to oyster soup.

## TOMATO SOUP.

### Mrs. J. Hudson.

One quart of tomatoes, one soup bone, one onion, one cucumber sliced, two ears of grated corn, salt, pepper and a trifle of cayenne pepper. Boil four hours, then add one tablespoon of corn starch dissolved in cold water; strain before serving.

## TOMATO SOUP.

### Mrs. G. W. Brayton.

For one gallon of soup, take two and a half quarts good beef soup, one medium sized carrot, one turnip, one beet and two onions peeled and cut in pieces; boil the vegetables in the beef soup three quarters of an hour; strain through a sieve; add a two quart can of tomatoes and boil fifteen minutes; strain again and add salt and pepper. While this is cooking, take a sauce-pan that will hold about six quarts and put in a quarter of a pound of butter and heat it to a light brown; add while hot three tablespoons of flour; take from the fire and mix well together, and thoroughly; add one desert spoon of sugar and stir until it boils; boil fifteen minutes and strain.

## TOMATO SOUP.

### Mrs. L. H. Smith.

Make one gallon beef stock. Take half peck ripe tomatoes, cut in halves, two carrots, two onions, one turnip cut fine; boil all together for one hour and a half, then strain all through a fine sieve; take a sauce-pan large enough to hold it and put it on the fire with half pound of butter; heat it until of a light brown color, and add two spoons of flour, mixing well together; add to this, two spoons of white sugar, salt and pepper to suit taste; stir well until it boils; let it boil and skim it for five minutes and serve very hot. This receipt serves a large family, usually prepare two quarts of beef stock for a small family, using half the quantity of ingredients.

## GREEN PEA SOUP.

### Anonymous.

Four pounds of lean beef cut in small pieces, one-half peck of green peas, one gallon of water; boil the empty pods of the peas in the water one hour; strain them out; add the beef and boil slowly one and a half hours. Half an hour before serving strain out the meat and add the peas; twenty minutes later add one-half cup of rice flour; salt and pepper to taste; and if you choose, one teaspoonful of sugar. After adding the rice, stir frequently to prevent burning.

## CORN SOUP.

### Mrs. W. P. Nixon.

One small beef bone, two quarts of water, four tomatoes, eight ears of corn; let the meat boil a short time in the water; cut the corn from the cob and put in the cobs with the cut corn and tomatoes; let it boil about half an hour and just before serving add the milk, which allow to boil for a few moment only; season with salt and pepper.

## CORN SOUP.

### Anonymous.

One quart of corn cut from the cob in three pints of water; when the grain is quite tender, mix with them two ounces of sweet butter rolled in a tablespoon of flour; let it boil fifteen minutes longer; just before taking up the soup, beat up an egg and stir in with pepper and salt.

## TURTLE BEAN SOUP.
### Mrs. A. N. Arnold.

Take a quart of black beans, wash them and put them in a pot with three quarts of water; boil until thoroughly soft; rub the pulp through a colander and return it to the pot; add some thyme in a clean cloth, and let it boil a few minutes for flavor; slice some hard boiled eggs and drop them into the soup; add a little butter, pepper and salt.

## BLACK BEAN SOUP.
### Mrs. John B. Adams.

Boil the beans and strain them; at the same time make your stock (of any kind of meat) saving the best for force meat balls; to be well seasoned and fried. Put the bean pulp in with the stock and boil; add red pepper, salt and a little thyme, tying it up in a bag to be taken out; cloves to your taste and a little wine. When ready to serve, put the fried balls into the tureen, with two or three sliced hard boiled eggs, and a lemon or two, according to the quantity of soup. Skim out bones and pieces of meat and pour over.

## BLACK BEAN SOUP.
### Mrs. H. L. Adams.

One pound of the round of beef, one-half pound of salt pork, and one quart of black beans; soak the beans twenty-four hours; chop the beef and pork and boil with the beans, one grated carrot and one onion five or six hours; strain and add hard boiled eggs, salt, pepper and sliced lemon.

## BLACK BEAN SOUP.
### Mrs. Andrews and others.

Take one quart of beans; cook them over night; put them in a pot with a large quantity of water; add a bone of beef or veal;

Tapioca Pudding without Eggs
& Milk —

Put one teacup of Tapioca and one
teaspoon full salt — into a pint and
a half of water; let them stand some
hours it will be quite warm but will not
cook. Two hours before dinner peel
six apples and take out the cores
without dividing the apples. Put
them in a pudding dish, fill the
holes with sugar, in which is grated
a little nutmeg or lemon peel. Add
a teacup of water, and bake an hour
turning the apples to prevent
their drying When the apples are
quite soft, pour over them the tapioca
and bake one hour —

To be eaten with hard sauce of
butter and sugar — Sago can be
used instead of Tapioca.

Floating Island
Beat the whites of eggs until very
stiff then put in one tablespoonful
of some acid jelly for each white,
and beat it a good while Boil
rich sweetened milk, put in a glass
dish, and when cold put the jelly
and eggs on the top.

## Ginger Tea

Pour half pint boiling water
on a teaspoon of ginger – add sugar
to taste.

## Sugar Cakes Mrs Bell

cup sugar 1½ milk 1½ butter 1½
teaspoonful saleratus, flour to roll

## To Prevent Moth

Put piece of camphor in a linen bag in
the drawers among linen or woolen
clothes and the moths will stay away.

## Gipsy Pudding

Cut stale cake in slices and lay
them in a pudding dish. Wet them
in a little wine. Boiled custard and
pour over the cakes, and let it stand
until cold.

## Cinnamon Muffins

One egg, little salt, one cup sugar, one
half cup butter, one and one half cup
sour milk, one teaspoon soda, one
teaspoon ground cinnamon, flour to
stiffen, so they will not run under the
rings.

## Tart Crust

One cup lard, one tablespoon white
sugar, the white of one egg beaten,
four tablespoons of water, mix,
as for pies, very flaky.

## Frosting without eggs

Dissolve one teaspoonfull gelatine in
tablespoonfull cold water, then add
one do of boiling water; if they do
not dissolve, set it on top of the
teakettle for a few moments; then
stir in gradually, nearly a teacup
of powdered sugar and spread on
the cake immediatly

stir frequently; when reduced to a pulp, strain through a colander and return to the fire, putting in a quantity of celery, some red pepper and onion. This should be done three or four hours before dinner is ready. The longer the soup simmers the **better**. Force meat balls are a great improvement.

## POTATO SOUP.
### M. A. T.

**Boil five** or six potatoes with a small piece of **salt pork and a** little celery; pass through a colander and add **milk or** cream (if milk, **a** little butter) to make the consistency of **thick** cream; chop a little parsley fine and throw **in**; let boil five minutes; cut some dry bread in small dice, fry **brown in** hot lard; drain them and place in the bottom of soup tureen, and pour the soup over; chop two onions and boil with the soup, if liked.

## FORCE MEAT BALLS FOR BLACK BEAN SOUP.
### Mrs. Baushar.

Take cold meat; **chop very fine**; add flour enough to make it stick together in balls about **the size** of a walnut; roll in flour **and fry until** brown, and add **to** the soup **just** before it is served.

## FORCE MEAT BALLS.
### Mrs. James S. Gibbs.

**Mix** with one pound of chopped **veal** or other meat one egg, a **little** butter or raw pork chopped fine, one **cup** or less of bread crumbs; the whole well moistened with warm water, or what is better, the water from stewed meat; season with salt and pepper; make in small balls and fry them brown.

## EGG BALLS FOR SOUP.
### M. A. T.

Boil four eggs; put into cold water; **mash** yolks with yolk of **one** raw egg, and one teaspoon of flour; pepper, salt and parsley; **make into** balls **and boil two** minutes.

## NOODLES FOR SOUP.

### Mrs. F. D. J.

Rub into two eggs as much sifted flour as they will absorb; then roll out until thin as a wafer; dust over a little flour, and then roll over and over into a roll; cut off thin slices from the edge of the roll and shake out into long strips; put them into the soup lightly and boil for ten minutes; salt should be added while mixing with the flour—about a salt spoonful.

# FISH.

> "The silvery fish,
> Grazing at large in meadows submarine,
> Fresh from the wave now cheers
> Our festive board."
>
> —ANON.

Fish are good, when the gills are red, eyes are full, and the body of the fish is firm and stiff. After washing them well, they should be allowed to remain for a short time in salt water sufficient to cover them; before cooking, wipe them dry dredge, lightly with flour, and season with salt and pepper. Salmon, trout and other small fish are usually fried or broiled; all large fish should be put in a cloth, tied closely with twine and then placed in cold water, when they may be put over the fire to boil. When fish are baked, prepare the fish the same as for boiling, and put in the oven on a wire gridiron, over a dripping pan.

## TO BOIL FISH.

### Mrs. C. G. Smith.

Put a small onion inside your fish and tie it up in a towel; cover it with cold water, salt and a little vinegar, and let it heat to the boiling point; from two to three minutes' boiling is sufficient for the largest fish, and a small one will not require more than one minute. Fish boiled in this way is incomparably better than when cooked longer.

A SUGGESTION.—Boiling salt water is best for salmon, as it sets the color.—M. A. T.

## BOILED WHITE FISH.
### Mrs. Andrews.

Lay the fish open; put it in a dripping pan, with the back down; nearly cover with water; to one fish put two tablespoons salt; cover tightly and simmer (not boil) one-half hour; dress with gravy, butter and pepper; garnish with sliced eggs.

For sauce use a piece of butter the size of an egg, one tablespoon of flour, one-half pint boiling water; boil a few minutes, and add three hard boiled eggs, sliced.

## TURBOT A LA CREME.
### Mrs. A. Keith.

Boil a large white fish; pick it up fine, taking out the bones; make a sauce of a quart of milk, a little thyme, a few sprigs of parsley, a little onion; simmer together till well flavored; wet two ounces of flour and stir in with a quarter of a pound of butter, stir until it thickens; then strain it on the yolks of two eggs; season with pepper and salt. Put some of the sauce in a pudding dish, then a layer of fish and so on until the dish is full, putting sauce on top; cover with rolled crackers and a little grated cheese, if to the taste; brown in the oven.

## SAUCE FOR BOILED FISH.

To one teacup of milk, add one teacup of water: put it on the fire to scald, and when hot stir in a tablespoonful of flour, previously wet with cold water; add two or three eggs; season with salt and pepper, a little celery, vinegar and three tablespoons of butter. Boil four or five eggs hard, take off the shells, and cut in slices, and lay over the dish. Then pour over the sauce and serve.

## BAKED HALIBUT OR SALMON.

Let the fish remain in cold water, slightly salted, for an hour before it is time to cook it; place the gridiron on a dripping pan with a little hot water in it and bake in a hot oven; just before it is done, butter it well on the top, and brown it nicely. The time of baking depends upon the size of the fish. A small fish will bake in about half an hour, and a large one in an hour. They are very nice when cooked as above and served with a sauce which is made from the gravy in the dripping pan, to which is added a tablespoonful of catsup and another of some pungent sauce and the juice of a lemon. Thicken with brown flour moistened with a little cold water. Garnish handsomely with sprigs of parsley and currant jelly.

## BAKED BLACK BASS.

### Mrs. P. B. Ayer.

Eight good sized onions chopped fine; half that quantity of bread crumbs; butter size of hen's egg; plenty of pepper and salt, mix thoroughly with anchovy sauce until quite red. Stuff your fish with this compound and pour the rest over it, previously sprinkling a little red pepper over it. Shad, pickerel and trout are good the same way. Tomatoes can be used instead of anchovies, and is more economical. If using them, take pork in place of butter and chop fine.

## BROILED WHITE FISH—FRESH.

### Mrs. G. E. P.

Wash and drain the fish; sprinkle with pepper and lay with the inside down upon the gridiron, and broil over fresh bright coals. When a nice brown, turn for a moment on the other side, then take up and spread with butter. This is a very nice way of broiling all kinds of fish, fresh or salted. A little smoke under the fish adds to its flavor. This may be made by putting two or three cobs under the gridiron.

## SALT MACKEREL.

### Mrs. F. D. J.

Soak the fish for a few hours in lukewarm water, changing the water several times; then put into **cold water** loosely tied in cloths, and let the fish come to a boil, turning off the water once, **and** pouring **over the** fish hot water from the tea kettle; let **this just** come to a boil then take them out and **drain** them, lay them on a platter, butter and pepper them, and place them **for** a **few** moments in the oven. Serve with sliced lemons.

## BOILED CODFISH—SALT.

Soak two pounds of codfish in lukewarm water over night or for several hours; change the water several **times**; about one hour before dinner put this into cold fresh water, and set over the fire; let it come to a boil, **or** just simmer, **for** fifteen minutes but not to boil hard, then take out **of** the water, drain and serve with egg sauce, or with cold boiled eggs sliced and laid over it, with a drawn butter or cream gravy poured over all.

## CROQUETTES OF FISH.

Take dressed fish of any kind; separate from the bones, mince it with a little seasoning, an egg beaten with a teaspoon of flour and one of milk; roll into balls, brush the outside with egg and dredge well with bread and cracker crumbs and fry them of a nice color. The bones, heads, tails, **an** onion, an anchovy and **a** pint of **water** will make the gravy.

## EELS.

### Mrs. P. B. Ayer.

**Skin** and par boil them; cleanse the back bone of all coagulations; cut them in pieces about three inches in length; dip **in** flour and cook in pork fat, brown.

## TONGUES **AND** SOUNDS.

### Mrs. P. B. Ayer.

Soak them thirty-six hours in cold water; scrape them thoroughly and boil tender; fry them brown or eat with butter and egg sauce.

## CHOWDER.

### Mrs. P. B. Ayer.

Five pounds of codfish cut in squares; fry plenty of salt pork cut in thin slices; put a layer of pork in your kettle, then one of fish; one of potatoes in thick slices, and one of onions in slices; plenty of pepper and salt; repeat as long as your materials last, and finish with a layer of Boston crackers or crusts of bread. Water sufficient to cook with, or milk if you prefer. Cook one-half hour and turn over on your platter, disturbing as little as possible. Clams and eels the same way.

## FISH CHOWDER.

### Mrs. R. A. Sibley.

Four pounds of fresh fish skinned and cut in pieces; put in a pot some of the fish, then some crackers and sliced potatoes, salt and pepper; another layer of fish, crackers and potatoes; cover the whole with water; add a little onion, if liked, and some fried pork or butter; boil until the potatoes are done, then add a quart of milk and let it boil. When dishing for the table, take out all the large bones. Cod fish or haddocks are the best; other fish will answer; use the head.

## POTTED FISH.

### Mrs. Gridley, Evanston.

Take out the back bone of the fish; for one weighing two pounds take a tablespoonful of allspice and cloves mixed; these spices should be put into little bags of not too thick muslin; put sufficient salt directly upon each fish; then roll in a cloth, over which sprinkle a little cayenne pepper; put alternate layers of fish, spice and sago in an earthern jar; cover with the best cider vinegar; cover the jar closely with a plate and over this put a covering of dough, rolled out to twice the thickness of pie crust. Make the edges of paste, to adhere closely to the sides of the jar, so as to make it air-tight. Put the jar into a pot of cold water and let it boil from three to five hours, according to quantity. Ready when cold.

# SHELL FISH.

## OYSTERS ON THE SHELL.

Wash the shells and put them on hot coals or upon the top of a hot stove, or bake them in a hot oven; open the shells with an oyster-knife, taking care to lose none of the liquor, and serve quickly on hot plates, with toast. Oysters may be steamed in the shells and are excellent eaten in the same manner.

## BROILED OYSTERS.

Drain the oysters well and dry them with a napkin. Have ready a griddle hot and well buttered; season the oysters; lay them on the griddle and brown them on both sides. Serve them on a hot plate with plenty of butter.

## CREAMED OYSTERS.

### Clara E. Thatcher.

To one quart of oysters take one pint of cream or sweet milk; thicken with a little flour, as if for gravy; when cooked, pour in the oysters with liquor; pepper, salt and butter the mixture. Have ready a platter with slices of nicely browned toast, pour creamed oysters on toast and serve hot.

## OYSTERS A LA CREME.

### Mrs. J. B. Lyon, Detroit.

One quart of oysters, one pint of cream; put the oysters in a double kettle, cook until the milk juice begins to flow out; drain the oysters in a colander; put the cream on the same way; when it comes to a boil, thicken with flour wet with milk as thick as corn starch, ready to mould; then put in the oysters and cook five minutes. Serve hot on toast.

## PANNED OYSTERS.

### Mrs. J. B. Lyon, Detroit.

Drain the oysters from the liquor; put them in a hot pan or spider; as soon as they begin to curl, add butter, pepper and salt. Serve on toast, or without, if preferred.

## STEWED OYSTERS.

### Mrs. Andrews.

In all cases, unless shell oysters, wash and drain; mix half a cup of butter and a tablespoon of corn starch; put with the oysters in a porcelain kettle; stir until they boil; add two cups of cream or milk; salt to taste; do not use the liquor of the oysters in either stewing or escaloping.

## ESCALOPED OYSTERS.

### Mrs. Andrews.

Butter the dish, (common earthen pie-plates are the best;) cover the bottom of the dish with very fine bread crumbs; add a layer of oysters; season with pepper and salt; alternate the crumbs and oysters until you have three layers; finish with crumbs; cover the top with small pieces of butter; finish around the edge with bread cut into small oblong pieces dipped in butter; bake half an hour; unless shell oysters wash them thoroughly and strain.

## ESCALOPED OYSTERS.

### Mrs. D.

Crush and roll several handfuls of friable crackers; put a layer in the bottom of a buttered pudding dish; wet this with a mixture of the oyster liquor and milk, slightly warmed; next a layer of oysters; sprinkle with salt and pepper, and lay small bits of butter upon them; then another layer of moistened crumbs, and so on until the dish is full. Let the top layer be of crumbs, thicker than the rest, and beat an egg into the milk you pour over them; put pieces of butter on top; cover the dish; bake half an hour.

## ESCALOPED OYSTERS.

### Mrs. Norcross.

Scald the oysters; butter the dish in which they are to be baked; put in first a layer of rolled crackers; take the oysters from the liquor one at a time, to be sure no shells are on them; then add a layer of oysters with butter, a little pepper, and continue adding a layer of crackers and oysters until the dish is full; have the top layer crackers; strain over the whole the liquor; bake half an hour.

## ESCALOPED OYSTERS.

### Clara E. Thatcher.

Roll one pound of crackers for one quart of oysters. Put a layer in the bottom of a buttered pudding-dish; next a layer of oysters; sprinkle with salt and pepper and lay small bits of butter upon them; then another layer of oysters, and so on till the dish is full; finish with a layer of crackers and small pieces of butter; then pour on the juice of the oysters, and one quart of water; bake three-quarters of an hour.

## OYSTER PIE.

Take a large dish, butter it, and spread a rich paste over the sides and around the edge, but not on the bottom. The oysters should be as large and fine as possible; drain off part of the liquor from the oysters; put them into a pan, and season them with pepper, salt, spice and butter; have ready the yolks of three boiled eggs chopped fine, and grated bread crumbs; pour the oysters with as much of their liquor as you please into the dish with the paste, strew over them the chopped egg and grated bread; roll out the lid of the pie and put it on, crimping the edges. Bake in a quick oven.

## OYSTER PATTIES.

### Aunt Maggie.

Make some rich puff paste and bake it in very small tin patty pans; when cool, turn them out upon a large dish; stew some large fresh oysters with a few cloves, a little mace and nutmeg; then add the yolk of one egg, boiled hard and grated; add a little butter, and as much of the oyster liquor as will cover them. When they have stewed a little while, take them out of the pan and set them to cool. When quite cold, lay two or three oysters in each shell of puff paste.

3

## OYSTER PATTIES.

### Mrs. Thos. Orton.

Stew the oysters; take the broth and allow the yolk of one egg to every dozen of oysters; turn off the broth and add the eggs; let it come to a boil; then turn back the oysters and fill the crust.

## TO FRY OYSTERS.

### Mrs. Edward Ely.

Roll a few crackers; beat two eggs, wash your oysters or not, according to your notion, but the bits of shell must be removed; dip your oysters into the egg, then into the rolled crackers; take half butter, and half lard in a spider, have it hot; (but not so hot that your oysters will burn;) fry them; then have a colander in a pan on the stove, and as soon as done, put into the colander to dry; when you have a dozen or so, take them out and put on a hot platter; salt to your taste.

## TO FRY OYSTERS.

### Mrs. D., and Mrs. T. V. Wadskier.

Use the largest and best oysters; lay them in rows upon a clean cloth and press another upon them, to absorb the moisture; have ready several beaten eggs; and in another dish some finely crushed crackers; in the frying pan heat enough butter to entirely cover the oysters; dip the oysters first into the eggs, then into the crackers, rolling it or them over that they may become well incrusted; drop into the frying pan and fry quickly to a light brown. Serve dry and let the dish be warm. A chafing dish is best.

## CORN OYSTERS.

### Mrs. W. P. Nixon.

One dozen ears of corn; two eggs; salt, pepper and a dredging of flour; grate the raw corn, over which dredge a little flour; season well; add the beaten eggs and fry quickly in buttter.

## FRICASSEED OYSTERS.

### Mrs. W. P. Brown.

For a quart can, drain the oysters dry as possible; put a piece of butter the size of an egg into your spider, and let it get quite brown; put in your oysters and as soon as they commence to cook, add as much more butter, which has been previously well mixed with a tablespoonful of flour; let it cook a moment and add one egg, beaten with a tablespoonful of cream; let this cook a moment and pour all over toasted bread.

## MACARONI WITH OYSTERS.

### Mrs. F. B. Orr.

Boil macaroni in salt water, after which drain through a colander; take a deep earthen dish or tin, put in alternate layers of macaroni and oysters; sprinkle the layers of macaroni with grated cheese; bake until brown. Delicious as a side-board dish at dinner.

## PICKLED OYSTERS.

### Mrs. C. G. Smith.

Wash them from their liquor and put them into a porcelain-lined kettle, with strong salt and water to cover them; let them come to a boil, and then skim them into cold water; scald whole peppers, mace and cloves in a little vinegar; the quantity of these must be determined by the number of oysters; when the oysters are cold, put them into a stone jar with layers of spice between them, and make liquor enough to cover them, from the liquor in which they were cooked; spice your vinegar and cold water to taste.

## LOBSTER CHOWDER.

### Mrs. Lamkin.

Four or five pounds of lobster, chopped fine; take the green part and add to it four pounded crackers; stir this into one quart of boiling milk; then add the lobster, a piece of butter one-half the size of an egg, a little pepper and salt, and bring to a boil.

## LOBSTER CROQUETTES.

### M. A. T.

The same mixture as given for stuffed lobster, without the cream; made into pointed balls, dipped in egg and then rolled cracker and fried in very hot lard; served dry and garnished with parsley.

## STUFFED CRABS OR LOBSTER.

### M. A. T.

Boil crabs and pick out meat; carefully preserving the shell whole; rub this with salad oil; add to meat one-fourth as much fine bread crumbs, very little nutmeg, cayenne pepper, grated rind and juice of lemon, butter and a little sweet cream, (if lobster, rub the coral with the cream;) replace in shells, dust lightly with bread crumbs and butter and brown in oven. Garnish with parsley and lemon.

## CLAM FRITTERS.

### M. A. T.

Twelve clams, chopped or not; one pint milk; three eggs; add liquor from clams; salt and pepper, and flour enough for thin batter. Fry in hot lard.

## TO DRESS CRAB.

### Mrs. Elia M. Walker.

Two or three shalots and a little parsley chopped very fine; one ounce of butter; a bunch of sweet herbs, a teacup of broth (or water); boil a few minutes, and take out the herbs, add the crumbs of a roll finely grated; one tablespoon of best sweet oil; one glass of sherry; the juice of half a lemon; cayenne pepper and salt to taste. Put in the crab to warm, then put all nicely into the shell, grate over some bread crumbs and put in the oven a few moments to brown.

## CLAM STEW.

### Mrs. M. L. S.

Lay the clams on a gridiron over hot coals, taking them out of the shells as soon as open, saving the juice; add a little hot water, pepper, a very little salt and butter rolled in flour sufficient for seasoning; cook **for five minutes** and pour over toast.

# Poultry and Game.

"Whoso seeks an audit here,
Propitious pays his tribute—game or fish,
Wildfowl or venison, and his errand speed."
—COWPER.

## BOILED FOWL.

**Take** a young fowl and fill the inside with oysters; place in **a** jar and plunge into a kettle of water; boil for one and one-half hours; there will be a quantity of gravy in the jar from the juice of the fowls and the oysters; make this into a white sauce with **the** addition of egg, cream, or **a little** flour **and** butter; add oysters **or serve up** plain with the **fowl.** This is very **nice** with the addition of a little parsley to the sauce.

## ROAST TURKEY OR CHICKEN.

**Having** picked and drawn the fowls, wash them well in two **or** three waters; wipe them dry; **dredge** them **with** a little flour inside and out, and **a** little pepper and salt; prepare a dressing of bread and cracker crumbs, fill the bodies and the crops of the fowls and then bake them for one or two hours; baste them frequently while roasting; stew **the** giblets **in a sauce** pan; just before serving, **chop** the giblets fine; after taking up the chicken, add the **water in** which the giblets were boiled, and the chopped giblets to the gravy of the roast fowl; thicken with a little flour, which has been previously wet with water; boil up, and serve in a gravy dish. **Roast** chickens and turkey should be accompanied with celery and jellies.

## BAKED CHICKEN.

### Anonymous.

Cut the fowls open and lay them flat in a pan, breaking down the breast and back bones; dredge with flour and season well with salt and pepper, with bits of butter; put in a very hot oven until done, basting frequently with melted butter; or when half done take out the chicken and finish by broiling it upon a grid-iron over bright coals; pour over it melted butter and the juices in the pan in which it was baked.

## CHICKEN FRICASSEE.

### Sarah Page, Albany, N. Y.

Cut up the chickens and put on the fire in a kettle with cold water sufficient to cover, add a little salt or salt pork sliced, if you like; boil until tender, and cut up and put in a part of a head of celery. When tender have ready hot baking-powder biscuits broken open and laid on a platter; on this place the chicken; thicken the gravy with flour moistened with water or milk, and pour it over the chicken and biscuits. If you prefer, use a good sized piece of butter to season instead of the salt pork.

## FRIED CHICKEN.

### Mrs. Bausher.

Cut the chicken in pieces, lay in salt and water, which change several times; roll each piece in flour; fry in very hot lard or butter, season with salt and pepper; fry parsley with them also. Make a gravy of cream seasoned with salt, pepper and a little mace, thickened with a little flour in the pan in which the chickens were fried, pouring off the lard.

## DRESSING FOR CHICKENS OR TURKEY.

### Mrs. F. D.

Chop bread crumbs quite fine, season well with pepper, salt and plenty of butter; moisten with a very little water, and add a few oysters with a little of the liquor, if you please.

## DRESSING FOR TURKEY.

### C. Kennicott.

One pint of soaked bread, two tablespoons of sage, two tablespoons of summer savory, two teaspoons of salt, two teaspoons pepper, butter size of an egg.

## CHICKEN CHEESE.

Two chickens boiled tender, chop, but not too fine; salt and pepper; three or four eggs boiled and sliced; line dishes or moulds with them; pour in the chicken and the liquor they were boiled in, when cold, slice.

## JELLIED CHICKEN.

### M. A. T.

Boil a fowl until it will slip easily from the bones; let the water be reduced to about one pint in boiling; pick the meat from the bones in good sized pieces, taking out all gristle, fat and bones; place in a wet mould; skim the fat from the liquor; a little butter; pepper and salt to the taste and one-half ounce of gelatine. When this dissolves, pour it hot over the chicken. The liquor must be seasoned pretty high, for the chicken absorbs.

## CHICKEN PIE.

### Mrs. H.

Stew chickens until tender; line the sides of a deep pie dish, with nice pastry; put in the chicken, and the water in which it has boiled, (which should be but half a pint); season with a large piece of butter, salt and pepper, and then cover loosely with a crust. While this is baking, have ready a quart can of fine oysters; put on the fire a pint of rich milk, (or the liquor of the oysters will do); let it come to a boil; thicken with a little flour, and season with butter, pepper and salt; pour this over the oysters boiling hot, and about fifteen minutes before the pie is done, lift the crust and pour the oysters and all, into the pie; then return to the oven to finish.

## CHICKEN LOAF.
### Mrs. W. H. Low.

Take two chickens, boil them in as little water as possible, until the meat will drop from the bones; cut it with a knife and fork; then put it back in the kettle; put in plenty of butter, pepper and salt; heat it thoroughly; boil an egg hard and slice it and place in the bottom of a dish; pour it in hot, place a weight upon it, and put it away to cool; it will come out in a form.

## CHICKEN CROQUETTES.
### Mrs. P. B. Ayer.

Two well cooked chickens chopped fine; one pound rice boiled not more than twenty minutes; an onion, if preferred; one-half pound old cheese grated; parsley chopped fine; very little cloves, mace and thyme; cayenne and black pepper to season. Mix this thoroughly with the yolks of ten eggs, well beaten; one pint of sifted crackers; beat six eggs, separately; form the first compound in a pointed wine glass; dip first in the egg and then in the sifted cracker and brown in hot lard. Heat before eating.

## CHICKEN CROQUETTES.
### Mrs. J. Young Scammon.

The proportions that we give below are for half a good sized chicken. After boiling, chop the meat fine, fry it with one ounce of butter; then add one-half teaspoon of flour; stir for half a minute, adding the chopped meat and a little more than a gill of meat broth; salt, pepper and a pinch of nutmeg; stir for five minutes, then take it from the fire and mix the yolks of two eggs with it; put on the fire again for one minute, stirring the while. Lastly, you may or may not add four mushrooms chopped, or two truffles, or both, according to taste. Turn the mixture into a dish and set it away to cool. When perfectly cold, mix it well, as the upper part is drier than the rest; put it in parts on the pasteboard a tablespoon for each part. Have bread crumbs on the paste-board, then make them into any form required. Dip each croquette in beaten egg; roll in bread crumbs again and fry in hot fat. Garnish each croquette with a sprig of parsley.

## CROQUETTES.
### Mrs. I. N. Isham.

Take cold fowl or fresh meat of any kind, with slices of ham, fat and lean; chop all together very fine; add half as much grated bread, and season with salt, pepper and nutmeg; one tablespoon of catsup, one teaspoon of made mustard and one lump of butter; mix well together, make up in little rolls or balls, dip in beaten yolks of eggs, cover with grated bread crumbs, and fry brown in lard.

## DUCKS.
### Miss S. P., Albany, N. Y.

When roasted; use dressing as for turkey, with the addition of a few slices of onion. Many cooks lay over the game slices of onions, which takes away the fishy flavor, removing the onion before serving. Make a sauce with the drippings in the pan, in which the game is roasted, into which are put the chopped giblets, which are previously well cooked; thicken the gravy with browned flour, moistened with water. Serve with currant jelly.

## ROAST GOOSE.

Stuff and roast in the same manner as ducks. Many cooks cover poultry with a paste of flour and water while baking, removing it before it is served.

## TO ROAST WILD FOWL.
### M. A. T.

Put an onion, salt and hot water into the pan, and baste for ten or fifteen minutes; change the pan; put in a slice of salt pork and baste with butter and pork drippings very often; just before serving dredge lightly with flour and baste. Ducks take from twenty-five to thirty-five minutes to roast, and woodcock and snips fifteen to twenty-five. Do not draw nor take of the heads of either. Garnish with fried or toasted bread, lemon, parsley and currant jelly.

## PRAIRIE CHICKENS, PARTRIDGES AND QUAILS.

Miss Sarah Page, Albany, N. Y.

Clean nicely, using a little soda in the water in which they are washed; rinse them and dry, and then fill them with dressing, sewing them up nicely, and binding down the legs and wings with cords. Put them in a steamer over hot water, and let them cook until just done. Then place them in a pan with a little butter; set them in the oven and baste them frequently with melted butter until of a nice brown. They ought to brown nicely in about fifteen minutes. Serve them on a platter, with sprigs of parsley alternating with currant jelly.

## QUAIL ON TOAST.

After the birds are nicely cleaned, cut them open down the back; salt and pepper them, and dredge with flour. Break down the brest and back-bones, so they will lie flat, and place them in a pan with a very little water and butter in a hot oven, covering them up tightly until nearly done. Then place them in a spider in hot butter, and fry a moment a nice brown. Have ready slices of baker's bread toasted, and slightly buttered upon a platter. The toast should be broken down with a carving knife, so that it will be tender. On this place the quails; make a sauce of the gravy, in the pan thicken lightly with browned flour, and pour over each quail and the toast.

## A SUGGESTION.

M. A. T.

Singe all poultry with alcohol and dip quails into clarified butter for boiling.

## PRESSED CHICKEN.

Mrs. C. H. Wheeler.

Cut up the fowls and place in a kettle with a tight cover, so as to retain the steam; put about two teacups of water and plenty of salt and pepper over the chicken, then let it cook until the meat cleaves easily from the bones, cut or chop all the meat (freed from skin, bones and grizzle) about as for chicken salad;

season well, put it into a dish and pour the remnant of the juice in which it was cooked over it. This will jelly when cold, and can then be sliced or set on the table in shape. Nice for tea or lunch. The nack of making this simple dish is in not having too much water; it will not jelly if too weak or if the water is allowed to boil away entirely while cooking.

## PIGEON PIE.

### Mrs. L.

Make a fine puff paste; lay a border of it around a large dish, and cover the bottom with a veal cutlet, or a very tender steak free from fat and bone; season with salt, cayenne pepper and mace. Prepare as many pigeons as can be put in one layer in the dish; put into each pigeon a small lump of butter, and season with pepper and salt; lay them in the dish breast downwards, and cut in slices a half dozen of hard boiled eggs, and lay in with the birds; put in more butter, some veal broth, and cover the whole with crust. Bake slowly for an hour and a half.

## MEATS.

——"Cook, see all your sawces
Be sharp and poynant in the palate, that they may
Commend you; look to your roast and baked meats handsomely,
And what new kickshaws and delicate made things.
—BEAUMONT AND FLETCHER.

## GENERAL RULES FOR COOKING MEATS.

All salt meat should be put on in cold water, that the salt may be extracted while cooking. Fresh meat which is boiled to be served with sauces at the table, should be put to cook in boiling water, when the outer fibres contract, the inner juices are preserved.

For making soup, put the meat over in cold water, to extract the juices for the broth.

In boiling meats, if more water is needed, add that which is hot, and be careful to keep the water on the meat constantly boiling.

Remove the scum when it first begins to boil. The more gently meat boils, the more tender it will become. Allow twenty minutes for boiling each pound of fresh meat.

Roast meats require a brisk fire. Baste often. Twenty minutes is required for roasting each pound of fresh meat. The variation in roasted meats consists simply in the method of preparing them to cook, before putting in the oven. Some are to be larded; some stuffed with bread dressing, and others plain, only seasoning with pepper and salt.

## HINTS FOR COOKING MEATS.

### E. E. Masey.

A tough piece of meat can be made tender by cooking for several hours, in water at a simmering heat. The fibre of meats is toughened by being subjected to a high temperature. It is upon this theory that Warren's Patent Cooker is constructed. The same results can be obtained by carefully watching the process of cooking, to prevent rapid boiling.

## ROAST BEEF.

Prepare for the oven by dredging lightly with flour, and seasoning with salt and pepper; place in the oven, and baste frequently while roasting. Allow a quarter of an hour for a pound of meat, if you like it rare; longer if you prefer it well done. Serve with a sauce, made from the drippings in the pan, to which has been added a tablespoon of Harvey or Worcestershire sauce, and a tablespoon of tomato catsup. Thicken with with browned flour, and serve in a gravy boat.

## BEEFSTEAK AND MUSHROOMS.

### Mrs Perry H. Smith.

Put in a sauce pan one ounce of butter, a small onion chopped fine, a little ground sage, and a little thyme, and put it over the

fire; when hot, shake in two tablespoons of flour, and when it
becomes brown, put in one gill of water, and let it boil for half
an hour. Then add three tablespoons of beef stock, a little salt,
a little nutmeg and one wine glass of sherry wine. But in one
can of mushrooms, and let it boil for ten minutes. Pour this
over a nicely broiled beefsteak.

## BROILED BEEFSTEAK.

Lay a thick tender steak upon a gridiron over hot coals, having greased the bars with butter before the steak has been put
upon it; (a steel gridiron with slender bars is to be preferred, the
broad flat iron bars of gridirons commonly used, fry and scorch
the meat, imparting a disagreeable flavor.) When done on one
side, have ready your platter warmed, with a little butter on it;
lay the steak upon the platter with the cooked side down, that
the juices which have gathered may run on the platter, but do
not press the meat; then lay your beefsteak again upon the gridiron quickly and cook the other side. When done to your liking,
put again on the platter, spread lightly with butter, place where
it will keep warm for a few moments, but not to let the butter
become oily, (over boiling steam is best;) and then serve on hot
plates. Beefsteak should never be seasoned with salt and pepper
while cooking. If your meat is tough, pound *well* with a steak
mallet on both sides.

## A LA MODE BEEF.

### Miss Sarah Page.

Take a piece of beef four or five inches thick, and with a small
knife make small holes entirely through it at small distances
apart. Then take strips of fat salt pork, roll them in pepper and
cloves. Lay on a pan, cover closely, and put over in a steamer,
and steam for three hours. When done, thicken the gravy in
the pan with a little flour. This is excellent when eaten as cold
meat.

## BEEF WITH TOMATOES.

### Mrs. P. B. Ayer.

Eight pounds fresh plate beef, second cut; boil tender two
quarts tomatoes, three cloves, plenty butter, pepper and salt;

when cooked nice and thick, strain through a colander and pour over your beef and serve hot or cold.

## MOCK DUCK.
### Mrs. C. C. Stratton, Evanston.

Take the round of beef steak, salt and pepper either side; prepare bread or crackers with oysters or without, as for stuffing a turkey; lay your stuffing on the meat; sew up, and roast about an hour; and if you do not see the wings and legs, you will think you have roast duck.

## BEEF OMELET.
### Mrs. S. B. Adams.

Four pounds of round beef, uncooked, chopped fine; six eggs beaten together; five or six soda crackers rolled fine, little butter and suet, pepper, salt and sage, if you choose; make two loaves, roll in cracker; bake about an hour; slice when cold.

## SPICED BEEF.
### Mrs. E. R. Harmon.

Four pounds of round of beef chopped fine; take from it all fat; add to it three dozen small crackers rolled fine, four eggs, one cup of milk, one tablespoon ground mace, two tablespoons of black pepper, one tablespoon melted butter; mix well and put in any tin pan that it will just fill, packing it well; baste with butter and water, and bake two hours in a slow oven.

## MEAT FROM SOUP BONES.
### Mrs. DeForest, Freeport.

Before thickening the soup or putting in the vegetables, take out a large bowl of the liquor; take the meat from the bones, chop it fine, season with catsup and spices; pour over the liquor, which should be thick enough to jelly when cold; put into molds and serve cold in slices.

## BEEF CROQUETTES.

### Mrs. J. B. R.

Chop fine some cold beef; beat two eggs and mix with the meat and add a little milk, melted butter, and salt and pepper. Make into rolls and fry.

## TO BOIL CORN BEEF.

### Mrs. A. W. D.

Put the meat in cold water; boil from five to six hours, then take out the bones; wrap it tightly in a towel; put on ice, with a weight to press it.

## PRESERVED BEEF.

### Mrs. Carter.

For preserving one hundred pounds beef: Six pounds salt, two ounces salt-petre, two tablespoonfuls soda, two pounds sugar, four gallons water; mix well together; sprinkle the bottom of the barrel with salt; put in the beef with a very little salt between each layer; pour over the brine and put on a weight to keep all well covered.

## TO CORN BEEF.

### Mrs. A. M. Gibbs.

To each gallon of cold water, put one quart of rock salt, one ounce of saltpetre and four ounces of brown sugar, (it need not be boiled;) as long as any salt remains undissolved, the meat will be sweet. If any scum should rise, scald and skim well; add more salt, saltpetre and sugar; as you put each piece of meat into the brine, rub over with salt. If the weather is hot, gash the meat to the bone, and put in salt. Put a flat stone or some weight on the meat to keep it under the brine.

Or this: To every four gallons of water allow two pounds of brown sugar, and six pounds of salt, boil about twenty minutes, taking off the scum; the next day turn it on the meat packed in the pickling tub; pour off this brine; boil and strain every two months, adding three ounces of brown sugar and half a pound of common salt. It will keep good a year. Sprinkle the meat

with salt the next day, wipe dry before turning the pickle over it.
Let it entirely cover the meat; add four ounces saltpetre. Canvas lids are excellent for covering as they admit the air and exclude flies. Mutton and beef may be kept sweet several weeks by simply rubbing well with dry salt and closely covering. Turn the pieces whenever the vessel is uncovered.

## BOILED TONGUE AND TOMATO SAUCE.

### Mrs. A. L. Chatlain.

Boil a pickled tongue till well done, then peel. For the sauce, one can of tomatoes, boil half down, then strain, rub together, one tablespoon of butter, one teaspoon of flour and a little salt, put these into the tomatoe, and let it come to a boil; then pour over the tongue and serve.

## BOILED LEG OF MUTTON.

### Mrs. J. Brown.

Boil well in clear water until tender, seasoning the water with salt; serve with egg sauce, and garnish with parsley, sliced lemons, or some sour jelly.

## MUTTON A LA VENISON.

### Mrs. J. B. L.

Take a leg of mutton and lard it well with strips of salt pork inserted in deep slits in the meat, which has been previously rolled in pepper and cloves; bake two hours or according to the size of the roast, basting frequently while in the oven; about an hour before serving, spread over it currant jelly, return to the oven and let it brown.

## MUTTON CHOPS.

Cut them nicely, clearing away all ragged ends and edges; fry for a few moments covered closely, and then dip each piece in cracker crumbs and beaten egg, or you may prepare them as for frying; then, lay them in a dripping pan, and put into the oven to bake; baste frequently with a little melted butter and water.

## ROAST VEAL.

### Mrs. D. S. F.

Prepare a leg of veal for the oven, by washing, drying, and larding it with strips of fat bacon or ham, and dredging it well with flour, and seasoning with salt and pepper; baste frequently and serve with the gravy thickened. A roast fillet of veal should be prepared by stuffing it with bread crumbs, seasoned with chopped ham, summer savory, pepper and salt. Dredge lightly with flour and bake.

## NECK PIECE OR SHOULDER OF VEAL.

### Mrs. C. C. Stratton, Evanston.

Put a piece of butter the size of an egg into a kettle; put it on the stove; when it begins to fry, put in the veal, season it and let it fry until brown; then add water sufficient to cook it. When done take cream and flour well stirred, and thicken as for fricasseed chicken, and you have a nice dinner, very like chicken and much cheaper. Two pounds of veal will make a dinner for six or eight, providing it is not all bone.

## VEAL PIE.

### Mrs. Houghteling.

Three pounds of lean veal; two slices of salt pork, chopped fine; one coffee cup of bread crumbs, two eggs, salt, pepper and herbs to taste; mix thoroughly and bake; use cold as a relish.

## PATTIE OF VEAL.

### Mrs. L. J. Tilton.

Three and one-half pounds of the leg of veal, fat and lean, chopped fine; six or eight small crackers rolled fine; two eggs, piece of butter the size of an egg, one tablespoon of salt, one of pepper and one of nutmeg; a slice of salt pork chopped fine. Work all together in the form of a loaf; put bits of butter and grate bread crumbs over the top. Bake two hours; to be cut in slices when cold.

4

## VEAL PATTIE.

### M. A. P.

Four pounds of veal and one and one-half pounds of salt pork chopped together, raw and very fine, with four rolled crackers; two well beaten eggs, one lemon and one small onion; salt, pepper and sweet herbs to taste; mix well and bake in a pan as you would a loaf of bread; requires three hours.

## VEAL CUTLETS, A LA FRIED OYSTERS.

### Mrs. A. M. Gibbs.

Cut the veal in small pieces three or four inches square; dry with a towel; season to taste; have ready a beaten egg and crackers rolled fine, each on separate dishes; dip each piece of the cutlet in the egg, then in the rolled cracker; have enough lard or butter hot in your spider so that it will nearly cover the cutlets when you put them in. A rich gravy can be made after the meat is done, by adding a little boiling water.

## VEAL LOAF.

### Mrs. Lamkin.

Three and one-half pounds of lean and fat raw veal, chopped fine; one slice of salt pork, six small crackers rolled fine, butter the size of an egg, two eggs, one tablespoon of salt, one tablespoon of pepper, one of sage, three of extract of celery; mix thoroughly. Pack tightly in a deep square tin; cover with bits of butter and sprinkle fine cracker crumbs over the top; cover with another tin. Bake two hours, uncover and brown the top.

## VEAL LOAF.

### Mrs. Chas. Duffield.

Six Boston crackers, three eggs, one tablespoonful of salt, pepper and sage, or summer savory; three pounds of veal. The veal must be raw and chopped fine; mix all well together and pack it hard in a **deep tin** pan; bake slowly **for one** hour; **a table-**spoonful of butter **improves it.** This is a nice relish for **tea, and** should be **sliced thin, when cold.**

## VEAL LOAF.

### Mrs. G. W. Brayton and others.

**Three pounds raw veal**; **one-half pound raw salt** pork chopped **fine;** three Boston crackers **rolled** fine, **or** bread crumbs; three **eggs, one** teaspoon black **pepper,** little sage, little mace **or nut-meg, one tablespoon** of salt. Make **in** a loaf and baste while baking **with butter size of an egg with** water, **and put on out-**side **of loaf a small quantity of** rolled crackers. **Bake about** three hours. **Is very nice cold, cut** in thin slices.

## SPICED VEAL.

### Mrs. C. E. Brown, Evanston.

Take four pounds veal, chop it fine and season highly with salt, pepper, **cloves and** cinnamon; add four small crackers rolled **out,** one egg, **and a** lump of butter **nearly the size of an egg;** **mix** throughly together and **press it in a baking tin, and bake** about two and a half hours. **When thoroughly** cold, slice for **tea.** Some prefer it in rolls, convenient **for slicing,** and baked **from** one half to three quarters of **an hour.**

## JELLIED VEAL.

### M. A. T.

**Boil the** veal tender, **pick** it up fine, **put in a mould, add the** **water it was boiled** in, and **set it in** a cold place; season with salt **and pepper to taste;** a layer of **hard boiled eggs** improves it.

## FRICANDEAU.

### Mrs. J. M. Brown, and Mrs. M. L.

Three and one half pounds of cold roast **veal** chopped fine, one table spoon of salt **and** one of pepper, one half a nutmeg, four or five rolled crackers, three eggs. **If the** veal is lean, add

a piece of butter half as large as an egg and tablespoon of cream.
Form all this in a large roll, and spot the roll over with bits of
butter; then strew over it the pounded crackers, (a little of the
cracker should be mixed with the meat;) put it in the oven, and
from time to time, add a little water.   Cook slowly two hours.
When cold slice thin, and it makes an excellent relish.

## CROQUETTES.
### Mrs. Dr. I. N. Isham.

Take cold fowl or fresh meat of any kind, with slices of ham,
fat and lean; chop together very fine, add half as much grated
bread, salt and pepper, nutmeg, one tablespoon catsup, one teaspoon made mustard, lump of butter; knead well together; make
up in little rolls or balls, dip in beaten yolks of eggs; cover with
grated bread and fry brown in lard; no butter is used, except
for chickens.

## CROQUETTES OF CHICKEN, VEAL OR SWEET BREAD.
### Mrs. Gen. N. J. T. Dana.

Put in a stew pan a piece of butter size of an egg, one spoonful of flour, a little pepper, salt and nutmeg; let it melt and mix
well; chop the meat, but not too fine; put in the mixture and
stir till well mixed; when cold, add the yolks of two eggs to bind
it; roll into oblong shape, dip it into egg beaten with a little pepper and salt; roll in crumbs of bread or powdered crackers and
fry in boiling lard.

## SWEET BREADS.

Scald in salt and water, take out the stringy parts; then put in
cold water a few minutes; dry in a towel; dip in egg and bread
crumbs and fry brown in butter; when done place in a hot dish;
pour into the pan a cup of sweet cream, a little pepper and salt,
and a little parsley chopped fine; add flour, and when boiling,
pour over the sweet breads; add mushrooms, if desired.

## SWEET BREADS, BROILED.

### Mrs. Bates.

Parboil, rub them well with butter and broil on a clean grid-iron; turn them often and now and then roll them over in a plate containing hot melted butter, to prevent them from getting hard and dry.

## CALF'S LIVER—FRIED.

Cut in thin slices; wash and drain them, roll them in corn meal or cracker crumbs, and fry in fresh or salt pork gravy or butter.

## CALF'S LIVER—STEWED.

Boil till partly done; take out of the sauce pan; chop in small pieces; put back in the sauce pan; skim well; stew until tender; season with butter, pepper and salt; thicken with a little flour, and serve over slices of toasted bread.

## TO ROAST VENISON.

### Mrs. Porter.

Wash a saddle of venison thoroughly in several waters, then rub it over with vinegar, red pepper and a little salt; lard with strips of salt pork rolled in seasoned bread crumbs; season if you like, with sweet marjoram and sweet basil, one teaspoonful each, also pepper; then rub the whole over with currant jelly, and pour over it one bottle of claret wine. Let it stand over night, and next morning cover the venison with a paste made of flour and water half an inch thick; then cover with soft paper, and secure well with strings; place it in the dripping pan with some claret, butter and water, and baste very often; half an hour before you take it up, remove paste and paper, baste it with butter and dredge with flour to make it brown.

For Sauce.—Take a pound and a half of scraps of venison, with three pints of water, a few cloves, a few blades of mace, one-half a nutmeg, and salt and cayenne pepper to taste; boil it down to a pint, skim off the fat and strain; add half a pint of currant jelly, one pint of claret and one-quarter pound of butter, divided into bits and rolled in flour.

## ROAST PIG.

See that the pig has been well scalded; put in the body a stuffing of dry bread crumbs, seasoned with sage, salt and pepper, and sew it up; skewer the legs back or the under part will not crisp; put in a hot oven after dredging well with flour, and baste it frequently while roasting with melted butter, or rub the pig with a cloth wet with melted butter. When done, serve whole on a platter, and garnish with parsley and celery tops alternately. Take off some of the fat from the gravy, set the rest on the top of the stove, thicken with a little flour, add a half a glass of sherry wine, and the juice of half a lemon and serve in a gravy boat.

## HEAD CHEESE.

### Mrs. C. Bradley.

To one head add one heart, one-half liver and one tongue; first clean the head very nicely, then put it in a brine for twenty-four hours; then boil it until it is very soft, pick out the bones and chop very fine; then add salt, pepper, four small onions and a little sage, if you wish; mix it very thoroughly and put it in a colander and set it over a kettle of hot water over night; in the morning put in the press and press it as cheese.

## SOUSE.

When the pigs' feet and ears are well cleaned and scraped, put in cold water, and over the fire to boil; when tender, put them in a jar; prepare a pickle of half a gallon of cider vinegar, whole black pepper, mace and cloves; boil up with the vinegar, and then pour over the pigs' feet. Let them stand for two or three days, when they will be ready for use.

## SAUSAGES.

### Mrs. C. Bradley and others.

Six pounds of lean fresh pork, three pounds of fat pork, twelve teaspoons of sage, and six teaspoons of pepper, six teaspoons of salt, (and two of cloves, and one nutmeg, if you prefer;) grind or chop very fine; mix these ingredients thoroughly, and pack in a jar, and pour hot lard over the top.

## HAM SANDWICHES.

### Mrs. W. Butterfield.

Take some boiled ham, and chop it very fine, mix it with a dressing composed of one dessert spoon of mustard, two of oil, one raw egg beaten very light, a little salt and pepper; cut and spread the bread very thin.

## HAM SANDWITCHES.

### Mrs. W. Butterfield.

Chop fine some cold boiled ham, a little fat with the lean; add tongue and chicken also chopped fine; make a dressing of one-half a pound of butter, three tablespoons of salad oil, three of mustard, the yolk of one egg, and a little salt; mix well together and spread over the meat smoothly on thin slices of bread. Very nice.

## BOILED HAM.

### Mrs. C. Waggoner, Toledo.

Take a ham weighing about eight or ten poinds; soak it for twelve or twenty-four hours in cold water; then cover it with boiling water, add one pint of vinegar, two or three bay-leaves, a little bunch of thyme and parsley, (the dried and sifted will do, or even the seeds of parsley may be used, if the fresh can not be procured); boil very slowly two hours and a half, take it out, skim it, remove all the fat, except a layer half an inch thick; cut off with a sharp knife all the black-looking outside; put the ham into your dripping pan, fat side uppermost, grate bread crust over it and sprinkle a teaspoon of powdered sugar over it; put it in the oven for half an hour, until it is a beautiful brown. Eat cold; cut the nicest portion in slices; the ragged parts and odds and ends can be chopped fine and used for sandwiches; or, by adding three eggs to one pint of chopped ham, and frying brown, you have a delicious omelet for breakfast or lunch. The bones should be put in a soup-kettle, the rind and fat should be rendered and strained for frying potatoes and crullers. Ham cooked in this way will go much farther than when cooked in the ordinary manner.

## VEAL OMELET.

### Mrs. J. S. Gano.

Three pounds of lean veal, two eggs, six small butter crackers, one tablespoon of thyme, one of salt, one of pepper, two of milk; knead it like bread and bake it two hours in a slow oven, basting it with butter often, then slice for tea.

## TRAVELING LUNCH.

### Mrs. J. L. B.

Chop sardines, ham and a few pickles quite fine; mix with mustard, pepper, catsup, salt and vinegar; spread between bread nicely buttered. This is to be cut crosswise, like jelly cake.

## OMELET.

### M. A. T.

Seven eggs beaten separately; add the yolks, one-half teacup sweet milk or cream, a teaspoon of flour, salt and pepper; after beating them very light, mix well; lastly, add the whites cut to a stiff froth; mix very lightly and only a little. Fry with butter on a quick fire. When brown, fold together and serve immediately. This will make two omelets.

Bread and Butter Pudding.
Cut the bread in thin slices, butter
each, place in a ... dish and
strew currants, raisins & citron or
... over it, then another layer of
... first, and so on until the dish be full.
Beat 6 eggs with 1 pint milk, a
little nutmeg, one teaspoonful rose-w-
sweeten to the taste, and pour over
mix, &c and let it soak one or two h-
Bake half an hour.

Coconut Pie.
1 Quart milk, 6 eggs, one coconut
grate the coconut fine, flavor with
lemon or vanilla or rose-water, ...
soft white sugar, strain the custa-
before, & stir in the coconut. This w-
makes 2 pies

Cherry Pie
Lay the cherries in a deep baking-
with plenty of sugar, and a little
of flour, place an inverted cup in th-
middle of the dish, and cover this w-
with crust. The cup prevents the ...
of the fruit from soaking the crust

Custard Pie

when together in the & line with.
Well the bottom. Bake in deep pie
plates, Bake the crust ve little before
volving the custard.

## Farina Pie —

3 eggs, 1 quart milk, one table-
oon full farina, half teaspoon
of white sugar to your taste
Put the milk on the & fire, let it simmer
and not boil, Soak the farina in a little
old milk. When the other milk is hot
stir in the farina add the eggs and
boil a little, till it thickens.
Then take it off the fire, and add the flavor
and pour it into pie crust.
Bake half an hour. Beat the white
of one egg, adding to it a table spoon
sugar, and a little flavoring
When the pie is baked, spread this
over the top, set it back in the oven for
a few minutes to brown

## OMELET.
### Miss E. C. Harris.

One cup of milk, one tablespoon flour stirred into the milk; four eggs, the yolks and whites beaten separately; one-half tablespoon of melted butter stirred into the mixture; a little salt. Stir in the whites before putting it into the spider. Cook on top of the stove about ten minutes, then set the spider in the oven to brown the top. To be eaten as soon as taken from the oven. Very nice. '

## OMELET SOUFFLE.
### Mrs. Lamkin.

One pint boiled milk, three spoonsful flour, yolks of seven eggs, beaten with the flour; season with pepper and salt, and add a piece of butter size of egg; mix well, then add whites well beaten; bake twenty minutes.

## FRIED OMELET.
### Mrs. F. B. Orr.

Three eggs, two gills milk, two tablespoons flour, a little salt and pepper, fried on hot griddle.

## FRIAR'S OMELET.
### Mrs. DeForest, Freeport.

Boil a dozen apples, as for sauce; stir in one-fourth pound of butter, ditto white sugar; when cold, add four well beaten eggs, and a few spoons of cream; put it into a baking dish, well buttered, and thickly strewn with bread crumbs on the bottom and sides; strew currants over the top. Bake forty-five minutes; turn on a platter, and sift sugar over it. Serve with sugar and cream, or a boiled custard; the latter is much the nicer.

## OMELET.

### E. V. Case, Elmhurst.

**Take** three eggs, beat the whites and yolks separately; to the yolks after they are beaten, add a half teaspoon of salt and a teacup of rich cream, in which a heaping teaspoon of flour has been smoothly rubbed; lastly, stir in the whites which have been beaten as for cake; have ready a spider in which has been melted a tablespoon of lard, and which is as hot as it can be and not be burned; pour in the mixture and let it stand till it is of a rich brown on the bottom.

## FRENCH OMELET.
### M.

One cup boiling milk with one tablespoon of butter melted in it; pour this on one cup bread crumbs, (the bread must be light); add salt, pepper and the yolks of six eggs well beaten; mix thoroughly; and lastly, add the six whites cut to a stiff froth; mix lightly and fry with hot butter; this will make two; when almost done, turn together in shape of half-moon.

## BOILED OMELET.
### E. M. Walker.

Four eggs well beaten up with a little pepper, salt, nutmeg, chopped parsley and chives; one-half pint of cream (or milk); half fill little well buttered cups or moulds and set them in boiling water; boil for ten minutes, then turn out. They may be served with a sauce.

## BAKED OMELET.
### Mrs. Edward Ely.

Take six eggs, two tablespoons of flour, a little salt, one cup of milk; take a little of the milk, and stir the flour into it; add the rest of the milk, and the yolks of the eggs; then beat the whites of the eggs to a stiff froth, and pour into the flour, milk and yolks; put a piece of butter the size of a small egg into an iron spider, and let it get hot, but not so the butter will burn; then pour the mixture in and put in a moderate oven to bake in the spider. It takes about ten minutes to bake. Then slip a knife under and loosen, and slip off on a large plate or platter.

## OMELET.

### (With ham, cold tongue and other meats.)

Any of these omelets are **nice,** laid upon minced meat, which has been previously **seasoned** with butter, pepper and salt, bound together with beaten **egg and a** little sweet cream, and warmed in **a pan.** Then **turn on the platter, and** lay the omelet over it.

## SALTING PORK.

### A. M. G.

**Cover the bottom of** the barrel with salt an inch deep; put down one layer of pork and cover that **with salt** half an inch thick; continue thus, until all your pork is disposed of; then cover the whole with strong brine; pack as tight **as** possible, the rind side down or next to the barrel; keep the **pork** always under the brine **by** using an inner cover and clean stones. **Should** any scum arise, **pour** off the brine, scald it, **and add** more **salt.** Old brine can **be** boiled down, well skimmed **and used for a** fresh supply.

## CURING **HAMS.**

### Mrs. Mulford.

Hang up the hams a week **or ten** days, the longer **the** tenderer **and** better, if kept perfectly sweet; **mix for** each good sized **ham, one** teacup of salt, **one tablespoon of molasses, one** ounce of **salt-petre; lay the hams in a clean** dry **tub;** heat the mixture and **rub well into the hams, especially** around the bones and recesses; repeat the process once or twice, or until all the mixture is used; then let **the** hams lie **two** or three days, when they must be put for three weeks in brine strong enough to bear an egg; then soak eight hours in cold water; hang up to dry in the **kitchen or other** more convenient place for a week or more; smoke from three to five days, being careful not to heat the hams. Corn cobs and apple tree wood are good for smoking. The juices are better retained if smoked with **the hock** down. Tie up carefully in bags for the summer.

---

*" White Russian" and "Mottled German"—Best Brands Known.*

## BOILED AND BAKED HAM.

Mrs. P. B. Ayer.

Boil your ham tender; cover it with the white of a raw egg, and sprinkle sugar or bread crumbs over it; put it in the oven and brown; it is delicious also covered with a regular cake icing and browned.

## TO BOIL A HAM.

M.

Wash and scrape the ham clean; put it on in cold water enough to cover it; put into the water two onions, two carrots, a head of celery, a dozen cloves and a handful of timothy hay; boil without stopping until the skin will readily peel from the ham; cover the ham with rolled crackers, or bread crumbs that have been browned and rolled, and bake in a slow oven for two hours.

## Sauces and Salads.

"To make this condiment, your poet begs
The powdered yellow of two hard-boiled eggs;
Two boiled potatoes, passed through kitchen sieve,
**Smoothness and** softness to the salad give;
**Let onions** atoms lurk within the bowl,
And, half suspected, animate the whole;
Of mordant mustard, **add a** single spoon;
Distrust the condiment that bites so soon;
But, deem it not, thou man of herbs, a fault
To add a double quantity of salt;
Four times the spoon with oil from Lucca crown,
And twice with vinegar, procured from town;
And lastly, o'er the flavored compound toss
A magic *soup con* of anchovy sauce.
O, green and glorious! O, herbaceous treat!
'T would tempt the dying anchorite to eat;
Back to the world he'd turn his fleeting soul,
And plunge his fingers in the salad bowl;
Serenely full, the epicure would say,
**'Fate cannot** harm me, I have dined to-day.'"

—SIDNEY SMITH.

### DRAWN BUTTER.

Drawn butter forms the basis of most sauces. From **this a** great variety may be made, by adding to **this** different flavors— anchovies, ochra, onions, celery, parsley, mint and relishes—us- ing those flavors, which are suitable **for** the meat, game or fish, with which the sauces are to be served.  A good standard recipe for drawn butter, is as follows:

Rub one tablespoon of flour, with one quarter of a pound of butter; when well mixed, put in a sauce pan with a tablespoon of milk or water; set it in a dish of boiling water, shaking it well until the butter melts and is near boiling.  It should not be set directly on the stove or over the coals, as the heat will make the butter oily and spoil it.

## MELTED BUTTER OR PARSLEY SAUCE.
### M. A. T.

One tablespoon of butter, one teaspoon flour, rubbed together; one tablespoon chopped parsley, first boiled five minutes in water and squeezed out; two tablespoons water; shake over a clear fire, *one way*, until it boils; add the parsley gradually.

## MINT SAUCE.
### M. A. T.

Two tablespoons green mint, cut fine; two of sugar, and one-half teacup vinegar.

## MINT SAUCE.
### Mrs. J. M. B.

Mix one tablespoon of white sugar to half a teacup of good vinegar; add the mint and let it infuse for half hour in a cool place before sending to the table.  Serve with roast lamb or mutton.

## CELERY SAUCE.
### Mrs. J. B. L.

Mix two tablespoons of flour with half a teacup of butter; have ready a pint of boiling milk; stir the flour and butter into the milk; take three heads of celery, cut into small bits, and boil for a few minutes in water, which strain off; put the celery into the melted butter, and keep it stirred over the fire, for five or ten minutes.  This is very nice with boiled fowl or turkey.

## EGG SAUCE.

Miss Hattie Buck, Adrian, Mich.

Take the yolks of **two eggs boiled** hard; mash them with **a** teaspoon of mustard, **a little** pepper and salt, three tablespoons of vinegar, and three of salad **oil**. A tablespoon of catsup im- proves this for some. Nice **for boiled** fish.

## TOMATO **SAUCE.**

Mrs. C. S. Horseman, **Rockford, Ill.**

**Thirty-six ripe** tomatoes, six green **peppers, two** onions chop- ped fine, **two cups** of sugar, **two tablespoons of salt, two tea-** spoons **of** ground cloves, two **teaspoons of mustard, two tea-** spoons **of** cinnamon, two cups **of vinegar, and** boil half a day.

## GREEN **TOMATO SAUCE.**

Mrs. Houghteling.

One peck **of** green tomatoes, cut in very thin slices; sprinkle with salt; press with a plate and leave to drain twenty-four **hours.** Then place in a porcelain kettle in **layers** with the following mix- ture :—six large **onions** cut in slices, one small bottle of mustard, one-quarter pound mustard seed, **two** teaspoons **cloves, four tea-** spoons black pepper, two **teaspoons ginger, four** teaspoons all- **spice.** Cover with vinegar and **simmer two** hours or **until** the tomato looks clear. All the spices should be ground.

## OYSTER SAUCE.

Mrs. L. T.

Take oysters out **of** their liquor and throw them into **cold wa- ter**; put the liquor **over the** fire with the beards of the oysters, and boil **with a bit of** mace and lemon **peel**; then strain the liquor; take the oysters out of **the water and** drain them, and put oysters and strained liquor into a saucepan, **with** sufficient butter and milk for your sauce; dust in to this **flour**; let it boil up; add a squeeze of lemon juice, and serve *hot.*

## ONION SAUCE.

Boil three or four white onions until they are tender, and then mince them fine; put one half pint of milk over to boil; add a piece of butter half size of egg, and a little salt and pepper; stir in the minced onion and a tablespoon of flour, which has been moistened with milk; let it cream over boiling water.

## CHILI SAUCE.

### Mrs. Henry M. Knickerbocker.

Twenty-four large ripe tomatoes, six green peppers, four large onions, three tablespoons salt, eight tablespoons brown sugar, six teacups vinegar. Chop the peppers and onions very fine; peel the tomatoes and cut very small; put all into a kettle and boil gently one hour.

## CHILI SAUCE.

### Etta C. Springer.

One peck ripe tomatoes boiled one hour; add a cup of salt, one quart of vinegar, one ounce whole cloves, one ounce cinnamon, one ounce allspice, one ounce ground white mustard, one quart of onions sliced, a little celery, a little horse-radish, one-half pound of sugar, six red peppers.

## CHILI SAUCE WITH SPICE.

### Mrs. Lamkin.

Eighteen tomatoes, (ripe ones;) one green pepper chopped fine; three onions, if that flavor is desired; two tablespoons of salt; one-half cup of sugar, two cups of vinegar, one teaspoon of each kind of spice; stew slowly; tomatoes to be sliced. Good without onion.

## CHILI SAUCE.

### Mrs. E. H. Dennison, Highland Park, Ill.

To nine large ripe tomatoes and three green peppers, add one onion chopped fine, two cups of vinegar, two tablespoons of sugar, and one of salt; steam one hour, then add one teaspoon of ginger, one of allspice, and one of cloves.

*For the Bath, Toilet, or Laundry,*

## HORSE-RADISH SAUCE.

Two teaspoons of made mustard, two of white sugar, half a teaspoon of salt, and a gill of vinegar; mix and pour over grated horse-radish. Excellent with beef.

## MADE MUSTARD.

Pour a very little boiling water over three tablespoons of mustard; add one saltspoon of salt, a tablespoon of olive oil, stirred slowly in, and one teaspoon of sugar; add the yolk of an egg, beaten well together, and pour in vinegar to taste. It is best eaten next day.

## SAUCE MAYONNAISE.

### Mrs. P. B. Ayer.

Yolks of two raw eggs, (not a particle of the white, or your sauce will curdle) and one and a half mustardspoons of made mustard, mixed together; add very slowly the best salad oil, stirring constantly until you can reverse the dish without spilling; then add one tablespoon of vinegar and cayenne and black pepper to taste, one-half teaspoon salt; stir briskly until quite light; colored, and serve on lobster, lettuce or fish.

## CURRY POWDER.

### Mrs. F. S. Page, Rockford, Ill.

Mix an ounce of ginger, one of mustard one of black pepper, three of cariander seed, three of turmeric, quarter of an ounce of cayenne pepper, half an ounce of cardamon, half an ounce of cummin seed and cinnamon; pound the whole very fine, sift and keep it in a bottle corked tight. To be used for gravies for ducks and other meats.

## MAITRE D' HOTEL SAUCE.

### Mrs. E. M. E.

Put one teacup of butter in an earthen dish; have ready two large tablespoons of parsley, which has been boiled for a few moments in water; chop fine and add to the butter the juice of two lemons; add cayenne pepper and salt to taste; let it boil a few moments. An excellent sauce for a variety of meats.

## CELERY VINEGAR.

Soak one ounce of celery seed in half a pint of vinegar; bottle it and use to flavor soups and gravies.

## GOOSEBERRY CATSUP.

### Mrs. Henry Stevens.

Eight quarts gooseberries, four pounds of sugar, one pint vinegar, one-half ounce cloves, one ounce cinnamon; boil four hours; careful not to let it burn.

## GOOSEBERRY CATSUP.

### Mrs. J. B. Adams.

Eight pounds ripe or partially ripe fruit, four pounds brown sugar; one pint good vinegar, two ounces each fine cloves and cinnamon tied in a bag; boil the berries and sugar for three or four hours, then add spice; boil a little more; put in a jar and cover well. Will keep two years, by occasionally scalding and adding little vinegar and spice.

## CUCUMBER CATSUP.

Take a dozen large ripe cucumbers; pare and cut them open, and take out all the seeds; then grate them; make a bag like a jelly-bag of some thin muslin cotton, and hang them up to drain over night; chop two or three onions and two or three green peppers, a tablespoon of salt, and thin substance left in the bag, with a quart of best vinegar. If made of good vinegar, will keep two or three years.

*For the Bath, Toilet, or Laundry,*

## CURRANT CATSUP.

### Mrs. Packard.

Three quarts currant juice, two pounds sugar, one ounce cinnamon, one tablespoon cloves, one tablespoon mustard, one tablespoon black pepper, one-half pint vinegar, one-half teacup salt; boil well together, care being taken not to scorch.

## CURRANT CATSUP.

### Etta C. Springer.

Five pounds of currants, three pounds of sugar, one pint of vinegar, two teaspoons of allspice, two teaspoons of cloves, two of mustard, one teaspoon cayenne pepper; boil two hours.

## TOMATO CATSUP.

### Mrs. J. B. King.

Boil one bushel of tomatoes until quite soft; strain through a seive and add half gallon vinegar, one and a half pounds salt, two ounces whole cloves, quarter pound allspice, two teaspoons red pepper, three teaspoons black peppers, five heads garlic, chopped fine; boil three or four hours.

## TOMATO CATSUP.

### Mrs. H. F. Waite.

One gallon ripe tomatoes, four tablespoons full of salt, four tablespoons full of black pepper, three tablespoons mustard, one-half tablespoon allspice, one-half tablespoon cloves, six red peppers; simmer the above in vinegar sufficient to cover the mixture three or four hours; then strain through a seive, and cork in bottles.

## TOMATO CATSUP.

### Mrs. N. P. Iglehart.

Slice your tomatoes as you do cucumbers; sprinkle salt on every two layers of tomatoes; let them stand twenty-four hours, after which strain them through a cloth or sieve; boil two gallons to one, or in that proportion; whatever quantity, boil down one-half; then add one ounce cinnamon, one ounce cloves, one ounce mace, one ounce black pepper, one ounce allspice, one nutmeg and one quart of port wine to two gallons of juice. The spices are to be ground. Boil all together, after the ingredients are added, one-half hour. This will keep seven years without fermenting. This quantity of spice is for one gallon of catsup.

## SPICED TOMATOES.
### Mrs. C. E. Browne, Evanston.

Take any quantity of tomatoes you choose; pour boiling water over them and remove the skins; add vinegar and sugar in about the same proportions as for sweet pickles, or to suit the taste; also salt, pepper, cloves, cinnamon and other spices if preferred; boil in porcelain or brass kettle, until the tomatoes are perfectly dissolved and the original quantity is diminished one-half. It is better not to add the spices until it is about half done. A favorite relish for cold meats.

## CHICKEN SALAD.
### Mrs. Morgan, Rockford, Ill.

Cut the white meat of chickens into small bits, the size of peas, (also the dark meat, if you like); chop the whole parts of celery nearly as small; prepare a dressing thus: Rub the yolks of hard boiled eggs smooth; to each yolk, put half a teaspoon of mustard, the same quantity of salt, a tablespoon of oil, and a wine glass of vinegar; mix the chicken and celery in a large bowl and pour over this dressing, with a little cream added. The dressing must not be put on till just before it is served.

## CHICKEN SALAD.
### Mrs. Higgins.

Two chickens, chopped coarse; eight heads of celery, three eggs, one pint vinegar, one tablespoon flour, one tablepoon sugar, one tablespoon melted butter, one-half tablespoon mustard, salt and pepper; mix the other ingredients thoroughly and stir in the vinegar boiling hot; a teacup of chopped ham and a little of the oil from the **chicken** improve the salad; when the dressing is cold, mix with **the** chicken and celery.

## CHICKEN SALAD.

### Mary Norton.

Take the breasts of four well boiled chickens, cut in small pieces, but not too fine; mix with the chicken eight teacups of celery cut also in small pieces, and with the above, the chopped whites of twelve hard-boiled eggs. For **dressing** the yolks of four raw eggs; beat into them half of **an** ordinary **sized** bottle **of** olive oil, beginning with a teaspoonful, and adding no more than that at a time, until it is all thoroughly mixed; then add the well mashed and pulverized yolks of twelve eggs, salt and pepper, **a** pinch of cayenne pepper, and a gill of vinegar; then stir this dressing thoroughly into the mixed chicken celery and whites of eggs.

## CHICKEN **SALAD.**

### Mrs. Chas. Duffield.

**The yolks of six** eggs, well beaten; one-half pint **of** melted butter, **or the** same quantity of olive **oil; three** tablespoons of mixed mustard, (or more, if it is not very strong;) salt to taste; **two** teaspoons **of** celery seed; mix thoroughly; then add three fourths of a pint of strong vinegar; **place** over the fire, stirring constantly **until** it becomes thick, like boiled custard. Turn the mixture over the chickens, which have previously been chopped (not very fine.) Just before bringing to the table, add four heads of chopped celery. If it is not strong enough of spice, add more mustard and cayenne pepper. This is enough for one boiled turkey, or three small chickens. The some dressing makes an excellent mixture for sandwiches, if used with finely chopped boiled ham or beef tongue, **but** should **not** be salted.

## CHICKEN SALAD.

### Mrs. Hobbs.

Three chickens chopped fine, both light and dark meat; the juice of two lemons; eight or ten eggs boiled hard; the whites chopped fine and the yolks mashed fine, moistened with six teaspoons melted butter, two of sweet oil; to which add one tablespoon of mustard, one of pepper, one of salt, one of sugar, three of cream; and last, add six large bunches of celery chopped fine, with sufficient vinegar to moisten the whole.

## SWEET BREAD SALAD.

### Mrs. D. C. B.

Four hard boiled eggs, one raw egg, three tablespoons of salad oil, one teaspoon of salt, one of pepper, two of sugar, two of mixed mustard, one half a tea cup of vinegar one calf's sweet bread, and two heads of lettuce. For dressing, mash the yolks and mix the oil thoroughly in them; then add the raw egg well beaten; mix the other ingredients in slowly and thoroughly, adding the vinegar last. Boil the sweet bread thoroughly until tender; pick it up in small pieces; break the lettuce also in small pieces, and then put in a dish alternate layers of lettuce, and sweet bread and dressing. Use the whites of the eggs sliced over the top.

For salmon salad, use the same dressing, omitting the sweet breads, and substituting salmon. Put the salmon on a platter, pour over it the dressing and garnish with celery leaves.

## LOBSTER SALAD.

### Mrs. S. I. D.

Two lobsters, picked fine; four heads of fresh lettuce, cut fine; put in a dish in layers with the lobsters; boil your eggs, mash the yolks, add three tablespoons of melted butter, a teaspoon of mustard, cayenne pepper and salt; two tablespoons of sugar, two cups of vinegar; heat together and pour over when served.

*For the Bath, Toilet, or Laundry,*

## FISH SALAD.

### M. A. T.

Boil tender a white fish or trout; chop fine; add same quantity chopped celery, cabbage or lettuce; season same as chicken salad.

## VEAL SALAD.

### Mrs. G. E. P.

Boil veal until very tender, chop fine and stir into it a nice salad dressing; put in a shallow dish and garnish with slices of lemon and celery; a little chopped cabbage or lettuce may be added, if desired. Boiled ham chopped and seasoned and served in the same manner, is a very nice dish.

## POTATO SALAD.

### M. A. T.

Sliced cold boiled potatoes; almonds blanched and quartered; hichory-nuts, also, if liked; (both of these may be omitted.) A very small quantity of chopped onions; pour over this any good salad dressing, not too much, and garnish with chopped parsley; cold boiled beets, sliced lemon, and anchovies, may be added to the salad, if liked.

## CUCUMBER SALAD.

### Mrs. King.

Take a dozen ripe "white spine" cucumbers; wash, pare and cut into strips, taking out the seeds; cut into pieces, like small dice; to each dozen cucumbers, take twelve large white onions chopped; six large green peppers, also chopped; one quarter pound each of black and white mustard seed, and a gill of celery seed; mix all well together; add a teacup of salt, and hang up in a cotton bag to drain for twenty-four hours. Then add enough clear cold vinegar to cover it; put into stone jars and fasten nearly air tight. In six weeks, it will be fit for use. Excellent.

## TOMATO SALAD.

### Miss Spruance.

Twelve tomatoes, peeled and sliced; four eggs, boiled hard; one egg (raw,) well beaten; one teaspoon salt; one-half teaspoon cayenne pepper; one teaspoon sugar; one teacup of vinegar; set on ice to become perfectly cold.

## DRESSING FOR SALAD.

### Mrs. Hoge.

Two raw eggs, one tablespoon of butter, eight tablespoons of vinegar; one-half teaspoon of mustard; put in a bowl over boiling water and stir until it becomes like cream; pepper and salt to your taste.

## SALAD DRESSING.

### M. A. T.

Take the yolks of two raw eggs, beat with them one teaspoon of made mustard; this mustard should be mixed with water, not vinegar; then add to this, drop by drop, olive oil, stirring constantly until the mixture becomes very thick; then add two teaspoonsful of powdered sugar and a scant one of salt; mix thoroughly; squeeze in the juice of one lemon; beat well, and if too thick, thin with a little sweet cream. If perferred, omit the lemon and cream, and use vinegar. This dressing with lettuce, celery or potato, makes a delicious salad. If used for chicken salad, the yolks of hard boiled eggs added make it richer. Garnish lettuce with nasturtium blossoms and sliced lemon. Garnish potatoes with cold boiled beets, chopped parsley and sliced lemon.

## DRESSING FOR LETTUCE.

### Mrs. H. E. Sargent.

Yolks of three hard boiled eggs; half teaspoon salt; one teaspoon made mustard; four teaspoons sweet oil; four tablespoons cream; three tablespoons vinegar; one raw egg beaten to a froth;

rub the yolks of the eggs to a fine powder, then add the salt, mustard and oil, mixing well together; then add the cream; and after that the vinegar and raw egg.

## DRESSED CABBAGE.
### Mrs. B. J. Seward.

One small teacup vinegar, one egg, two tablespoons sugar, one teaspoon salt, butter half the size of an egg; beat the egg before mixing; stir till boils; cool, then pour over chopped or shaved cabbage.

## HOT SLAW.
### Anonymous.

Cut cabbage in fine shreds; boil in clear water until tender, allowing so little that when done there will be very little left in the stew pan; just before dishing, add a teacup of vinegar, a tablespoon of butter, a little salt and pepper.

## COLD SLAW.
### Carter.

Shave hard white cabbage very fine; for one quart of this slaw take yolks of three eggs; beat them well, stir into them one tumbler and a half of good vinegar, two teaspoons of thick sweet cream, a small piece of butter, a teaspoon of mixed mustard; salt and pepper to taste; mix all together with the yolks and put into a stew pan where it will boil; add the cabbage and let it boil five minutes, stirring all the time; dish the slaw and set it where it will get cold; if the vinegar is very strong, use less in proportion. Add two teaspoons of sugar, if liked.

# Breakfast and Supper.

"Dinner may be pleasant;
So may social tea;
But yet, methinks the breakfast
Is best of all the three." 
—Anon.

## RELISHES.

### OYSTER STEW.
Mrs. A. S. Ewing.

Strain the juice from the oysters placed in the colander into a stew pan; let it come to a boil; remove the scum and a clear liquor will remain; turn cold water upon the oysters, and rinse thoroughly; add them to the liquor, with a cup of cream or milk, butter, salt and cayenne pepper. Have ready buttered dice-shaped pieces of toast upon a meat dish; pour the oysters over, garnish with parsley, and serve hot.

### TOAST.

Toast the bread very quickly, dip each slice in boiling water, (a little salt in the water,) as soon as you have toasted it; then spread it with butter; cover and keep hot as you proceed. Make milk toast in the same way, keeping the milk at nearly boiling heat; it is better to spread the butter on to the bread after it is dipped in hot milk, than to melt it in the milk; thicken what milk is left very little, and pour over the toast when sent to the table.

## FRENCH TOAST.
### Mrs. M. J. Savage.

To one egg thoroughly beaten, put one cup of sweet milk and a little salt. Slice light bread, and dip into the mixture, allowing each slice to absorb some of the milk; then brown on a hot buttered griddle; spread with butter and serve hot.

## TONGUE TOAST.
### M. A. P.

Take cold boiled tongue, mince it fine; mix it with cream or milk, and to every half pint of the mixture, allow the well beaten yolks of two eggs; place over the fire and let it simmer a minute or two; have ready some nicely toasted bread; butter it; place it on a hot dish and pour the mixture over; send to the table hot.

## LEMON TOAST.
### E. A. Forsyth.

Take the yolks of six eggs, beat them well and add three cups of sweet milk; take baker's bread not too stale and cut into slices; dip them into the milk and eggs, and lay the slices into a spider, with sufficient melted butter hot to fry a nice delicate crown; take the whites of the six eggs, and beat them to a froth, adding a large cup of white sugar; add the juice of two lemons, heating well, and adding two cups boiling water; serve over the toast as a sauce, and you will find it a very delicious dish.

## FRIED BREAD IN BATTER.
### M. A. T.

Take one tablespoon sweet light dough; dissolve it in one cup sweet milk; add three or four eggs, one and a half cups flour, one teaspoon of salt; cut some thin slices of light bread, dip in this batter; and fry in hot lard; sprinkle with powdered sugar, and garnish with jelly.

## COD-FISH BALLS.

### Mrs. Banks.

Take four cups of mashed potatoes; three cups of boiled cod-fish minced fine; add butter; mix well together; then add two well beaten eggs, beating it up again thoroughly; drop by spoon-fulls into hot lard and fry the same as doughnuts.

## COD-FISH HASH.

### Mrs. N. P. Wilder.

One pint boiled picked codfish well freshened, one quart cold boiled chopped potatoes mixed well together, three slices salt pork freshened, cut in very small pieces and fried brown; re-move half the pork, and add your fish and potatoes to the re-mainder; let it stand and steam five minutes without stirring; careful not to let it burn; then add one-third cup milk and stir thoroughly; put the remainder of the pork around the edge of the spider, and a little butter over it; simmer it over a slow fire for half an hour, until a brown crust is formed, when turn it over on a platter and serve.

## BEEF HASH.

Chop fine cold beef, either boiled or baked; have ready cold boiled potatoes; to one pint of meat, put one pint and a little more of potatoes, chopped fine; have ready a spider, with a good piece of butter in it; put in the hash; season with pepper and salt, and then add rich milk or cream. Milk is a very great improvement.

## BREAKFAST STEAK.

A nice steak of beef or veal; pound it with a steak mallet, if tough; lay in a baking tin, dredge it lightly with flour, season

with salt and pepper, and if you like, a little chopped parsley;
then put in the oven, and bake for twenty or thirty minutes, or
until sufficiently well done; take it up, put it on the platter, spread
with butter, and dredge **into the** juices **of** the meat in the baking pan, **a little flour,** and season with butter; **let this** boil **up,
and pour over** steak. This is very nice.

## SIDE DISH.

R. A. Sibley.

**Chopped cold meat** well seasoned; wet with gravy, if conven-
**ient, put** it on a platter; then take cold rice made moist with
milk and **one** egg, season with pepper and salt; **if not** sufficient
rice, add powdered bread crumbs; place this around the platter
quite thick; **set in** the oven to heat and brown.

## ANOTHER SIDE DISH.

R. A. Sibley.

Cold turkey, chicken or any cold meat, chopped fine, seasoned with salt, pepper and gravy; lay pie crust round the edge of
the platter, and cover the same; bake a nice brown in the oven.
**Very little** meat makes quite a dish for several persons.

## HAM AND EGGS.

Anonymous.

Take pieces of cold ham chopped, and after cooking, add
beaten eggs to suit your taste.

## A NICE BREAKFAST DISH.

H. N. Jenks.

Mince cold beef or lamb; if beef put in a pinch of pulverized
cloves; if lamb, a pinch of summer savory to season it, very
little pepper and some salt, and put it in a baking dish; mash
potatoes and mix them with cream and butter and a little salt,

and spread them over the meat; beat up an egg with cream or milk, a very little; spread it over the potatoes, and bake it a short time, sufficient to warm it through and brown the potatoes.

## POTATO PUFFS.

### S. S. Peirce.

Take cold roast meat, (either beef, veal or mutton;) clear it from gristle; chop fine; season with pepper and salt; boil and mash some potatoes, and make them into a paste with one or two eggs; roll it out with a little flour; cut it round with a saucer; put your seasoned meat on one-half; fold it over like a puff; turn it neatly around, and fry it a light brown. Nice for breakfast.

## RICE CAKES.

### Mrs. A. M. Gibbs.

One teacup of soft boiled rice, the yolk of one egg, a pinch of salt, two tablespoons of sifted flour, beaten well together; add sweet milk until it is about the consistency of sponge cake or thick cream, and just before baking stir in lightly the beaten white of the egg. The less flour used the better for invalids.

## CHICKEN CROQUETTES.

### Mrs. Chaffee, Detroit.

One plump chicken, two pounds veal cut from the round. Boil chicken and veal separately in cold water, just enough to cover; pick to pieces and chop. Cut up one-third of a loaf of bread and soak in the broth of the chicken while warm; put all in a chopping bowl; season with salt, pepper, mace and nutmeg; beat three eggs light and mix with the above ingredients; make up in oblong balls; fry brown in hot lard and butter equal parts.

# BREAKFAST CAKES.

### LAPLANDERS FOR BREAKFAST.
#### Mrs. A. L. Chetlain.

Three eggs, three cups of flour, three cups sweet milk, one tablespoon of melted butter, and a little salt; beat well together, then bake in iron moulds.

### BREAKFAST GEMS.
#### Mrs. Brown.

One cup sweet milk, one and a half cups flour, one egg, one teaspoon salt; beaten together five minutes; bake in *hot* gem pans, in a hot oven about fifteen minutes.

### BREAKFAST BUNS.
#### Mrs. J. W. Preston.

Two cups of flour, three-fourths cup of corn meal, three-fourths cup of butter, one-half cup of sugar, two eggs unbeaten, one cup of milk, three teaspoons baking powder; bake in hot oven twenty minutes.

### QUICK SALLY LUNN.

One cup of sugar, one-half a cup of butter; stir well together, and then add one or two eggs; put in one good pint of sweet milk, and with sufficient flour to make a batter about as stiff as cake; put in three teaspoons of baking powder; bake and eat hot with butter, for tea or breakfast.

## BREAKFAST CAKE.

### Mrs. C. Bradley.

One pint of flour, three tablespoons of butter, three table-spoons of sugar, one egg, one cup sweet milk, one teaspoon cream tartar, one-half teaspoon soda; to be eaten with butter.

## RYE CAKES FOR TEA.

### Harriet N. Jenks.

Two teacups of rye flour, one of wheat flour, one of sour milk, one-half teaspoon of soda, put in the sour milk, and while foam-ing stir it in the flour and rye, with one-half teaspoon of salt, one-half teacup of molasses; make it stiff and turn it into a but-tered pan; spread it smooth with a spoon dipped in hot water; bake one-half hour.

## RYE GRIDDLE CAKES.

Stir into sour milk sufficient rye flour to make a batter for griddle cakes; add salt, and a little soda, and bake on a hot griddle. These are very simple, but very nice.

## JOLLY BOYS.

### Jeannie Brayton.

One quart of corn meal; scald and cool; one pint of flour, two eggs, one teaspoon soda, two of cream-tartar, a little milk, salt; make as thick as pancakes, and fry in hot lard. Nice for breakfast.

## GRAHAM BREAKFAST CAKES.

### Mrs. A. M. Gibbs.

Two cups of Graham flour, one cup of wheat flour, two eggs well beaten; mix with sweet milk, to make a very thin batter; bake in gem irons; have the irons hot, then set them on the upper grate in the oven; will bake in fifteen minutes.

*For the Bath, Toilet, or Laundry,*

## TEA CAKE.

### Mrs. H. P. Stowell.

One egg, one cup sugar, one cup sweet milk, piece **of butter** size of an **egg,** one teaspoon cream-tartar, one-half teaspoon soda, one pint of flour. Eaten warm.

## COTTAGE CHEESE.

### Mrs. A. M. Gibbs.

**Pour** boiling water on the **thick** milk in **the** pan **in** which it **has** turned, stirring while you pour; **as** soon as the milk separates from **the** whey and begins to appear cooked, let it settle; in a minute **or** two most of the water and whey can be poured off; if not sufficiently cooked, more hot water may **be** used; set the pan on edge and with your **spoon** or hand draw **the curd** to the upper side, pressing **out** as much **water as possible;** if desired, it can stand a few moments in **cold water; when** squeezed dry, work the curd fine, rolling **it** between the hands; add salt and cream to taste; in very warm weather when the milk has turned quickly, it is very palatable without the addition of cream.

# VEGETABLES.

See dying vegetables life sustain;
See life dissolving, vegetate again.
—POPE.

## BOILED POTATOES.

Old potatoes are better for being peeled and put in cold water an hour before putting over **to** boil. They should then be put into fresh cold water, when set over the fire. New potatoes should always be put into boiling water, and it is best to prepare them just **in time for** cooking.

## POTATOES AND CREAM.

Mince **cold** boiled potatoes fine; **put them into a** spider with melted **butter in** it; let them fry **a little in the butter** well covered; then put in a fresh piece of butter, season with salt and pepper, and pour over cream or rich milk; let it boil up **once and** serve.

## POTATOES FRIED.

### Mrs. A.

Pare potatoes; **cut in** pieces one-half inch square, and as long as the potato; keep them in cold water till wanted; drop in boiling lard; when nearly done, take them out **with** a skimmer and drain them; boil up the lard again, **and drop** them back, and **fry till done**; this makes them **puff up**; sprinkle with salt and serve very hot.

## SARATOGA FRIED POTATOES.

**Cut into thin slices; put them in cold** water over night with **a** small piece alum **to make them** crisp; rinse in cold water, and dry with **crash towel; fry light** brown in boiling lard.

## PARSNEPS.

Boil until tender in a little salted water; **then** take up; skim them, cut in strips, dip in beaten egg, and fry in melted butter or hot lard.

## BAKED SQUASH.

Cut in pieces, scrape well, bake **from** one to one and a half hours, according **to the** thickness **of** the squash; **to** be eaten with salt and butter **as** sweet potatoes.

## FRIED SQUASHES.

### Mrs. F. M. Craigie.

Cut the squash **into thin** slices, and sprinkle it with salt; **let it** stand a few moments; then beat two eggs, and dip the squash into the egg, then fry it brown in **butter.**

## GREEN-CORN OYSTERS.

To a pint of grated corn add two **well** beaten eggs; one-half cup of cream, **and** a half **cup of** flour, with one-half spoonful of baking powder stirred in it; season with pepper and salt, and fry in butter, dropping the batter in spoonsful; **serve a** few at a time, **very hot, as** a relish with meats.

## GREEN-CORN **PATTIES.**

### M.

Grate as much **corn as will make** one pint; **one teacup flour,** one-half teacup butter, one egg, **pepper and salt to taste. If too** thick, **add** a little milk, and fry in butter.

## SUCCOTASH.

One pint **of green corn cut from the cob,** and two-thirds of **a** pint of Lima beans; let them stew in just enough water to cover them until tender, then season with butter, pepper, salt and a little milk; simmer together a few moments and serve.

## BOSTON BAKED BEANS.

**Soak over** night one pint of beans **in** clear water; **in the** morning parboil the beans, and at the same time, **in** another dish, **parboil a** piece of salt pork, about three inches long **and** wide **and** thick; **drain** off the water from the beans and pork; put both **together in a** deep pan with the pork at top; season with one tablespoon of molasses, and bake for several hours. Add a little **water** when they are put in to bake.

## ASPARAGUS.

**Cut off the green** ends, and chop up **the remainder of the** stalks; boil these until tender, and season **with** salt **and pepper;** have ready some toasted bread in a deep dish; mix together equal parts of flour and butter **to a** cream; add to this slowly, enough of the asparagus water or clear hot water, to make a sauce; boil this up once; put the asparagus on the toast, and pour over all the sauce.

## BAKED CABBAGE.

Boil a cabbage, then put in a colander and drain it until perfectly dry; then chop fine; put in pepper, salt and a little cream, and put in an earthen baking pan, and into the oven. Bake one hour.

## ESCALOPED TOMATOES.

Put in an earthen baking dish, a layer of cracker crumbs and small bits of butter; then a layer of tomatoes with a very little sugar sprinkled over them; then another layer of cracker crumbs seasoned with butter, and a layer of tomatoes, until your dish is full, with the cracker crumbs at the top; pour over all this a little water to moisten, and bake half an hour.

## FRIED EGG PLANT.

### Mrs. F. M. Cragie.

Slice the egg plant, at least half an inch thick; pare each piece carefully, and lay in salt and water, putting a plate upon the topmost, to keep it under the brine, and let them remain for an hour or more. Wipe each slice, dip in beaten egg, then in cracker crumbs, and fry in hot lard until well done and nicely browned.

## MACARONI.

### Mrs. M. C. Gridley, Evanston.

Cook macaroni in water until soft; then put in a deep dish, with alternate layers of grated crackers and cheese, a little salt; fill up the dish with milk and bake one hour.

## YANKEE BAKED BEANS.

### Mrs. Higgins.

Boil the beans until they begin to crack, with a pound or two of salt fat pork; put the beans in the baking pan; score the pork across the top, and settle in the middle; add two tablespoons of sugar or molasses, and bake in a moderate oven two hours; they should be very moist when first put into the oven, or they will grow too dry in baking; do not forget the sweetening if you want Yankee baked beans.

## BAKED TOMATOES.
### Mrs. F. B. Orr.

Pare and slice, cover the bottom of a dish sprinkled with bread crumb or crackers; put in a layer of tomatoes and sprinkle crumbs over them; fill up the dish, with crumbs upon the top; season the whole with salt and pepper.

## FRIED TOMATOES.

Cut a large Feejee tomato in half, flour the cut side, heat very hot, and put the floured side down; when brown on one side, turn; when done, pour over a tea cup of hot cream or rich milk.

## TOMATO HASH.

Butter the dish well; put in a layer of sliced tomatoes, a layer of cold meat, sliced thin; then a layer of bread and butter, and so on until the dish is full, seasoning well with pepper and salt, and beaten eggs poured over the top.  Bake brown.

# Puddings and Pies.

*" And solid pudding against empty praise."*

## PIE CRUST.
### Mrs. A. M.

One large cup of butter, one large cup of lard; stir together with a knife to get all the lumps out; sift one quart of flour, and mix into it with (ice water), to made it the consistency to roll out, saving flour enough from the quart for that purpose; *avoid kneading it; use hands as little as possible.*

## PIE CRUST.
### Mrs. C. Bradley.

To four cups of flour, one full cup of lard, or half lard and half of butter, rubbed well into the flour; then add cold water enough to roll; add white of one egg beaten to a stiff froth.

## CREAM PIE.
### Mrs. Higgins.

One cup sweet cream, one egg, one teaspoon flour, two tablespoons sugar.

## CREAM PIE.
### Mrs. F. M. Craigie.

Roll out the under crust and cover the plate; then roll out the upper crust and spread it over the under crust, placing little

---

wedges of paste between, to prevent them from sticking together; after these are baked, take off the upper crust and pour in your cream; replace the upper crust, and it is ready for the table. The cream is made by taking two eggs, one pint of milk and one tablespoon of flour; sweeten to taste and flavor with essence of lemon; boil them well together in a tin set in boiling water until like thick cream, stirring all the time. This makes two pies.

## CREAM PIE.
### Mrs. S. Cornell.

Butter the size of an egg; one cup sugar and two eggs stirred together; then add one-third cup milk, two cups flour, with two teaspoons baking powder, stirred in before sifting into the mixture; bake in two pie tins for two pies. For the filling—one pint milk, taking out enough to wet one-half cup flour, and boil the rest; two-thirds cup sugar and yolks of two eggs; stir the filling mixture together, and boil three minutes; when cold flavor with lemon or vanilla, and spread between the upper and lower crusts; when cut smothly apart. This makes two very delicious pies.

## CREAM PIE.
### Mrs. Bartlett.

One cup powdered sugar, one cup flour, one teaspoon cream-tartar and one-half teaspoon soda, five eggs beaten separately; grated rind of lemon. Cream—set in hot water one-half pint of milk; when scalding hot add one-half cup sugar, a little salt and one egg beaten together; stir until thick, and when cool, add one tablespoon vanilla; put between cakes.

## PHILADELPHIA BUTTER PIE.
### Mrs. A. N. Arnold.

Cover a pie plate with crust, as for a custard pie; take a peice of butter the size of an egg, two-thirds of a cup of sugar, one cup sweet cream, one tablespoon of flour; stir butter, flour and sugar together; then stir in the cream; pour in the plate; bake until brown.

## SQUASH PIE.

### Mrs. P. B. Ayer.

One small cup of dry maple sugar dissolved in a little water, two cups of strained squash stirred in the sugar; add four eggs, two teaspoons of allspice, two cups of milk; one teaspoonful of butter, and two of ginger, added last.   This makes two pies.

## SQUASH PIE.

### Mrs. Rice.

One pint of squash, one pint of milk, three eggs, one-half of a nutmeg, one teaspoon of cinnamon; one teaspoon of vanilla, two cups of sugar; put everything into the squash; the milk last.

## SQUASH PIE.

### Mrs. L. H. Davis.

Two teacups of boiled squash, three-fourths teacup of brown sugar, three eggs, two tablespoons of molasses, one tablespoon of melted butter, one tablespoon of ginger, one teaspoon of cinnamon, two teacups of milk, a little salt.   Makes two plate pies.

## CUSTARD PIE.

### E. E. Macey.

Make a custard of the yolks of three eggs with milk, seasoned to the taste; bake it in ordinary crust; put it in a brick oven, that the crust may not be heavy, and as soon as that is heated remove it to a place in the oven of a more moderate heat, that the custard may bake slowly, and not curdle; when done, beat the whites to a froth, add sugar and spread over the top, and return to the oven to brown slightly; a small pinch of salt added to a custard, heightens the flavor; a little soda in the crust prevents it from being heavy.   Very nice.

*Charles Harms, General Caterer,* 955 *Wabash Ave., near* 22d.

# WASHINGTON PIE.
### Mrs. A. M. Chetlain.

One and one-half cups of sugar, one-half cup of butter, one-half cup of sweet milk, three eggs, two and one-half cups of flour, two teaspoons of baking powder; bake in three layers, in jelly cake tins; pare and grate two large apples; add one cup of sugar, grated rind and juice of one lemon; put this on the stove and let it steam until it forms a jelly; then take it off and stir in the yolk of one egg. When the cake and jelly are both cold, put them together.

# WASHINGTON PIE.
### Mrs. D.

One cup of sugar, three eggs, one and one-half cups of flour, one teaspoon of baking powder; flavor to taste; bake as for jelly cake in layers, and spread between the layers raspberry jam.

# COCOANUT PIE.
### Mrs. E. P. Thomas, Rockford, Ill.

Grate fresh cocoanut; to one cup of cocoanut, add one and one-half cup of sweet milk, the yolks of four eggs, a little salt, and sweeten to taste; one tablespoon of melted butter; beat the whole five or six minutes; beat the whites of the eggs to a stiff froth, and put over the top just long enough to slightly brown before taking the pie from the oven. If you use desiccated cocoanut, soak it in the milk over night.

# COCOANUT PIE.
### Mrs. Taylor, Fort Wayne.

One and one-half pints of milk, six eggs, one cocoanut, three cups sugar, one-half cup butter; mix sugar and butter, then the eggs, then the cocoanut, and lastly the milk.

*Charles Harms, General Caterer, 955 Wabash Ave., near 22d.*

## POLISH TARTLETS.

Roll some good puff-paste out thin, and cut it into two and a half inch squares; brush each square over with the whites of an egg, then fold down the corners, so that they all meet in the middle of each piece of paste; slightly press the two pieces together, brush them over with the egg; sift over sugar; bake in a quick oven for a quarter of an hour; when they are done, make a little hole in the middle, and fill with jam or jelly.

## LEMON TARTS.

Mix well together the juice and grated rind of two lemons, two cups of sugar, two eggs, and the crumbs of sponge cake; beat it all together until smooth; put into twelve patty pans, lined with puff paste, and bake until the crust is done.

## LEMON RAISIN PIE.

### Anonymous.

One cup of sugar, one lemon, one cup of raisins, one cup water; chop lemon and raisins fine, cook in the water three-quarters of an hour.

## LEMON PIE.

### Mrs. A. M. Chetlain.

One tablespoon of corn starch stirred in a little cold water; add one cup of boiling water, let it come to a boil, then add seven tablespoons of sugar, yolks of four eggs, grated rind and juice of two lemons; bake with a bottom crust, then beat the white of four eggs and a little sugar, pour this over the top, and then brown.

## LEMON PIE.

### Mrs. L. Bradley.

One lemon, grate the rind and squeeze the juice; three eggs, one tablespoon of butter, three tablespoons of sugar, one cup of milk; beat the white of eggs and stir in after the rest are mixed.

## ACID PIE.

M. A. Bingham, Elgin, Ill.

One cup of soft bread or crackers, one cup of sugar, two cups of water, little lemon, one egg, one teaspoon of tartaric acid.

## LEMON PIE

Mrs. H. L. Adams and others.

One tablespoon of corn starch, boiled in a cup of water; one egg, one cup of sugar, juice and rind of one lemon; bake in a crust. This will fill one shallow plate.

## LEMON PIE.

Mrs. J. W. Preston.

Six eggs, (less two whites,) two cups of white sugar, one cup of sweet milk, two tablespoons of corn starch dissolved in the milk; two large lemons, juice and rind; bake slowly until set. Meringue for the top: White of two eggs beaten with six table-spoons of powdered sugar; bake to a light brown, after having spread over the surface of the pie.

## LEMON PIE.

Mrs. G. L. Dunlap.

Yolks of six eggs, two cups of pulverized sugar, beaten well together, two and a half cups of milk, three lemons (only juice), a little salt, mix well, bake; then take the whites of the eggs, add one-half cup of pulverized sugar, beaten well together, then spread over the top of pies and brown. This receipt will make two good sized pies.

## LEMON PIE.

Miss Annie Slocum.

Two lemons, five eggs, one cup of sugar, one cup of water, two tablespoons corn starch; grate the outside of the lemon rinds into a dish, then cut in half and remove the seeds, scooping the pulp and juice into the dish with a silver spoon; add the sugar and water, wetting the starch with some of the water; mix it in with the yolks and one white of an egg, (the eggs well beaten first,) pour into two tins lined with pastry, and bake; beat the remaining whites; gradually stir in ten tablespoons of pulverized sugar, and when the pies are done, spread the snow over them, and place in the oven until brown.

### LEMON PIE.
#### M.

For three pies, take the rind and juice of four lemons, the yolks of nine eggs, nearly one cup of butter, two cups of sugar, one-half cup of sweet milk; beat the whites of six eggs with six ounces of sugar; put on the top, after baking, and brown slightly.   Very rich.

### LEMON PIES.
#### Mrs. Beyer and others.

For one pie, take one large lemon, the yolks of two eggs, one cup of sugar, one-half cup of cold water, one teaspoon of butter. Icing for the same:  Whites of two eggs, two tablespoons of pulverized sugar; brown it nicely in the oven.

### MINCE MEAT.
#### Mrs. Higgins.

Six pounds of beef and six pounds of apples, chopped fine; four pounds of sugar, two of citron, three of raisins, three of currants, one of suet, two quarts of boiled cider, one-half cup of salt, two nutmegs, two tablespoons of ground cloves, two of allspice, two of cinnamon; when used, enough sweet cider should be added to make the mixture quite moist.

### MINCE MEAT
#### Mrs. J. M. Durand.

Two pounds of raisins, one of currants, one of suet, two and one-half of sugar, one-quarter of citron, one-eighth of cinnamon, two chopped pippins, three lemons, two nutmegs; wine, **brandy** and cloves to taste.

## MINCE PIE.

### Mrs. Pulnise.

**Two** pounds of suet (chopped fine,) **four pounds** of mince **meat, three** cups of raisins, **three cups of** currants, **two** pieces of citron, twelve cups of fine **chopped apples, five** large teaspoons **of cloves,** four large teaspoons **of** ginger, **four** nutmegs, **one quart of syrup, four** quarts **of cider,** five teaspoon of cinnamon, **one teaspoon of** pepper, salt **to taste,** one cup **of sugar,** two lemons (juice, and rind grated;) **stir** all together; **let** come to a boil, then **put** in a jar; when making pies put a tablespoon of brandy **to** a pie.

## MINCE PIE.

### Mrs. James Morgan.

Boil beef until tender, (three **pounds** after it is boiled,) **when** cold, chop fine; add three pounds **of fine** chopped suet, **and mix** with the beef; add a tablespoon **of salt,** six pounds **of apples, four** pounds of currants, **six pounds** of raisins, two pounds **of** citron; season to taste with **powdered** cinnamon, mace, cloves **and** nutmeg; add boiled cider, brandy and **wine until** quite soft; **mix well** and pack **in stone** jars, pour brandy **over** the top and **cover tightly.** This **will** make about **five** gallons. Add two **pounds** sugar.

## MINCE PIE.

### C. Kennicott.

Three pints apples, one pint boiled beef, one-half pint of butter or beef drippings, one pint of molasses, one-half pint of water, one and a half teaspoons allspice, one teaspoon cinnamon, one teaspoon salt, three-fourths teaspoon cloves, two and a half large spoons of vinegar, one-half of a nutmeg. Young housekeepers will find this recipe a great comfort.

## MOCK MINCE PIE.

### Mrs. G. F. DeForrest, Freeport, Ill.

One egg, three or four large crackers, or six or eight small
ones, one-half cup molasses, one-half cup sugar, one-half cup
vinegar, one-half cup strong tea, one cup chopped raisins, a
small piece of butter, spice and salt.

## SHAM MINCE PIE.

### Eliza Wormley.

Ten crackers, made fine; two cups of water, one of vinegar,
one-half of butter, one of molasses, five eggs; add raisins; beat
the eggs, butter and sugar together; spices and sugar to taste.

## MINCE PIE.

### Mrs. J. R. Adams.

Boil and chop three pounds of lean beef, two pounds of suet,
four of good raisins, four of currants, one of citron, four of sugar,
grated rind and juice of three lemons, and two sweet oranges,
three large tablespoons of cinnamon, three grated nutmegs, two
tablespoons of cloves, two of mace, one quart of cooking brandy, some wine, four tablespoons of salt; pack it down tightly in
a jar, and stir well before using. In making a pie, take nearly
two-thirds of apples and more than one-third meat; add enough
cider to make very juicy, and enough sugar to make very sweet.

## VINEGAR PIE.

### Ella Guild.

One cup of sugar, one-half of vinegar, two teaspoons of flour,
one of butter, one of cinnamon, two cups of water; boil all together till thick, and bake as you would a custard pie. This is
very nice.

## RICE PIE.

### Mrs. A. S. Ewing.

One quart of milk, boiled; one small teacup of rice flour mixed in a little cold milk; add to the boiling milk two table-spoons of butter; when cold, add five eggs well beaten; sweeten to taste; flavor with vanilla, and bake.

## FRUIT PIE.

### Mrs. M. P. Carroll.

Must be baked in a two quart tin basin; to give it the right shape the basin must be of nearly the same size top and bottom; first make a nice pie-crust; put a layer of it in the bottom, but not around the sides of the dish; then a layer of chopped sour apples, two inches thick; then a layer of chopped raisins; sprinkle sugar over this, pieces of butter, and any spice you like—cloves and nutmeg are nice; another layer of crust and fruit, &c., until your dish is full; put a crust on top; bake slowly for two hours; when done, turn bottom upwards on a plate, and before putting it on the table sprinkle fine sugar over it. It is quite as good when warmed again as when first baked. It takes one pound of raisins, ten or twelve good sized apples, two large cups of sugar, more if you like.

## TRANSPARENT PIE.

### Mrs. Perry Smith.

Five eggs, butter the size of a large egg, two coffee cups of sugar, three tablespoons of thick cream; divide the sugar, beat half with the butter, and the other half with the yolks; add the whipped cream; whip the cream and lay it on a sieve, so that the thin part sifts through; put sponge cake in a mould, dipping the edges of each piece in the white of eggs, so they will stick together; put sponge cake over the top of the mould.

*Charles* Harms, *General Caterer, 955 Wabash Ave., near 22d.*

## EVE'S PUDDING.

### Mrs. L. Bradley and Mrs. D. S. Munger.

If you want a good pudding, mind what you are taught;
Take eggs six in number, when bought for a groat;
The fruit with which Eve her husband did cozen,
Well pared, and well chopped, at least half a dozen ;
Six ounces of bread, let Moll eat the crust,
And crumble the rest, as fine as the dust ;
Six ounces of currants, from the stem you must sort,
Lest you break out your teeth, and spoil all the sport ;
Six ounces of sugar, won't make it too sweet ;
Some salt, and some nutmeg, will make it complete ;
Three hours let it boil, without any flutter ;
But Adam won't like it, without wine and butter.

## SUET PUDDING.

### Mrs. E. R. Harmon.

One cup of suet chopped fine, one cup chopped raisins, one cup of molasses, one cup of sweet milk ; three teaspoons of baking powder; spice to your taste; four cups of flour; mix and steam three hours.

## SUET PUDDING.

### Mrs. Bartlett.

One cup suet, one cup sugar, one cup milk, one cup chopped raisins, three cups flour, one teaspoon salt, one teaspoon soda ; spice to taste ; boil three hours.

## SUET PUDDING.

### Mrs. J. H. Brown.

Two cups of chopped suet, two of raisins, two of molasses, four of flour, one of milk, three teaspoons of baking powder; boil three and one-half hours; eat while hot. Sauce for same : One cup of sugar, one-half of butter, one egg, one tablespoon of wine or vinegar; beat fifteen minutes and heat to a scald.

## SUET PUDDING.
### Mrs. Henry Stevens.

One teacup of suet chopped fine, one teacup of molasses, one teacup of sweet milk, three and a half teacups of flour, one cup fruit, one teaspoon soda; steam two hours. Sauce for same: One coffee cup pulverized sugar, one-half teacup butter; stir these to a cream; place the dish in a kettle of boiling water; stir in white of one egg beaten to a stiff froth; one teaspoon of vanilla; serve hot.

## SUET PUDDING.
### Mrs. S. A. Tolman.

One cup sugar, one-half cup raisins, one cup suet, one cup sweet milk, two eggs, one teaspoon cream-tartar, one-half teaspoon soda, cinnamon, ten whole cloves. Sauce: One tablespoon of butter; boil in a pint of water, add flour, sugar and nutmeg.

## SUET PUDDING.
### Mrs. W. Butterfield.

One cup of suet, one cup of molasses, one cup of milk, one cnp of raisins, three and half cups of flour, one egg, one tablespoon of cloves, one tablespoon of cinnamon, one nutmeg, a little salt, one teaspoon of soda (dissolve in the milk;) steam three hours.

## FRUIT PUDDING.
### Mrs. Taylor, Fort Wayne.

One quart of flour, two tablespoons of butter, one teaspoon of salt, two teaspoons of baking powder; make a soft dough of milk or water, roll out thin and spread with fruit; roll it up and boil three quarters of an hour.

## POOR MAN'S PUDDING.
### Mrs. C. H. Wheeler.

One cup of suet, one cup of molasses, three cups of flour, one egg, one cup raisins seeded, one teaspoon of soda dissolved in a cup of sweet milk, spices to suit the taste; steam three hours, and serve with liquid sauce.

## PLUM PUDDING.

### Mrs. H. E. Houghton.

One cup suet, one cup sweet milk, one cup molasses, one cup sugar, one cup currants, two and a half cups raisins, four cups flour, one teaspoon cinnamon, one teaspoon cloves, one teaspoon spice, one teaspoon soda; boil three hours.

## PLUM PUDDING.

### Mrs. H. S. Towle.

One pint chopped suet, one pint sour apples, one pint raisins, one pint currants, one-half pint sugar, one-half pint sweet milk, one cup of citron; beat eight eggs and mix with the above, and add sufficient flour to make it stick together; boil three hours in a cloth bag; serve with brandy sauce.

## ENGLISH FRUIT PUDDING.

### Mrs. H. S. Bristol.

One pound currants, one pound stoned raisins, one pound sugar, one pound suet, two pounds of grated or soaked bread, six eggs, one-half teaspoon saleratus, one teaspoon salt, and one grated nutmeg; crumb the soft part of the bread fine; soak the crust with boiling milk, or water will do; beat up the eggs and put all together, mixing thoroughly with the hands; take a square piece of cotton cloth and lay in a tin pan, put the pudding into the cloth and tie down close; put into a pot full of boiling water, and boil five hours; as the water boils away, keep adding more.

## ENGLISH PLUM PUDDING.

### M. Walker.

One pound raisins, (stoned), one pound of currants, one pound suet very finely chopped, one pound flour, seven eggs, two wine glasses brandy, **three of sweet wine,** sugar and spice to taste; (it **may** require **a little sweet milk) tie it** tightly in a well floured cloth, which should be first dipped in hot **water, and boil** for four hours; **or** it may be boiled in a pudding form.

## PLUM PUDDING.

### Mrs. E. Hempstead.

One pint raisins, one pint currants, one pint **suet,** one pint **flour, one-half pint** bread **crumbs, one cup** milk, **five** eggs, spices **to taste, a little** candied orange and lemon; **mix** all together **and boil three hours.** To be eaten with wine **sauce.**

## BLACK PUDDING.

### Mrs. H. M. Kidder, Cranston, Ill.

**One teacup of molasses, one teacup of butter,** one teacup of sugar, two teacups of flour, one teacup **sour milk,** four eggs, one nutmeg, **one teaspoon** soda; **mix** butter **and sugar to a** cream, **add** eggs **well beaten,** then **molasses, then nutmeg,** then flour **and sour** milk; **last,** soda dissolved **in a little warm water; steam** three hours. **This** pudding **can be made Saturday** and heated **over again for Sunday. Sauce for same: Half** cup **butter,** one of **sugar,** worked thoroughly together to a cream; put a teacup and **a half of water in** sauce **pan, and when** it boils, thicken with **flour to the consistency of** cream; take from the fire and stir **rapidly into it the butter** and sugar; **it** will be like white foam; **flavor** to taste. This **is** an excellent sauce for all puddings.

## BIRD'S NESTS.

### Mrs. F. M. Craigie.

Pare **six or** eight large apples, (Spitzenbergs **or** Greenings are best,) **and** remove the **core** by cutting **from** the end down into the middle, **so as to leave the** apple **whole,** except where the core has been removed; place them as near together as they can stand with the open part **upward, in** a deep pie-dish; next make a thin batter, using one quart sweet milk, three eggs with sufficient flour, and pour it into the dish around the apples, also filling the cavities in them; bake them in a quick oven; eat them with butter and sugar.

## CHOCOLATE PUDDING.

### Mrs. Packard.

One quart milk, three tablespoons sugar, four tablespoons corn starch, two and a half tablespoons chocolate; scald the milk over boiling water; dissolve the corn starch in a little scalded milk, and before it thickens add the chocolate dissolved in boiling water; stir until sufficiently cooked. Use with cream, or sauce of butter and sugar, stirred to a cream.

## COCOANUT PUDDING.

### C. A. Tinkham.

One quart sweet milk, ten tablespoons grated cocoanut, one cup powdered sugar, and whites of ten eggs; bake one hour, evenly and slowly; to be served cold, with sugar and cream.

## A DELMONICO PUDDING.

### Mrs. De Forrest.

Three tablespoons of corn starch, the yolks of five eggs, six tablespoons of sugar; beat the eggs light, then add the sugar, and beat again till very light; mix the corn starch with a little cold milk, mix all together, and stir into it one quart of milk, just as it is about to boil, having added a little salt; stir it until it has thickened well; pour it into a dish for the table, and place it in the oven until it will bear icing; place over the top a layer of canned peaches, and it improves it to mix the syrup of the peaches with the custard part; beat the whites to a stiff froth, with two tablespoons white sugar to an egg, then put it into the oven till it is a light brown.

## QUEEN'S PUDDING.
### Mrs. A. P. Wightman, Evanston.

One quart of sweet milk, one pint of bread crumbs, five eggs, one teaspoon of corn starch, one large, or two small, lemons, one cup of common sugar, and one of pulverized sugar; bring the milk to a scald, pour it over the bread crumbs and let it cool; beat the yolks of the eggs and one cup of common sugar together, and mix in the cornstarch also; just before putting in to bake, add the grated rind of the lemon, and bake twenty minutes. Beat the whites of the eggs and one cup of pulverized sugar together, and add the lemon juice; when the pudding is done, put this on the top and set it in the oven again for a few minutes; to be eaten cold.

## QUEEN OF PUDDINGS.
### Mrs. L. H. Clement.

One pint of nice bread crumbs, one quart of milk, one cup of sugar, the yolks of four eggs well beaten, the rind of one lemon grated, and butter the size of an egg; bake three-quarters of an hour; beat the whites of the eggs to a stiff froth, adding a cup of powdered sugar and the juice of the lemon; spread this over the pudding when done and replace in the oven until slightly browned.

## ROLY-POLY.
### M.

Take one quart of flour; make good biscuist crust; roll out one-half inch thick and spread with any kind of fruit, fresh or preserved; fold so that the fruit will not run out; dip cloth into boiling water, and flour it and lay around the pudding loosely, leaving room to swell; steam one or one and one-half hours; serve with boiled sauce; or lay in steamer without a cloth, and steam for one hour.

## RAILROAD PUDDING.

### E. Gage.

Cook a dozen apples soft, then stir in about a pint of Graham flour; salt it; then eat with sugar, cream and butter; it is very simple, and good for people troubled with dyspepsia.

## RICE PUDDING.

### E. Gage.

One quart of milk, with two tablespoons of rice; let it come to a boil, then pour it over two tablespoons of sugar, one-half cup of raisins, a little lump of butter, flavor with ground cinnamon. Bake until thick.

## RICE PUDDING WITHOUT EGGS.

### Mrs. C. H. Wheeler and others.

Two quarts of milk, half a teacup of rice, a little less than a teacup of sugar, the same quantity of raisins, a teaspoon of cinnamon or allspice; wash the rice, and put it with the rest of the ingredients into the milk; bake rather slowly from two to three hours; stir two or three times the first hour of baking. If properly done, this pudding is delicious.

## COTTAGE PUDDING.

### Mr. G. S. Whitaker.

One cup of sugar, one cup of sweet milk, one pint of flour, two tablespoons of melted butter, one teaspoon of soda, two teaspoons of cream tartar, one egg.

## COTTAGE PUDDING.

### M. G. Rand.

One teacup of white sugar, one-half cup of butter, (or little less,) one cup sweet milk, one egg, a little nutmeg, one pint of flour, three teaspoons of baking powder; rub the butter, sugar and egg together until light, add the nutmeg and milk, stir the baking powder into the flour while dry, and add just as the pudding is to be put in the oven; bake in a quart basin, very slowly; bring to the table hot, cut like cake, and serve with sauce made according to the following directions: Rub one tablespoon of flour in a little cold water until smooth, then turn it into one pint of boiling water, letting it cook five minutes, stirring constantly; add sugar, salt and nutmeg to suit the taste.

## COTTAGE PUDDING.
### Mrs. D. C. Norton.

One cup of sugar, butter the size of a large egg, one cup sour milk, one teaspoon saleratus, (sweet milk is just as good if two teaspoons of baking powder is used instead of saleratus,) two eggs, two heaping cups of flour, a little salt.

## PUDDING IN HASTE.
### Mrs. F. E. Stearns.

Three eggs, three cups of milk, and three cups of flour; bake in patty tins or cups, and serve with hot sauce.

## MINUTE PUDDING.
### C. Kennicott.

One-half cup milk, five large spoons flour, three eggs, one-half teaspoon of salt, stirred smoothly together; stir this into one pint of boiling milk.

## A QUICK PUDDING.
### Mrs. A. W. D.

One-half pint of milk, one-half pint of cream, three eggs beaten separately, little over one-half pint flour; season with lemon or vanilla.

## BOILED INDIAN PUDDING.

### Mrs. A. W. D.

Three cups of raisins, one cup of chopped suet or butter, one pint of Indian meal, four sour apples, one quart of milk, one egg, and a little salt.

## BAKED INDIAN PUDDING.

### Mrs. A. W. D.

Seven spoons of Indian meal, two spoons of butter, one-half teaspoon salt, one teacup molasses, ginger or cinnamon to your taste; pour into these a quart of milk while boiling hot; mix well and put in a buttered dish; just as you put it in the oven, stir in a teacup of cold water, which will produce the same effect as eggs. Bake three-quarters of an hour.

## BOILED INDIAN PUDDING.

### Mrs. De Forest.

One quart of good butter milk or thick sour milk, two table-spoons of sweet cream, three eggs, one teaspoon soda, three handsful of flour, a little salt, Indian meal to make a rather thin batter.

## INDIAN PUDDING.

### Mrs. Benham.

One quart of milk, four tablespoons (heaping) of Indian meal, one tablespoon flour, one teaspoon of ginger, one of cinnamon, one lemon peel, one teaspoon salt, two eggs, one cup molasses; bake three hours, not in too hot an oven; boil the meal in half the quantity of milk, one cup raisins, one cup of suet, (not too full), add the remainder of milk before the eggs.

## GRAHAM PUDDING.

### Thos. G. F. De Forest.

One and a half coffee cups Graham flour, one-half coffee cup molasses, one-fourth coffee cup butter, one-half coffee cup sweet milk, one egg, one even teaspoon soda, one good half cup raisins, one good half cup currants; salt and spice to taste; steam two and a half or three **hours; serve** with liquid sauce.

## SUNDERLAND PUDDING.

### Mrs. C. M. Dickerman, Rockford.

Eight tablespoons flour, **four** eggs, three pints sweet milk, **one** tablespoon melted butter, one-half **nutmeg; bake in** a pie **tin;** serve with pudding sauce.

## DANDY JACK.

### Mrs. Benham.

**One pint** milk, yolks of three eggs, **two** heaping tablespoons corn starch, one-half cup sugar; flavor **as you like;** for top, the whites of the eggs and a little sugar.

## PRETTY PUDDING.

### Mrs. Charles Bradbury.

**One** tablespoon flour wet with **one-half cup of cold** milk, the yolks of three eggs beaten, **one small** cup of sugar; mix these together; put one quart of milk **in a kettle, and set it in** boiling **water; when the milk is at** the boiling **point, stir in the** above mixture **with** vanilla or rose flavoring; **stir** till it begins to thicken, **then take it off** and let it cool a little; pour it into a pudding dish **or** cups; **then beat** the whites of the eggs to a stiff froth, add a teaspoon of **fine** white sugar, and drop it on the top of the custard in **rounds** about as large as an **egg;** put **a small** spoon of currant **or** other tart jelly on the middle of **each round; serve** cold.

## WEBSTER PUDDING.

### Mrs. O. L. Wheelock.

One cup molasses, one cup milk, one cup suet, one-half cup brandy, or wine if you like, one teaspoon saleratus, one teaspoon cloves, one teaspoon cinnamon, one-half nutmeg, two cups currants, one teaspoon salt; mix as soft as pound cake, and steam it two hours. Serve with hard sauce.

## SPONGE PUDDING.

### Mrs. Ada Sturtevant, Delaware, Wis.

One-half cup of butter, or one cup of chopped suet, one-third cup molasses, one-half cup wine, one-half cup sweet milk, three cups flour, one teaspoon soda, raisins and such spices as you prefer, about one-half spoonful of each; dried cherries are nice, instead of raisins, or it is good without any fruit; steam two hours and serve hot with sauce.

## POUND CAKE PUDDING.

### Mrs. E. L. Nichols.

One cup of sugar, one-half of butter, rub to a cream, add one cup of milk, three eggs, the yolks and whites beaten separately, one teaspoon of soda in the milk, two teaspoons of cream tartar in the flour; fruit; bake or steam an hour.

## ROME PUDDING.

### Mrs. M. J. Woodworth.

Eight good sized apples stewed and strained, the yolks of five eggs, one-quarter pound of butter, one lemon chopped fine, one-half pound sugar, one gill of cream; put a thin paste on a plate, as for custard pie, and bake.

## ASTOR HOUSE PUDDING.

### Mrs. Lamkin.

Two-thirds of a cup of rice, three pints of milk, one cup of sugar, a little salt, a piece of butter one-half the size of an egg; let it come to a boil; bake one and one-half hours in a slow oven.

## BATTER PUDDING.

Mrs. H. L. Bristol.

One pint of milk, four eggs, the yolks and whites beaten separately, ten tablespoons of sifted flour, a little salt; beat in the whites of the eggs the last thing before baking; bake half an hour.

## BATTER PUDDING.

Mrs. Booth.

Seven eggs, two pint cups of milk, eight spoons of flour, (large iron spoon), a pinch of salt; beat the yellow of the eggs, then add the flour and one cup of milk to beat the lumps out; add the rest of the milk, and last of all, the whites of the eggs well beaten; bake one hour; this will do for ten persons.

## BAKED BATTER PUDDING.

One quart of sweet milk, seven tablespoons of flour, (heeping) six eggs well beaten, (whites separated,) one tablespoon brandy; put the whites of the eggs in the last thing, and bake half an hour. To be eaten with brandy sauce.

## STEAMED BATTER PUDDING.

Mrs. L. H. Davis.

Two eggs and one tablespoon of sugar beaten together, one cup of milk, two cups flour, one tablespoon melted butter, half teaspoon soda, one teaspoon cream tartar; beat well, and pour the batter over either sliced apples or peaches, and steam one hour and a quarter; this will fill a three pint basin. Serve with hot sauce.

## AMHERST PUDDING.

Mrs. F. M. Craigie.

Three cups of flour, one of suet, one of milk, one of molasses, two of raisins; salt and spice to your taste; one teaspoon of saleratus; boil it in a bag three hours. For sauce: One cup of sugar, one-half of butter, one egg.

## CORN PUDDING.

### Mrs. F. M. Craigie.

One dozen ears of corn, one pint of milk, two eggs, salt, two teaspoons of sugar, two of flour; bake one hour in quick oven.

## BREAD PUDDING.

### Mrs. Freeman.

Soak a pint of bread crumbs in milk for an hour, then squeeze with the hands to a pulp, and mix well with a gill of milk, then add three tablespoons of sugar, one-quarter pound of raisins, one-quarter pound of melted butter, and the yolks of four eggs; then beat the whites of the eggs to a froth and mix with the rest; turn the mixture into a dish and bake; bake about forty minutes. Serve with wine sauce, hot or cold, according to taste.

## BREAD PUDDING.

### Mrs. C. M., Winnetka, Ill.

Put a pint of scalded milk to a pint of bread crumbs and add the yolks of four eggs well beaten, a teacup of sugar, butter the size of an egg, and the grated rind of a lemon; bake, and then beat the whites of the eggs into a cup of powdered sugar and the juice of one lemon; cover the pudding with it, and set it in the oven till it is a brownish yellow.

## BAKED CRACKER PUDDING.

### Mrs. H. P. Stowell.

Two quarts of sweet milk, seven Boston butter crackers, rolled, three eggs, a little nutmeg, a little salt; sweeten with sugar to taste. Bake two hours and a half in a moderate oven.

## APPLE BREAD PUDDING.

### Mrs. O. L. Wheelock.

Pare, core and chop one-half dozen sour apples; dry bread in the oven until crisp, then roll; butter a deep dish and place in it a layer of crumbs and apples alternately, with spice, and one-half cup of beef suet chopped fine; pour in one-half pint of sweet milk, and bake till nicely browned; serve with hard sauce.

## APPLE PUDDING.

### Mrs. W. Guthrie.

Five eggs, one pint milk, four tablespoons flour, four apples grated; bake one hour and a quarter; serve with sweetened cream or pudding sauce.

## APPLE PUDDING.

### Etta C. Springer.

Five large sour apples chopped, one cup raisins, one cup sugar, one cup sweet milk, one cup flour, one-half cup butter, two eggs, little salt, butter and sugar worked together; bake one hour; any sauce you please.

## HUCKLEBERRY PUDDING.

### Mrs. B. J. Seward.

One teacup molasses, one dessert spoon saleratus, stirred thoroughly in the molasses; as much flour as can be stirred in with one quart of huckleberries. To be steamed four hours in a basin, or boiled in a pudding bag. Serve with liquid sauce. An excellent dessert.

## HUCKLEBERRY PUDDING.

### Mrs. Bartlett.

One brick loaf, wet it with boiling milk, say one pint, four eggs, little salt, and one quart of berries. Boil one and a half hours. Serve with wine sauce.

## FIG PUDDING.

### Mrs. E. Wood.

One pound suet chopped fine, one pound wheat flour, one-half loaf of wheat bread, one pound figs chopped, one and a half

cups molasses, one teaspoon soda, one teaspoon cream tartar.
To be eaten with sauce.

## FIG PUDDING.
### E. M. Walker.

One-half pound figs, one-quarter pound greated bread, two
and a half ounces powdered sugar, three ounces butter, two
eggs, one teacup of milk. Chop the figs small and mix first
with the butter, then all the other ingredients by degrees; butter a mould, sprinkle with bread crumbs, cover it tight and boil
for three hours.

## CURRANT PUDDING.
### Mrs. Bartlett.

Slice a baker's loaf, add butter, stew and sweeten three pints
of currants, turn over the bread, and set away until cold; serve
without sauce, slice the bread thin.

## MUSKMELON PUDDING.
### Mrs. De Forest.

One-half cup butter, one pint milk, two eggs, three teaspoons
baking powder, nearly one quart of flour. Steam two hours,
serve with a liquid sauce.

## FRUIT PUDDING.
### Mrs. S. W. Cheever, Ottawa, Ill.

One cup milk, one cup sugar, two eggs, two teaspoons cream
tartar, one teaspoon soda, flour, dried fruit; steam two hours.
Sauce: To a pint of milk, add a lump of butter size of a small
egg, let this come near to a boil; save out from the pudding half
teacup batter, thin it, and stir into the hot milk, stir all the time
till it begins to thicken; sweeten and flavor to the taste.

## SWEETMEATS PUDDING.

### Mrs. C. E. Browne.

Make a nice pie crust, little or much, as you may desire, and roll it out in a long oval shape; spread thickly with raspberry or currant jam, or with stewed fruit, cherries, or plums, then wet the edges of the dough with cold water, and roll it up, closing the edges tightly. Steam it for an hour or more, and serve in slices with a sauce of butter and sugar beaten well together, with nutmeg or other flavoring.

## CHERRY PUDDING.

### Mrs. H. S. Towle.

One pint flour, one pint sweet milk, one quart cherries, four eggs, a little butter and salt, baking powder; steamed; serve with cream and sugar.

## JELLY PUDDING.

### Mrs. C. H. Wheeler.

One quart of milk, one pint of bread crumbs, yolks of four beaten eggs, one half cup of sugar; bake about half an hour; when cool, spread jelly over the pudding, beat the whites with a little sugar, and spread on top for frosting; set back in the oven a few minutes after the whites have been spread on the pudding; excellent for Sunday dinners, as it may be eaten cold.

## BAKEWELL PUDDING.

### E. M. Walker.

Cover a dish with thin puff paste, and put over it a layer of any kind of firm jelly, one-half inch thick; take the yolks of four eggs, and one white, one-quarter pound sugar, one-quarter pound butter, twelve sweet, and eight bitter almonds, well pounded; beat all together to a froth, pour over the jelly and bake one-half hour in a moderate oven.

## KISS PUDDING.

Mrs. F. B. Cole.

One quart milk, three tablespoons of **corn starch**, yolks of four eggs, half cup sugar, and a little **salt**; put part of the milk, salt and sugar on the stove and let it boil; dissolve the corn starch in the rest of the milk; **stir into the milk, and** while boiling add the yolks. Flavor **with vanilla.**

FROSTING—Whites of four eggs beaten to a stiff froth, half a cup of sugar; flavor with lemon, spread it on the pudding, **and** put it into the oven to brown, saving a little of the frosting to moisten the top; then put on grated cocoanut to give it the appearance of snow flake.

## MERINGUE PUDDING.

Mrs. C. A. Rogers.

One pint of stale bread crumbs, one quart of milk, the yolks of four eggs, butter the size of an egg, a small cup of sugar, **salt,** the grated rind of one lemon; bake. When cool, spread the top with preserves or jelly; beat the whites of the eggs with five tablespoons of pulverized sugar; spread on the pudding and brown in a quick oven; eat with cream.

## CORN STARCH LEMON PUDDING.

Glen Cove Starch Co.

Grate the rind of two lemons, add the juice and rind to six ounces of sugar and three ounces of the improved corn starch. Stir this well into some cold water, sufficient to make it smooth. Place three pints of milk on the fire; when boiling add the above, stirring all the time until it thickens. Remove it from the fire, and add one ounce of butter and four eggs. Stir again while on the fire, taking care not to allow it to burn; as soon as it becomes thick, remove it and fill out some small cups or forms, previously dipped in cold water. Place them aside; in one hour they will be fit to turn out. Cream and sugar or any sauce preferred.

SAUCE.—**One** ounce of the improved corn starch in **a little** cold milk; **blend** till smooth; then pour **a pint** of boiling milk on it. Beat the **white of four** eggs in three ounces of sugar, one glass of brandy; **add this to the** sauce, and allow it to remain **on** the fire a **short time,** stirring all **the** while. The sauce **can be** served hot **or cold.** May **be flavored** with anything to fancy.

## ORANGE PUDDING.

### Mrs. J. G. Hamilton.

Peel and cut five **sweet** oranges into **thin slices,** taking out the seeds; pour over them a coffee cup **of** white sugar; **let** a pint of milk get boiling hot, by setting it in **a** pot of boiling water; add the yolks of three eggs, well **beaten, one** tablespoon of corn starch, made smooth with a little cold milk; stir all the time; as soon as thickened, pour over the fruit. Beat the whites to **a** stiff froth, adding a tablespoon of sugar, and spread over the top for frosting; set it in the oven for a few minutes to harden; eat cold or hot, (better cold,) for dinner or supper. Berries or peaches can be substituted for oranges.

## CREAM PUFFS.

### Mrs. Watson Thatcher.

**One** and one-half cups of flour, two-thirds of a cup of butter, one-half pint of boiling **water;** boil butter and water together and stir in the flour while boiling; let it cool and add five well beaten eggs; drop on tins and bake thirty minutes in a quick **oven;** fill them with the following: **One pint of milk, one cup** of sugar, two-thirds of a cup of flour, two eggs; **beat** the eggs, flour and sugar together, and stir them in the milk while it is boiling. When partially **cool,** flavor with lemon. These are favorites in bake shops.

8

## DESSERT PUFFS.
### Mrs. N. C. Gridley, Evanston.

One pint sweet milk, scant pint flour, three eggs, (whites and yolks beaten separately;) bake in cups. To be eaten with liquid sauce.

## PUFF PUDDING.
### Mrs. C. A. Rogers.

Five tablespoons of flour, five tablespoons of milk, five eggs stirred smooth; turn on a pint of boiling milk, and bake twenty minutes. To be eaten with hard sauce.

## MOLLY PUFFS.
### Mrs. George B. Cushing.

One cup Indian meal scalded; when it cools, add two cups of rye meal, two eggs, one tablespoon of brown sugar, and a small half teaspoon of soda; fry them, dropped from a spoon in boiling lard.

## GERMAN PUFFS.
### H. M. Brewer.

One pint sweet milk, five tablespoons flour, one tablespoon melted butter, six eggs, leaving out the whites of three; bake in buttered cups, half filled, twenty minutes, in hot oven.

FOR SAUCE.—Beat the whites of five eggs to a stiff froth, and one coffee cup powdered sugar, and the juice of two oranges; turn the pudding from the cups on to a platter, and cover with the sauce, just before sending to the table.

## DUMPLING FOR ANY KIND OF POT-PIE.
### Mrs. E. R. Harmon.

One quart of flour; mix in it three teaspoons of baking powder; rub in a piece of butter about the size of an egg, and mix very soft with sweet milk; roll about an inch thick; cut in

squares; put in steamer over the pot; cover tightly with cloth
before you put cover on, keeping it air-tight; steam for half an
hour.

## A SIMPLE DESSERT.

### A. S. Ewing.

Put a teacup of tapioca into sufficient cold water; boil until
the lumps become almost transparent; squeeze the juice of two
lemons partially into the mixture, then slice them into it, sweet-
en or not, then eat when cold, with cream and sugar.

## GERMAN PUDDING.

### A. S. Ewing.

Beat six eggs separately until very light; add one pint milk to
the yolks, six tablespoons flour, one-half spoon butter, one-half
nutmeg and salt spoon salt; stir in whites of eggs last. Bake
half an hour.

SAUCE.—Six tablespoons sugar, one-half pound butter worked
to a cream, one egg, one wineglass wine, one-half nutmeg; put
on the fire and let it come to a boil.

## AN EXCELLENT DESSERT.

### Mrs. J. Young Scammon.

One can or twelve large peaches, two coffeecups of sugar, one
pint of water and the whites of three eggs; break the peaches
with and stir all the ingredients together; freeze the whole into
a form; beat the eggs to a froth.

## CHOCOLATE PUDDING.

### Mrs. E. Wood.

One and a half quarts milk, boiled, one-half cake of chocolate
stirred in milk, small cup of corn starch dissolved in little water,
add too eggs, with one cup sugar, a little salt. Cream for sauce.

*Enquire for Duryea's "Improved Corn Starch." It is pure.*

## CHOCOLATE PUFFS.

### Mrs. O. L. Parker.

One pound sugar sifted, one of chocolate scraped very fine, mix together; beat the white of one egg, and stir in your chocolate and sugar; continue to beat until stiff paste; sugar your paper, drop them on it and bake in a slow oven.

## SNOW BALLS.

### Mrs. A. W. D.

One pint of flour, one-half of sugar, one-third of a cup of milk, three eggs, two teaspoons of cream tartar, one of soda, a piece of butter the size of an egg rubbed into the flour. Roll out; sift over lightly with flour; double over and cut out with a wine glass. When fried, roll in pulverized sugar.

## CHERRY PUDDING.

### H. N. Jenks.

A pint of bread crusts or soft crackers, scalded in a quart of boiling milk, piece of butter the size of an egg, one teaspoon of salt, three eggs, one and a half teacups of sugar if eaten without sauce, and if with sauce a tablespoon of sugar; a pinch of pulverized cinnamon, and a quart of stoned cherries; bake quickly.

## WIDOW BEDOT PUDDING.

### Mrs. J. J. McGrath.

One cup of suet chopped fine, one cup of raisins, one cup of sweet milk, spice to taste, flour to make a thick batter; steam one hour and serve with butter and sugar sauce.

## FRUIT PUDDING.

Place in a tin basin fruit of any kind, (raspberries, peaches and apples are the best,) put sugar over them, and a little water; if peaches are used put them in after paring them, whole; have

ready a biscuit crust, made of one pint of flour, with a small
piece of butter or lard, a little salt, two teaspoons of baking
powder, and water or milk to make a dough; then roll out crust,
and place over the top of your fruit in the tin; cover with another
two quart basin, to give room for the crust to rise, and set it on
the stove; as the fruit stews the crust will steam done.  Serve
with cream and sugar.

## GIPSY PUDDING.
### L. Osgood.

Cut stale sponge cake into thin slices; spread them with currant jelly or preserves; put two pieces together like sandwiches,
and lay them in a dish; make a soft custard, pour over while it
is hot, let cool before serving.

## CRACKED WHEAT PUDDING.
### Mrs. A. M. Lewis.

Cook cracked wheat enough for two meals; stir in a few minutes before taking up, raisins, dates, or any dried fruit; next
day prepare a custard as usual, and stir thoroughly through the
wheat, and bake just long enough to bake the custard; thus you
have two desserts with but little trouble.  Very palatable and
nutritious.

## LEMON PUDDING.
### Mrs. White.

Put in a basin one-fourth pound of flour, the same of sugar,
same of bread crumbs and chopped suet, the juice of one good
sized lemon, and the peel grated; two eggs, and enough milk to
make it the consistency of porridge; boil in a basin for one hour;
serve with or without sauce.

## ORANGE PUDDING.
### Nellie.

Line the bottom of a pudding dish with stale sponge cake,
slice upon the cake six oranges; make a custard of one quart of

milk and five eggs, leaving out the whites of four; beat the whites to a stiff froth, adding sugar, put on top of pudding, and put in the oven until brown.

## APPLE SAGO PUDDING.

### Mrs. K.

One cup sago in a quart of tepid water, with a pinch of salt; soaked for one hour; six or eight apples, pared and cored, or quartered, and steamed tender, and put in the pudding dish; boil and stir the sago until clear, adding water to make it thin, and pour it over the apples; this is good hot with butter and sugar, or cold with cream and sugar.

## GERMAN PUFFS.

### Mrs. E. P. Thomas, Rockford, Ill.

One pint sweet milk, four eggs, five tablespoons flour, and a little salt.   Bake three-quarters of an hour.

## RICE SNOW BALLS.

Boil a pint of rice in two quarts of water, with a teaspoon of salt, until quite soft, then put it in small cups, having them quite full; when perfectly cold, turn them into a dish, take the yolks of three eggs, one pint of milk, one teaspoon corn starch; flavor with lemon, and cook as you do soft custard; turn over the rice half an hour previous to eating it.   This is a nice dessert in hot weather.   Sweet meats are a good accompaniment.

## FOAMING SAUCE.

### Mrs. King.

One-half tea cup of butter, the same of sugar; beat to a froth; put into a dish and set in a pan of hot water; add a tablespoon of hot water, or if preferred, a little vanilla; stir one way until it comes to a very light foam.

## WINE PUDDING SAUCE.

One cup of sugar, one-half cup of butter, one-half cup of wine, one egg; beat butter, sugar and egg together; set it on the stove and heat, pour in the wine, add a little nutmeg; pour from one dish to another a few times, and send to the table.

## WINE SAUCE.

### M. A. T.

Two teacups of sugar, one teacup of butter; stir to a cream; beat two eggs very light, and stir all together; add one teacup of wine; mix and set on top of teakettle of boiling water. It must not be put on the stove, nor boil.

## PUDDING SAUCE.

### Mrs. B. P. Hutchinson.

Two eggs well beaten, one cup pulverized sugar; when mixed pour over one cup of boiling milk, and stir rapidly; flavor as you please.

## PUDDING SAUCE.

### Mrs. Andrews.

One cup of sugar, one-half cup of butter, yolks of three eggs; one teaspoon of corn starch or arrow root; stir the whole until very light; add sufficient boiling water to make the consistency of thick cream; wine or brandy to suit the taste.

## SAUCE FOR APPLE PUDDING.

### M.

Boil good molasses with a little butter, and serve hot.

## HARD SAUCE FOR PUDDINGS, RICE, &c.

### M.

Take one teacup sugar, one-half teacup butter; stir together until light; flavor with wine or essence of lemon; smooth the top with a knife, and grate nutmeg over it.

---

*Enquire for Duryea's "Improved Corn Starch." It is pure.*

## COLD TAPIOCA PUDDING.

### Mrs. H. F. Waite.

One cup tapioca in five cups water, one cup sugar and one lemon. Wash the tapioca; add the water; put it in a tin pail, in a kettle of water; let it boil two hours or more and until it is perfectly clear; just before taking up, add a teaspoon of salt, one cup sugar and rind and juice of a lemon; stir thoroughly; place to cool; eat with cream and sugar.

## TAPIOCA PUDDING.

### Mrs. Rice.

Cover three tablespoons tapioca with water; stand over night; add one quart milk, a small piece of butter, a little salt and boil; beat the yolks of three eggs with a cup of sugar and boil the whole to a very thick custard; flavor with vanilla; when cold cover with whites of egg beaten.

## TAPIOCA PUDDING.

### Mrs. Frances M. Thatcher.

Soak one cup of tapioca in milk; add one quart of milk, one cup of white sugar, two eggs, butter the size of an egg, nutmeg and raisins to suit taste; steam two hours.

## CREAM TAPIOCA PUDDING.

### Mrs. A. T. Hall.

Soak three tablespoons of tapioca in water over night; put the tapioca into a quart of boiling milk, and boil half hour; beat the yolks of four eggs with a cup of sugar; add three tablespoons of prepared cocoanut; stir in and boil ten minutes longer; pour into a pudding dish; beat the whites of the four eggs to a stiff froth, stir in three tablespoons of sugar; put this over the top and sprinkle cocoanut over the top and brown for five minutes.

*Enquire for Duryea's "Improved Corn Starch." It is pure.*

## APPLE TAPIOCA PUDDING.

### Mrs. C. Duffield.

One cup of tapioca soaked over night in six cups of water; next morning add about **six** large tart apples, chopped very fine, (or more, according **to** the size,) then one cup of white sugar; bake slowly about four hours; to be eaten either warm **or cold,** with cream. Very delicate for invalids.

## SNOW PUDDING.

### Mrs. D.

One-half package Coxe's gelatine; **pour** over **it a cup of cold** water **and** add one and one-half cup of sugar; **when** soft, add one cup boiling water, juice of one lemon and the whites of four well beaten eggs; beat all together until very light; put in glass dish and pour over it custard made as follows :—one pint milk, yolks four eggs and **grated** rind of one lemon; boil. Splendid.

# CUSTARDS, CREAMS, etc.

## MRS. GRAVE'S CUSTARDS.

Six eggs, one pint milk, one **and a** half cups sugar, one tea-**spoon** of vanilla; beat sugar and eggs together, and stir into the hot milk; when done, strain; **cook** very slowly, not to boil; pour into cups.

ANOTHER WAY.—Instead of boiling, put the mixture into cups; set them in **a** dripping pan half full of water and bake in the oven till done.

*Enquire for Duryea's "Improved Corn Starch." It is pure.*

## RICE CUSTARD.

### Mrs. C. M. Dickerman, Rockford.

To half a cup of rice, add one quart of milk, and a little salt; steam one hour, or until quite soft; beat the yolks of four eggs with four tablespoons of white sugar; add this just before taking off the rice; stir in thoroughly, but do not let it boil any more; flavor with vanilla. Beat the whites of the eggs to a stiff froth, with sugar; after putting the mixture into the pudding dish in which you serve it, put the whites over it and let it slightly brown in the oven.

## RICH CUSTARD.

### Mrs. Morgan, Rockford, Ill.

One quart of cream, the yolks of six eggs, six ounces of pow-dered white sugar, a small pinch of salt, two tablespoons of brandy, one tablespoon of peach water, half a tablespoon of lemon brandy, an ounce of blanched almonds pounded to a paste; mix the cream with the sugar, and the yolks of the eggs well beaten; scald them together in a tin pail in boiling water, stirring all the time until sufficiently thick; when cool, add the other ingredients, and pour into custard cups.

## BOILED CUSTARD.

### Mrs. R. M. Pickering.

One quart of milk, eight eggs, one-half pound of sugar; beat to a good froth the eggs and sugar. Put the milk in a tin pail and set it in boiling water; pour in the eggs and sugar and stir until it thickens.

## CHOCOLATE CUSTARD.

### Mrs. Higgins.

Three ounces Baker's chocolate, three pints milk, four table-spoons white sugar, two tablespoons brown sugar; prepare a soft custard of the milk and the yolks of five eggs and the white of one; dissolve the chocolate in a cup of warm milk and heat it to boiling **point**; when cool, sweeten it **with** brown sugar and flavor with **the extract of** vanilla; **pour** the whole into a dish and cover with the **whites of** the **five** eggs beaten stiff, with a **little** sugar; **brown** slighty and serve cold.

## SAGO CUSTARD.
### C. D. Adams.

Three tablespoons **of** sago **boiled in a** little water till **clear**; **add** one quart of milk, let it come to a boil, then add five **or six well** beaten eggs and sugar to taste. Put the vessel **containing** the **custard** in a kettle of boiling water; **stir it** briskly, **till it** thickens a little; **flavor** with vanilla after it **is partly** cool.

## APPLE CUSTARD.
### Mrs. F. B. Orr.

Pare, **core and** quarter one dozen tart apples, strew into it the grated rind of one lemon; stew until tender in very little water; then mash smooth with back ·**of a** spoon. To one and a half pints of strained apple add one and a quarter pounds sugar; leave it until cold; beat six eggs light and stir alternately into one quart milk with the apples; put into cups or deep dish and bake twenty minutes; to be eaten cold.

## APPLE CUSTARDS.
### Mrs. C. M. Dickerman, Rockford.

Take six tart apples, pare and quarter them, put into a baking dish with one cup water; cook until tender, **but** not to pieces, then turn them into a pudding dish and sprinkle sugar over to cover them; beat eight eggs with sugar and **mix** with them three pints of milk, a little nutmeg; turn it over the apples, and bake twenty-five minutes.

*Enquire for Duryea's* "Improved Corn Starch." *It is pure.*

## CARAMEL CUSTARD.

### Mrs. Perry Smith.

One quart of milk, one cup of white sugar, one cup of brown sugar, two tablespoons of corn starch, pinch of salt and vanilla. Place the milk with the white sugar and salt in a farina kettle, over the fire; if you have not such a kettle, a tin pail set in a pot of hot water will answer the purpose; beat the eggs, without separating, in a large bowl, and wet the corn starch with a little cold milk; put the brown sugar in a tin pan and set over the fire; stir until it is thoroughly scorched, but not burned; then turn the scalding milk on the eggs; put the mixture in the kettle again over the fire; stir in the corn starch until it thickens; lastly, stir in the scorched sugar and remove from the fire; then add a generous amount of vanilla. The scorched sugar falls into the custard in strings, but these will dissolve with vigorous stirring, after removal from the fire. Turn into custard glasses and serve cold.

## APPLE SOUFFLE.

### Mrs. A. N. Arnold.

Stew the apples; add a little grated lemon peel and juice; line the sides and bottom of the dish about two inches thick. Make a boiled custard with one pint of milk and two eggs; when it is cool, pour it into the center of the dish. Beat the whites of the eggs and spread it over the top; sprinkle sugar over it, and bake a few minutes in the oven.

## FLOATING ISLAND.

### E. E. Macey.

One-half package of gelatine, one pint of water; soak twenty minutes; add two cups of sugar, set it on the stove to come to a boil; when nearly cold, add the whites of four eggs beaten stiff, the juice and rind of two lemons, and pour into a mold. Make a custard of the yolks of four eggs, a quart of milk, and a small tablespoon of corn starch, sweetened to taste.

---

*Enquire for Duryea's "Improved Corn Starch." It is pure.*

## APPLE FLOAT.

### Mrs. O. L. Parker.

To one quart of apples, **partially stewed** and well mashed, put the whites **of** three eggs, well beaten, and four heaping tablespoons of loaf sugar; beat them together for fifteen minutes, and eat with rich milk and nutmeg.

## ORANGE FLOAT.

### Mrs. M. E. Kedzie, Evanston.

One **quart of** water, the juice and pulp of two lemons, one coffee cup of sugar; when boiling add to it four tablespoons **of** corn starch mixed in water; let it boil, stirring it fifteen minutes; when cool, pour it over four or five sliced oranges; over the top spread the beaten whites of three eggs, sweetened, and a few drops of vanilla. Eaten with **cream.**

## SPANISH CREAM.

### Mrs. J. P. Booker.

One pint milk and one-half box gelatine, heated together; yolks of three eggs, and five tablespoons sugar beaten together added to the above; take off as soon as it thickens, then stir **in** the whites of three eggs beaten **to** a stiff froth; flavor **with va-**nilla; to be served with cream and sugar.

## SPANISH CREAM.

### Mrs. J. H. Brown.

Boil one ounce of gelatine in one pint of new milk until dissolved, **add** four eggs well beaten and half a pound of sugar; stir it over **the** fire until the eggs thicken, take it off the fire and add a full wine-glass of peach water, and when cool pour it into moulds; serve with cream.

*Enquire for Duryea's "Improved Corn Starch." It is pure.*

## VELVET CREAM.

### Mrs. R. Harris.

Nearly a box of gelatine, soaked over night in a cup of wine; melt it over the fire, with the sugar; when it is warm, put in a quart of cream or new milk and strain it into moulds. If the wine is too hot, it will curdle the milk.

## CHOCOLATE CREAM.

### Mrs. Spruance.

Soak one box of Cox's English gelatine (in cold water sufficient to cover) one hour; one quart of milk boiled; scrape two ounces of French chocolate, mix with eight spoons of white sugar; moisten this with three spoons of the boiling milk; then stir in the gelatine and the yolks of ten well beaten eggs; stir three minutes briskly; take off, strain and add two teaspoons of vanilla; strain and put in moulds to cool. Serve with sugar and cream.

## CHOCOLATE CREAM.

### Mrs. King.

Half a cake of chocolate dissolved in a little hot water; put in a cup of milk and when it boils have five eggs well beaten and mixed with two cups of milk; pour the hot chocolate into the eggs and milk; stir well and boil all together for a few minutes; sweeten to your taste. To be eaten cold.

## APPLE CREAM.

### Mrs. Mann.

One cup thick cream, one cup sugar, beat till very smooth; then beat the whites of two eggs, and add; stew apples in water till soft; take them from the water with a fork; steam them if you prefer. Pour the cream over the apples when cold.

## CARAMEL CREAM.
### Mrs. Anna S. Ogden.

Three pounds sugar browned in the oven to a liquid, but not burned; sixteen eggs, seven quarts of milk, and one of cream; the milk should be boiled and be frozen like ordinary ice cream.

## BAVARIAN CREAM.
### Mrs. Chas. Duffield.

One pint of milk, yolks of four eggs, one-fourth pound of sugar, one-half ounce of gelatine; put all over the fire, and stir until the gelatine is dissolved, then strain through a fine sieve, and when cool, add one pint of cold cream; flavor with vanilla.

## ITALIAN CREAM.
### E. V. Case, Elmhurst.

Take one quart of cream, one pint of milk sweetened very sweet, and highly seasoned with sherry wine and vanilla; beat it with a whip dasher, and remove the froth as it rises until it is all converted into froth. Have ready one box of Cox's sparkling gelatine, dissolved in a little warm water; set your frothed cream into a tub of ice; pour the gelatine into it, and stir constantly until it thickens, then pour into moulds, and set in a cool place.

## ICE CREAM.
### M.

One pint milk, yolks of two eggs, six ounces sugar, one table-spoon corn starch; scald until it thickens; when cool, add one pint whipped cream, and the whites of two eggs, beaten stiff; sweeten, flavor and freeze.

## ICE CREAM.
### Mrs. A. P. Iglehart.

Have ready two quarts of rich cream; take out three pints and stir into the pint left one pound of white sugar; flavor with lemon or vanilla, after mixing this well add it to the three pints and freeze it.

## ICE CREAM.

### Mrs. W. H. Ovington.

Scald one quart of milk with one sheet of Isinglass, (broken,) and a vanilla bean; when cool, strain, mix with one pint of cream whipped to a froth; sweeten to taste.

## TAPIOCA MERINGUE.

### Mrs. Spruance.

One teacup of tapioca soaked in one and a half pints of warm water three hours; peel and core eight tart apples; fill apples with sugar, grating a little nutmeg or moistening with wine; one hour before needed, pour the tapioca over the apples and bake, serving in the dish baked in; the addition of the whites of four well beaten eggs spread over the top and browned slightly, improves it.

## SPANISH MERINGUES.

### M.

Take the whites of eight eggs; beat until stiff; add one-half pound of powdered sugar and a pinch of salt, and beat well; grease some paper and lay on a board; drop the meringues on it, and bake in a slow oven; when done, remove with a knife and place the two together; sprinkle with powdered sugar before baking.

## SWISS MERINGUES.

### M.

Use the same mixture as above, formed in a ring, using whipped cream with sugar and vanilla to the taste, for the centre.

## MELANGE.

### Mrs. W. Guthrie.

Line a deep pie dish with pie crust, and spread on a thin layer of tart apple sauce, then a layer of buttered bread; on this another layer of apple. Bake until the crust is done; when done, spread on the whites of two eggs beaten to a froth and sweetened; brown slightly. Serve with pudding sauce of butter and sugar stirred to a cream, seasoned with lemon.

## LEMON SPONGE.

### Mrs. Lamkin.

Two ounces of gelatine; pour over one pint of cold water; let it stand fifteen minutes; add half a pint of boiling water, three-quarters of a pound of white sugar, and the juice of four lemons. When the gelatine is cold, before it begins to get firm, add the well beaten whites of three eggs; beat the whole fifteen minutes, until the mixture is quite white, and begins to thicken; then put in a mould first wet in cold water.

## LEMON SPONGE.

### Mrs. B.

Two ounces isinglass, one and three-fourths pints water, three-fourths pound powdered sugar, juice of five lemons and rind of one, whites of three eggs; dissolve isinglass in water, strain, add sugar, lemon rind and juice; boil the whole ten or fifteen minutes; strain again; let it stand until it is cold and begins to stiffen; beat the whites of the eggs, add them to the mixture; beat until quite white, then mould and let it stand.

## SNOW SOUFFLE.

### Mrs. J. Louis Harris, Keokuk, Iowa.

Beat the whites of two eggs to a stiff froth; dissolve one-half box of gelatine in a little more than a pint of hot water, two cups of sugar, and the juice of two lemons; when this is dissolved and cooled, stir into it the eggs you have beaten, beat the whole together until it is white and stiff; mould and pour around it soft custard.

*"Richards' Queen Baking Powder" makes Biscuit very light.*

9

## SNOW AND ICE PUDDING.
### Mrs. W. R. Cornell, Hyde Park.

In one pint of boiling water dissolve one-third of a package of Cox's gelatine, three-fourths of a teacup of sugar, juice of two lemons; when nearly formed into jelly, stir in lightly the whites of two eggs, beaten to a stiff froth; then place in a mould and serve with a boiled custard, poured over the snow and ice mould of jelly.

## SNOW PUDDING.
### Mrs. McDowell.

One-half box of Cox's gelatine; pour over it one pint of boiling water; then add two cups of sugar and the juice of two lemons; when cool, add the whites of three eggs, well beaten, and pour into a mould to harden.

FOR SAUCE.—The yolks of three eggs and one pint of milk sweetened to taste; place in a vessel of hot water to boil, stirring constantly; when nearly cold, add a little salt, and flavor with vanilla.

## SNOW PUDDING.
### Mrs. E. R. Harmon.

Pour one pint of boiling water to half a box of gelatine, two cups sugar, juice of two lemons; when nearly cold, strain it and beat with whites of three eggs half an hour until perfectly light and thick. Put it in a glass dish, then make soft custard with the yolks of the three eggs and one pint of milk; flavor with vanilla and pour over it.

## SNOW PUDDING.
### Mrs. Henry Stevens.

One-half box of Cox's gelatine, dissolve in one pint of boiling hot water; when nearly cool, add one cup sugar, juice of one lemon; strain; add whites of three eggs beaten to a stiff froth; beat all thoroughly and quickly pour into mould. Serve cold with soft custard made of the yolks of the three eggs, and one-

*The excellence of the above receipts can only be realized by*

half teaspoon of corn starch stirred in one pint of boiling milk ;
sweeten to taste.

## SNOW PUDDING.

Mrs. L. H. Smith, Kenwood.

One-third box Cox's gelatine, soaked ten minutes in one-half
pint cold water, and afterwards add one-half pint boiling water,
juice of two good sized fresh lemons, one and a half cups powdered sugar ; allow this to stand over a slow fire only a few moments; then strain it through a flannel bag into your pudding
dish and set away to cool; then make a smooth custard of the
yolks of five eggs with one and a half tablespoons corn starch ;
sweeten to taste and cook it a few minutes in a tin pail, set in a
kettle of boiling water, stirring all the while; when sufficiently
cooked and partially cooled, flavor with vanilla extract, and
when entirely cold, pour this custard over the jelly already in
the dish, and beat to a stiff froth the whites of the five eggs,
adding a little sugar and pour over the top of the custard, and it
is then ready to serve. This is considered an excellent and delicate dessert, if properly and carefully made.

## CHARLOTTE RUSSE.

M.

One pint cream and whites of six eggs, beaten to a stiff froth
separately; one-fourth ounce of gelatine soaked in one gill of
milk; set on back of stove to dissolve. Mix cream and eggs,
sweeten and flavor; stir in gelatine; when cool, place on sponge
cake and set away to get firm; or you can use two eggs (whites)
and one-half ounce gelatine. Good.

## APPLE CHARLOTTE.

Mrs. A. M. Gibbs.

Put a layer of bread, cut in thin slices and buttered on both
sides, in the bottom of your pudding dish, and on this a layer of
apples cut as for a pie, seasoning with sugar and a dust of cinna-

mon, alternating the bread and apples until the dish is filled, having a layer of bread on top.   Bake one-half hour.   If the bread is in danger of becoming too brown and hard, cover with a plate until the apples are cooked.   To be eaten with cream.

## CHARLOTTE RUSSE.
### Mrs. W. Butterfield.

Take one-third of a box of gelatine, soak it ten minutes in enough cold water to cover it, then add a little hot water to dissolve it; whip up one pint of cream, very light, with a wire spoon or whip churn; mix it thoroughly with the gelatine; add two tablespoons of sugar and flour with vanilla.

## CHARLOTTE RUSSE.
### Mrs. E. Wood.

Two quarts cream, sweeten with white sugar to taste; put cream in pan of ice and whip until light; one package of gelatine to one and a half quarts water; add to the whipped cream while boiling hot, stirring it all the time; dish out with a slice of sponge cake.

## CHARLOTTE RUSSE.
### Mrs. A. M. Gibbs.

Whip one quart rich cream to a stiff froth, and drain well on a nice seive.   To one scant pint of milk add six eggs beaten very light; make very sweet, flavor high with vanilla.   Cook over hot water till it is a thick custard.   Soak one full ounce Cox's gelatine in a very little water, and warm over hot water. When the custard is very cold, beat in lightly the gelatine and the whipped cream.   Line the bottom of your mould with buttered paper, the sides with sponge cake or lady-fingers fastened together with the white of an egg.   Fill with the cream, put in a cold place or in summer on ice.   To turn out, dip the mould for a moment in hot water.   In draining the whip cream, all that drips through can be re-whipped.

## CHARLOTTE RUSSE.

### S. Osgood.

One-third of a box of gelatine, put in a pint of sweet milk and let it cool; beat four eggs and stir in, but do not let the milk boil; one cup of sugar, stir in with the yolks; when cool, add one quart of cream and the whites of the four eggs, well **beaten.** Stir all together, flavor the cream with vanilla before **mixing.**

## CHARLOTTE RUSSE.

### Mrs. J. P. Hoit.

**Take one quart of thin cream,** sweeten and flavor; whip the cream until all in **froth;** then take half box of gelatine, put in as little **cold** water as possible to soak, and **set on** the stove to melt; have the gelatine cool before putting into **the** cream; have **a** dish already lined with cake or lady-fingers, pour the cream into it and set on ice until ready for use.

## CHARLOTTE.

### Mrs. W. W. Kimball.

One quart of **rich cream, three** tablespoons of Madeira wine, whites of two eggs beaten to a stiff froth, one teacup of powdered sugar, half a box of gelatine dissolved in half **a cup** of sweet milk; flavor with vanilla; beat the cream and wine **together;** add **the** eggs, then the sugar, and **last, the** gelatine.

## RICE CHARLOTTE.

### E. M. Walker.

Blanch one-fourth pound of rice, and boil in one quart of milk, with a little sugar and vanilla; when soft, let it cool, and then mix it **with** one pint of whipped cream; oil a mould and fill with a layer of **rice** and preserves, or marmalade, alternately; let it stand until stiff, and then turn it out.

## FRUIT BLANC-MANGE.

### Mrs. T. V. Wadskier.

Stew nice fresh fruit, (whatever you may please, cherries and raspberries being the best,) strain off the juice, and sweeten to taste; place it over the fire in a double kettle until it boils; while boiling, stir in corn starch wet with a little cold water, allowing two tablespoons of starch for each pint of juice; continue stirring until sufficiently cooked, then pour into moulds wet in cold water; set them away to cool    This, eaten with cream and sugar, makes a delightful dessert.

## CHOCOLATE MANGE.

### S. D. F.

One box of Cox's gelatine dissolved in a pint of cold water, three pints of milk; put over to boil, with one cup of French chocolate; when the milk is just scalded, pour in the gelatine; sweeten to taste; boil five minutes, then take from the fire, flavor with vanilla, pour into moulds.    When cold, serve with powdered sugar and cream.

## MOUNT BLANC.

### Mrs. T. B. Orr.

One-third box of gelatine, grated rind of two lemons, two cups of sugar, one pint boiling water; before the mixture gets stiff, stir in the whites of five eggs beaten to a stiff froth.    Eat with custard, boiled, made with yolks of eggs and one pint of boiling milk.    Sweeten to taste, flavor with vanilla.    Excellent.

## GELATINE BLANC MANGE.

### C. D. Adams.

Soak one-half box Cox's gelatine in one and a half pints of milk for an hour; put it over a kettle of boiling water, and when it comes to the boil, add the beaten yolks of three eggs and four tablespoons of sugar, stirring it briskly for a few moments; when partly cool, add the whites of the eggs, beaten very light; flavor with vanilla; cool in a mould and serve with sugar and cream.

*You can only realize the excellence of the above receipts by*

# BREAD AND YEAST.

Bread is the staff of life.
—SWIFT.

The bread she daily offers me,
Is that perpetual feast of sweets
Where no crude surfeit reigns.
—ANON.

## GENERAL DIRECTIONS FOR MAKING BREAD.

In the composition of **good bread**, there are three important **requisites**: Good flour, good **yeast, and** strength to knead it well. Flour should be white **and dry**, crumbling easily again after it is pressed **in the** hand.

A **very good method of** ascertaining the quality **of** yeast, **will be to add a** little **flour** to a very small **quantity, setting** it in a **warm** place. **If in the** course of ten **or** fifteen minutes it rises, **it** will do to use.

When **you make** bread, first set the sponge with warm milk or water, keeping it in **a** warm place until quite light. Then mould this sponge, by adding flour into one large loaf, kneading it well. Set this to rise again, and then when sufficiently light,

*Using Richards' Queen Baking Powder and Extracts of Fruit.*

mould into smaller loaves; let it rise again, and then bake.    Care should be taken not to get the dough too stiff with flour ; it should be as soft as it can be to knead well.

To make bread or biscuits a nice color,  wet the dough over top with water just before putting in the oven.    Flour should always be sifted.

## YEAST.

### Mrs. E. S. Chesebrough.

Put two tablespoons of hops in a muslin bag and boil them in three quarts of water for a few minutes; have ready a quart of hot mashed potatoes; put in one cup of flour, one tablespoon of sugar, one of salt ; pour over the mixture the boiling hop water, strain through a colander, put a pint or less of fresh baker's yeast or two cakes of yeast in while it is warm, and set it in a warm place to rise.    This yeast will keep three or four weeks, if set in a cool place.    In making it from time to time, use a bowl of the same to raise the fresh with.

## YEAST.

### Mrs. M. L., Evanston.

Six good potatoes grated raw, a little hop tea, one quart boiling water, three-fourths cup of brown sugar, one-half teaspoon salt; when cool, add yeast to rise; keep covered and in a cool place.

## POTATO YEAST.

### Mrs. J. B. Adams.

Boil, steam and mash a few potatoes; pour slowly on some boiling water, in which a bag of hops has been boiled; stir immediately in sifted flour enough to thicken; when lukewarm, add compressed yeast (dissolved,) or raise with potato or baker's yeast.

## GOOD YEAST.

### Mrs. N. P. Iglehart.

On one morning boil two ounces of best hops in four quarts of well water half an hour, strain it and let the liquor cool to the consistency of milk; then put in a small handful of salt, and half pound of brown sugar; beat up one pound of good flour with some of the liquor; then mix all well together, and let it stand till next day; when strained, bottle it, (it must be frequently stirred while it is making and kept near the fire.) Before using it, shake the bottle well; it will keep in a cool place two months. Use the same quantity for bread as other yeast.

## YEAST.

### Mrs. W. C. Harris.

Boil in separate pans, one-half cup of hops, and two potatoes; strain both liquids boiling hot on a large cup of flour, one spoon of salt, half cup sugar, a cup of yeast. Pour it into a jug and set it in a cool place.

## YEAST.

### Mrs. Freeman.

Boil two ounces of hops in four quarts of water twenty minutes, strain through a sieve and add one coffee cup of sugar to the hop water. When so cool as not to scald, stir in one coffee cup of flour. Let this mixture stand in a warm place three days, stirring frequently. The third day boil three potatoes, press them through the colander and stir gradually into the hop water, adding a handful of salt; let it stand till next morning, then put into a jug. Shake well every time before using. Use a teacup full for six loaves. To your sponge next morning add three good sized potatoes pressed through the colander, with the water they are boiled in.

## GOOD YEAST.

### S. S. Peirce.

Eight potatoes boiled and mashed fine, four tablespoons of flour put in with the potatoes, two tablespoons of salt, two of sugar; pour on one quart of boiling water; stir carefully while pouring, so as to dissolve, and add one quart of cold water;

*We advise the use of "Richards' Queen" for making light biscuit.*

then strain, and when cold, add one cup of yeast and set in a warm place to rise; as soon as it is light, put it in a jug or bottle and cork tight.

## YEAST.

### Mrs. John C. Corthell.

Six large raw potatoes grated into a stone jar, one handful of dry hops in two quarts of water; boil a few minutes and add one tablespoon of salt, one teacup of sugar; strain the liquor on the potatoes while boiling hot; stir six yeast cakes in cold water until dissolved, then add to the yeast when cool; let it stand two days before using. Use one-half a cup to four loaves of bread.

## YEAST THAT WILL NOT SOUR.

### Mrs. J. B. Adams.

Boil two ounces of hops in two quarts of water; put one cup of brown sugar in a jar; boil and strain the hops and pour into the jar. Add one cup of flour stirred smooth; let it stand in a warm kitchen till it ferments. Add six potatoes boiled and mashed, and one cup of salt.

## YEAST.

### Mrs. Anna Marble.

Two quarts of wheat bran, one of Indian bran, two gallons of boiling water; simmer an hour or so; put in a handful of hops. As soon as the water boils, add one tea cup of molasses and one tablespoon of ground ginger. When cold, put in a teacup of yeast and cork tightly. Keep cool.

## YEAST.

### From the Prairie Farmer.

A handful small of fragrant hops deposit in a kettle;
Then add a pint of Adam's ale, and boil them till they settle.
Then if you wish to brew good yeast, lively and sweet, you'd
    oughter
Take four potatoes, medium sized, and wash them well with water;

Divest them of their jackets next,—in common parlance, skin 'em,
And faithfully dig out the eyes, there's dirt imbedded in 'em.
Then make assurance doubly sure, and banish all pollution,
By subsequently giving them another grand ablution;
Then boil them,—half an hour perhaps, of course your judg-
   ment using,—
Or steam them, if you like it best; the method's of your choosing.
But whether boiled or cooked by steam, the process should be
   rapid;
Potatoes moderately cooked are heavy, sogged, vapid.
Then mash them thoroughly, each lump with vigor pulverizing;
And put them in a vessel which leaves ample room for rising;
A cup half filled with sugar add; 'twill sweeten it enough;
It needs the same amount of salt; you'll find it quantum stuff.
The hop infusion strain in next, a pint, you mind, by measure,
Then with two quarts of water warm, dilute it at your pleasure,
And gently keep it moving from circumference to center;
Never fail to bid your silver spoon its hidden depth to enter;
Then add two brimming cups of yeast and quickly take occasion
The fragrant mixture to subject to brisk manipulation.
And when the entire ingredients are mingled well together,
Then give the opportunity to rise, according to the weather—
In winter set it near the stove, and oft renew the fire,
In summer, place it further off, the temperature is higher—
Then patiently the issue wait, while time his flight is winging,
Its status scanning now and then; and when you hear it singing,
And see upon its surface—now here now there—a bubble,
You'll feel a thousand fold repaid for all your toil and trouble.
Give to the wind all idle fears; all doubts, all scruples banish;
And when the bubbies thicken fast, and crowd, and break and
   vanish,
The yeast is prime, your toil is o'er, success has crowned per-
   sistence,
And loaves of tender, light, sweet bread are looming in the dis-
   tance.

*When in haste you wish to make delicate light and white bread.*

## BREAD.
Mrs. E. S. Chesebrough.

Take four quarts of sifted flour and a tea cup of yeast; a
pinch of salt, and wet with warm milk and water stiff enough to
knead. Work it on the board until it requires no more flour.
If made at night, the bread will be light enough to work over
and put in pans early in the morning. This quantity will make
two large loaves. One-third of the lump may be taken for rolls,
which can be made by working in butter the size of an egg, and
setting aside to rise again; when light the second time, make
out in oblong shapes, cover them with a cloth, and let them
rise again. As soon as they break apart, bake them in a quick
oven. They will not fail to be nice if they are baked as soon as
they seam. This is the great secret of white, flaky rolls. Two
or three potatoes will improve the bread. Good housekeepers
always have flour sifted in readiness for use, and never use it in
any other way.

## BREAD.
M. E. B. Lynde.

The sponge is made over night in the centre of a pan of flour,
with milk and warm water and a cup of home-made hop and potato yeast to about four loaves. The yeast is put in when about
half the flour and water are mixed, and then the remainder of
the water is added and the sponge beaten with a wooden spoon
for fifteen minutes and left to rise over night in a moderately
warm place. In the morning, the bread-dough mixed and
kneaded for half an hour, adding flour to make a stiff dough,
and left to rise in a mass. It is then made into small loaves,
being kneaded with as little flour as possible, and put in pans to
rise the second time, all the while kept moderately warm, and
when light, bake in a moderately hot oven. The important
part of said recipe is the beating of the sponge fifteen minutes,
as given. Bread made after this recipe received first premium
at Wisconsin State Fair, 1872.

*We wish to impress upon all the neccessity of using*

## EXCELLENT BREAD.

Mrs. Geo. W. Pitkin.

Four potatoes mashed fine, four tea spoons of salt, two quarts of luke warm milk, one-half cake of compressed yeast, dissolved in one-half cup of warm water; flour enough to make a pliable dough; mould with hands well greased with lard; place in pans, and when sufficiently light, it is ready for baking.

## SUPERIOR BREAD.

Mrs. D. C. Norton.

Scald one quart of sour milk; when cool enough, set your sponge with the whey; take about three quarts of flour, make a hole in the centre, put in the whey, about a good teaspoon of salt, one teacup of good hop yeast (home made is best,) and stir quite stiff with a spoon; wrap in a thick cloth, so as to keep as warm as possible, (in cold weather,) in summer it is not necessary. In the morning knead well, adding flour until stiff enough, and keep warm until light; then set it in pans to rise; no saleratus is needed. Bread made in this way will never fail to be good, if good flour and yeast are used.

## WHEAT BREAD.

Mrs. D. W. Thatcher, River Forest.

Take a pan of flour, and put in a small handfull of salt and a bowl of soft yeast and one pint of luke warm milk, mix stiff with flour, and let it rise. Then knead it into pans, and let it rise, and if wanted very white, knead it down two or three times; this makes it whiter, but loses its sweet taste; bake forty-five minutes.

## RICE BREAD.

Mrs. E. S. Chesebrough.

Boil a teacup of rice quite soft; while hot, add butter the size of an egg, one and a half pints of milk, rather more than one-half

pint of bolted corn meal, two tablespoons of flour, two eggs, and
a little salt.  Bake just one hour.  The bread should be about
two inches thick.

## MRS. FURLONG'S BROWN BREAD.

Three cups of corn meal, one cup of flour, one cup of syrup,
one cup of sour milk, two cups of sweet milk; one teaspoon of
soda, one teaspoon of salt; steam four hours.

## BROWN STEAMED BREAD.
### Mrs. G. B. Griffin.

Two cups corn meal, one cup Graham flour, one cup white
flour, one cup molasses, two cups sour milk, one cup sweet milk,
one teaspoon saleratus; steam four hours.

## RYE AND INDIAN BROWN BREAD.
### Mrs. Messer.

One quart of rye meal, unbolted, one quart of Indian meal,
yellow, one cup molasses, two-thirds cup of yeast, one-half teaspoon of soda; wet up with milk or water, not very stiff.

## BROWN BREAD.
### Mrs. G. F. DeForest, Freeport, Ill.

One and a half pints of thick sour milk, one and a half cups
Graham flour, one and a half cups rye flour, two cups two-thirds
full of Indian meal, one-half cup molasses, salt, one heaping
teaspoon soda beaten into the milk before adding the other ingredients.   Steam five hours.   Very fine.

## STEAMED BROWN BREAD.
### Mrs. C. G. Smith.

One pint of sweet milk, four tablespoons of molasses, one cup
of Indian meal, two cups of rye or Graham flour, one teaspoon

of salt, **one of** saleratus; mix with a spoon, **and steam** three hours, and bake half an hour or more.

## BROWN BREAD.
### Mrs. Lamkin.

One and one-half cups of rye meal, one and one-half of **Indian meal,** one-half **cup** of molasses, two and one-half of cold water, **even** teaspoon of soda, a little salt; steam four and a half **hours, then put** it in the oven for a very few minutes, just **to take the moisture from the** top.

## BROWN BREAD.
### Mrs. A. L. Chetlain.

One quart of bread sponge, one pint of Graham flour, (perhaps a little **more,**) one egg, one cup of molasses, one tablespoon of melted butter, a trifle of salt; mix well together, let rise and bake.

## BROWN BREAD.
### Mrs. Spruance.

Three cups of corn meal, one of flour, three of sweet milk, one **of sour** milk, two-thirds of molasses, one teaspoon of soda, one of salt, whites of two eggs beaten to a froth. **Steam four** hours; eat while hot. Excellent.

## BROWN BREAD.
### Mrs. Banks.

Two cups **of Graham** flour, **one of** wheat **flour,** two large spoons of molasses, **a** little salt, **one yeast** cake **or** half cup of yeast, warm water enough to make **a very** stiff batter. Put it in the bake-tin, and when light **enough,** bake in **a good** oven three-fourths of an **hour.**

*Using "**Richards'** Queen;" it makes Biscuit delicate and light.*

## BOSTON BROWN BREAD.
### Mrs. F. E. Stearns.

One and one-half cups of Graham flour, two cups of corn meal, one-half cup of molasses, one pint of sweet milk, and one-half a teaspoon of soda; steam three hours.

## BROWN BREAD.
### Mrs. Kent.

Three and one-half cups of Graham flour, two of corn meal, three of sour milk, one-half of molasses, one and one-half teaspoons of soda; steam two and one-half hours, and put in the oven for fifteen minutes.

## BROWN BREAD.
### Mrs. E. Wood.

One quart of Graham flour, one pint of wheat flour, one-half cup of brown sugar, one pint of yeast, a little salt; let rise, put in pans, stand short time to rise and then bake.

## BOSTON BROWN BREAD.
### Mrs. L. Gilbert, Evanston.

Three teacups Graham flour, two teacups corn meal, one-half teacup molasses, one pint sour milk, one pint water, one teaspoon soda, one teaspoon salt, put into a tin pail, covered tightly and boil four hours in a kettle.

## BROWN JOE.
### Mrs. O. L. Wheelock.

Two cups of Indian meal, two of flour, one of molasses, one pint of milk; one teaspoon of soda, same of salt; steam six hours.

## TRAVELER'S BREAD.

Take Graham flour, (unsifted,) and currants, figs, dates or raisins may be used by chopping them; stir quite stiffly with the coldest water as briskly as possible, so as to incorporate air with it; then knead in all the unbolted wheat flour you can; cut in cakes or rolls one-half inch thick, and bake in a quick oven.

## STEAMED BREAD.

### Sophia B. Irmberg.

One cup flour, one cup rye meal, one cup corn meal, one-half cup molasses, one and a half cups of sour milk, one egg, little salt, one teaspoon soda. Steam for three hours; then set the pan in the oven for ten or twenty minutes before sending it to the table.

## STEAMED CORN BREAD.

### Mrs. Jane Conger.

Take three cups of meal, and one of flour, scald two cups of the meal with boiling water, add the other cup of meal and flour, two cups of sour milk, one cup molasses, one teaspoon of soda, a little salt. Steam three hours.

## STEAM LOAF.

### Mrs. Dickinson.

Four cups Indian meal, two cups of flour, two cups of sweet milk, two cups of sour milk, one and a half cups molasses, one teaspoon of soda and a little salt. Steam three hours.

## CORN MEAL BREAD.

### Mrs. A. M. Chetlain.

For a small family, one quart of meal run through sieve, one teaspoon salt, three eggs broken in the meal and well mixed; add one teaspoon of saleratus, and sour milk enough to make a stiff batter; mix in this about three tablespoons of melted butter, and bake in a hot oven. If baking powder is preferred, use two teaspoonsful mixed in the meal while dry, and the same quantity of other ingredients, but use sweet milk.

---

*"Richards' Queen Baking Powder;" it makes Biscuit very light.*

## CORN BREAD.

### Mrs. Juliet L. Strayer, a Southern Lady.

One-half pint of butter milk, one-half pint of sweet milk; sweeten the sour milk with one-half teaspoon of soda; beat two eggs, whites and yolks together; pour the milk into the eggs, then thicken with about nine tablespoons of sifted corn meal. Put the pan on the stove with a piece of lard the size of an egg, when melted pour it in the batter; this lard by stirring it will grease the pan to bake in; add a teaspoon of salt.

## CORN BREAD.

### Mrs. O. F. Avery.

One pint Indian meal, one pint sour milk or buttermilk, two eggs, whites and yolks beaten separately, whites put in last thing; two tablespoons sugar, one tablespoon melted butter, a little salt, half a teaspoon saleratus.

## CORN BREAD.

### Mrs. Wm. H. Low.

Two tablespoons of sugar, one tablespoon butter, two eggs; stir all together, add one cup of sweet milk, three teaspoons of baking powder, and three-fourths of a cup corn meal; flour to make it quite stiff.

## INDIAN BREAD.

### Mrs. G. H. L.

Five cups Indian meal, yellow, five cups sour milk, three cups rye flour, one-half cup molasses, one tablespoon saleratus.

## INDIAN BREAD.

### Mrs. A. T. Hall.

One pint of meal, one pint of flour, one pint of milk, one tea-cup of molasses, one teaspoon of soda, one-half of cream tartar; steam two hours and bake half an hour.

*You can only realize the excellence of the above receipts by*

## GRAHAM BREAD.

### Mrs. B. J. Seward.

One pint **sweet milk, one** half cup molasses, one teaspoon saleratus, one teaspoon salt. Mix thin enough **to pour.**

## GRAHAM BREAD.

### Mrs. J. B. Hobbs.

**For** one loaf, take two cups of white bread sponge, to which add two tablespoons of brown sugar, and Graham flour to make **a** stiff batter; **let it rise,** after which add Graham flour sufficient to knead, but **not** very stiff; then put in **the pan to rise and bake.**

## GRAHAM BREAD.

### Mrs. H. P. Stowell.

Set sponge of fine flour, same as for wheat bread; when sufficiently raised, instead of mixing with fine flour, mix with Graham to the usual consistency; mould with fine flour a little, raise once, **then it is** ready for the oven. Sweeten with syrup or sugar, **if** desired, though **I think it** better without either.

## GRAHAM BREAD.

### Mrs. Ludlam, **Evanston.**

**One** cup wheat flour, three cups Graham **flour,** two tablespoons of molasses, one teaspoon salt, yeast enough **to make it rise;** mix and put in baking tins at night. It will be ready to bake in the morning.

## ROLLS.

### Mrs. H. F. Waite.

To the quantity of light bread dough that you would take **for** twelve persons, **add the** white of one egg well beaten, two tablespoons of white sugar, and two tablespoons of butter; work these **thoroughly together;** roll **out** about half an inch thick; cut the **size desired,** and spread one with melted butter, and lay another upon the top **of it.** Bake delicately, when they have risen.

## PARKER HOUSE ROLLS.
### Mrs. A. H. Dashiell, Bricksburg, N. J.

One quart sifted flour, one-half cup of yeast, two tablespoons of sugar, salt, two tablespoons butter and one of lard; pour one pint of boiling milk over the ingredients, except yeast, and add that when lukewarm; mix early in the morning, and knead at noon, adding sufficient flour to make as stiff as biscuit; when light knead into rolls; roll out rather thin, cut with a biscuit cutter and then roll oblong, spread a little butter on one end and fold over; let them rise on the pans before baking. They ought to bake in ten or fifteen minutes. In cold weather the sponge should be made at night.

## PARKER HOUSE ROLLS.
### Alice M. Adams, Mrs. J. P. Hoit and others.

Two quarts flour, make a hole in the top, put in a piece of butter the size of an egg, a little salt, and a tablespoon of white sugar; pour over this a pint of milk previously boiled and cooled, and one-half teacup of good yeast. When the sponge is light, mould for fifteen minutes, let it rise again and cut into round cakes, butter one side and turn over on itself, bake in a quick oven.

## PARKER HOUSE ROLLS.
### Mrs. L. J. Tilton.

Boil one pint of sweet milk, and when partly cooled melt in it half a cup of white sugar and one tablespoon of lard or butter; when lukewarm, add half a cup of yeast; make a hole in two quarts of flour and pour this mixture in. If for tea, set to rise over night, in the morning mix well and knead for half hour, then set to rise again; about four o'clock knead again for ten or fifteen minutes; roll out thinner than for biscuit, rub melted butter upon half the surface and fold it upon the other; set to rise once more in pans, and when light, bake twenty minutes in a hot oven.

*No Biscuit so delicate as that made with "Richards' Queen.*

## DETROIT ROLLS.

### Mrs. A. M. Gibbs.

Put one pint warm milk in the middle of two quarts flour, beat up a thick batter, a little stiffer than pancakes, and add one-half cake German compressed yeast. When light, knead up like bread, kneading the dough out in a long roll and folding over like pie crust, doing this six or seven times. When again light, add a piece of butter size of a large egg, pulling it through the dough, then work in two eggs, and one tablespoon sugar that has been beaten together very light. Knead again same way as before. Roll out on your bread board with rolling pin, cut with small round or oval cutters, dipping cutter occasionally in a cup of melted lard or drippings instead of flour, and put in pans to rise. When creamy light, bake. It will expedite the rising, to set the pans over hot water.

## FRENCH ROLLS.

### Mrs. Thos. Orton.

Take one-half cup of yeast, rub a small one-half cup of butter in the flour, (you will have to guess the quantity), then add the yeast, and water enough to wet; mix as for soda biscuit. Let it rise till morning. Roll in thin sheets, and cut into squares, spread a very little butter on each, and sprinkle a little flour on to roll up. Put in the pan when light, bake twenty minutes. Nice.

## FRENCH ROLLS.

### Etta C. Springer.

One quart flour, add two eggs, one-half pint milk, tablespoon of yeast, knead it well; rise till morning. Work in one ounce of butter, and mould in small rolls; bake immediately.

## YPSILANTI EGG ROLLS.

### Mrs. A. M. Gibbs.

Allow one egg for each person, two cups milk for three eggs, four tablespoons flour; beat whites and yolks separately; eggs are added last.   Put a very little of the mixture into a hot frying pan, well greased with butter, roll as you would omelet, and pile a number on a platter; send in hot.   For breakfast or tea.   Can be eaten with sugar.

## BROWN ROLLS.

### Mrs. Melancthon Starr, Rockford, Ill.

One quart Graham flour, milk enough to make a stiff batter, one-third cup of yeast, and mix over night; in the morning add two eggs, one large tablespoon of sugar, one-fourth teaspoon of soda, piece of butter half the size of an egg, and a little salt; put into cups, and let stand twenty minutes before baking.

## CORN MEAL ROLLS.

### Mrs. A. H. Dashiell, Bricksburg, N. J.

To one quart of mush, add, when hot, one-half cup unmelted lard, salt it well; when lukewarm, add one-half cup of yeast; make this at noon, and at night add a small teaspoon of soda, and knead in wheat flour as for biscuit.   In the morning mould into biscuit, and let them rise in the pan before baking.   Bake in a quick oven.

## GRAHAM ROLLS.

### Mrs. M.

Three teacups Graham flour, two teaspoons cream tartar, one teaspoon soda, one tablespoon melted butter, milk to wet it with.

## TREMONT BISCUIT.

### Brought from Boston by Mrs. O. B. Wilson.

One and a half pints of warm milk, one tablespoon lard, two tablespoons white sugar, a little salt, one yeast cake, (Twin Bro's,) a cup of home-made yeast or half a cake of compressed yeast as is most convenient; two quarts of sifted flour.   To mix—make a hole in the flour and mix in all the ingredients to make a sponge; set in a warm place to rise; when quite light, work in all the flour and set the dough once more to rise; when well risen, work a little more, and roll out about one-third of an inch thick, and cut with a biscuit cutter. Moisten one edge with melted butter, then fold together in the middle like rolls. Place them in a bread pan about one inch a part; set to rise for about half an hour in a warm place, and when light, bake in a quick oven, allowing from ten to fifteen minutes if the oven is just right. Make up about ten o'clock in the morning, if wanted for tea; if wanted for breakfast, make up about nine o'clock in the evening, and work in all the flour at the first mixing, then add as soon as you are up in the morning, one-half teaspoon of soda, mould your biscuit and they will be ready for baking when the oven is hot. With compressed yeast, about six hours all together is required. These are very delicate and delicious when properly made.

## VIRGINIA BISCUITS.
### Mrs. J. G. Hamilton.

Rub a teaspoonful of lard into a quart of flour, put the flour into a sifter and sift a teaspoon of soda with the flour, one teaspoon of salt, and one pint of butter milk to moisten the flour; after beating the mixture with a spoon until thoroughly mixed, turn it out on a biscuit board, work until smooth, cut it out with a cutter and bake with a steady heat.

## GREEN MOUNTAIN BISCUITS.
### Mrs. Lamkin, Evanston.

Three cups milk, two cups sugar, one cup butter; make a stiff batter at night with two tablespoons yeast; one-half the sugar and one-half the butter melted; in the morning add the other half of sugar and butter, and make it not quite as stiff as yeast bread; two hours before tea make up the biscuits and set them to rise.

*When in haste you wish to make delicate light and white bread.*

## LIGHT BISCUITS.

### Mrs. A. R. Edwards.

One pint of sweet milk, one-half pint of lard (not melted,) one-half pint of home-made yeast; add salt and flour to mix soft, rise once, then put in tins.

## FRENCH BISCUITS.

### Mrs. Lind.

Two cups of butter, two cups of sugar, one egg (or the whites of two,) half a cup of sour milk, half a teaspoon of soda, flour to roll; spinkle with sugar.

## RAISED BISCUITS.

### Hannah Johnson; endorsed by Mrs. A. N. Sheppard.

Take one and one-half pints of milk, one spoon of lard, two of white sugar, and one yeast cake or one-half a package of compressed yeast, and two quarts of flour; make a hole in the flour and put in all the ingredients; set in a warm place to rise until morning, then mix all together and set to rise again; when well risen, roll out rather thin, cut them out like biscuits, wet one edge with melted butter, and fold together like rolls; when well risen, bake in a quick oven about twenty minutes. If made with compressed yeast, six and one-half hours will be sufficient to raise them in winter.

## TEA BISCUITS.

### Mrs. Norcross.

One cup of hot water, two of milk, three tablespoons of yeast; mix thoroughly; after it is risen, take two-thirds of a cup of butter and a little sugar and mould it; then let it rise, and mould it into small cakes.

## TEA BISCUITS.

### Mrs. O. L. Parker.

Make a good soda or cream biscuit; mould it and roll it out half the thickness of common biscuit; spread it over with three

or four spoons of melted butter; then over this sprinkle half a coffee cup of the best sugar; roll up as compactly as you would a roll of jelly cake; slice your roll off into inch thick slices; lay these flat on your tins and bake as biscuits. They are very nice cold.

## RAISED BISCUITS.

### Mrs. C. H. Wheeler.

Make a sponge of one pint of milk, a little salt, and half a cake of compressed yeast—any other will do; when light, take a piece of butter the size of an egg, one-quarter of a cup of sugar, and one egg; beat them up together and stir into the sponge, adding flour to make a stiff batter; stir it well and leave to rise; then take with a spoon the light dough just enough for each biscuit and work softly into shape; lay into pans and bake after standing a short time to rise again.

## GRAHAM BISCUITS.

### Mrs. A. W. D.

Three cups of Graham flour, one of wheat flour, one egg, butter the size of an egg, one tablespoon of sugar, two of cream tartar, one of soda; salt and milk to mix.

## GRAHAM BISCUITS.

### M.

One quart of Graham flour, three and one-half heaping teaspoons of baking powder, one teaspoon of salt, one of butter; make into soft dough with milk.

## GRAHAM BISCUITS.

### Mrs. Phelps.

Three cups of Graham flour, one cup white flour, three cups milk, two tablespoons lard, one heaping tablespoon white sugar, one salt spoon of salt, one teaspoon of soda, two teaspoons of cream tartar; mix and bake as you do the white soda biscuit.

*"Richards' Queen"* in making Biscuits, Cakes, Bread or Rolls.

## RYE BISCUITS.

### Mrs. Lamkin.

Two cups rye meal, one and a half cups flour, one-third cup molasses, one egg, a little salt, two cups sour milk, two even teaspoons saleratus.

## BUNS.

Two coffee cups bread dough, two eggs, one cup sugar, spices, a few currants; mould like rusk and let them rise before baking.

## BUNS.

### M.

Take one large coffee cup of warm milk, one-quarter cake of yeast and salt; make sponge, let rise; when light, work into a dough, adding one-half teacup sugar, one egg, butter twice size of an egg; let rise, roll into a sheet, butter it, cut into strips three inches wide and six inches long; fold not quite in the middle; let rise again and bake; when in a dough, if it rises before you are ready, push it down.    Excellent.

## RUSKS.

### Mrs. P. B. Ayer.

To one tumbler of warm milk, add a half gill of yeast, three eggs and a coffee cup of sugar, beaten together; two ounces of butter rubbed into flour, of which use only enough to enable you to mould it; let it raise over night; when very light, roll and put on tins to raise again; after which, bake in a quick oven twenty minutes.

## RUSKS.

Milk enough with one-half cup of yeast to make a pint; make a sponge and rise; then add one and a half cups of white sugar, three eggs, one-half cup of butter; spice to your taste; mould, then put in pan to rise.    When baked, cover the tops with sugar dissolved in milk.

*The excellence of the above receipts can only be realized by*

## SODA BISCUITS.

### M.

To each quart of flour add one tablespoon of shortening, one-half teaspoon of salt and three **and a** half heaping teaspoons of Price's Cream **Baking Powder;** mix baking powder thoroughly through **the flour, then add** other ingredients. Do not knead, and bake quick. To use cream-tartar and soda, take the same proportions without the baking powder, **using** instead three **heaping** teaspoons of cream-tartar and **one of** soda. If good, **they will bake** in five minutes.

## SODA BISCUITS.

### Mrs. A. M. Gibbs.

Three heaping tablespoons of sour cream; put **in a bowl· or** vessel containing a quart and fill **two-thirds** full of sweet milk, four teaspoons of cream-tartar, two teaspoons of soda, a little salt; pour the cream in the flour, mix soft and bake in a quick oven.

## STRAWBERRY SHORTCAKE.

Make good biscuit crust; bake in two **tins of same shape and** size; mix berries with plenty of sugar; **open the** shortcake, but-**ter** well and place berries in layers, alternated **with** the crust; have the top layer **of berries** and over all put charlotte russe or whipped cream.

## ORANGE SHORTCAKE.

### M.

Make a nice shortcake; spread **in** layers of sliced oranges with sugar and **a** little cream. To be eaten with sweetened cream.

## APPLE SHORTCAKE.

### M.

Season apple sauce with butter, sugar, &c.; make a nice short-cake, open and butter it and put the apple sauce in layers. Serve with sweetened cream.

*Using "Richards' Queen;" it makes Biscuit **delicate and light.***

## SALLY LUNN.

### Mrs. J. H. Brown.

One quart of warm milk, one-half cup of butter, one of sugar, five eggs and one cup of yeast; flour enough for stiff batter. Bake one hour.

## SALLY LUNN.

### M.

Take one **pint of** milk, three of flour, three eggs, a **little salt,** two tablespoons **of** butter, and two of **sugar.** Yeast enough to **raise.**

## SALLY LUNN.

### Mrs. C. H. Wheeler.

One pint of milk, a piece of lard or butter the size of an egg warmed in the milk; take **from the** stove and add three well beaten eggs, three pints of flour, **one** cup of yeast; let it stand about three hours or until **light;** then pour into flat pans without working or **kneading,** and let it stand an hour before baking; when baked, split and butter; eat while hot.

## SALLY LUNN.

### Mrs. I. W. Preston, Highland Park.

One quart of flour, butter the size of an egg, two eggs, **two** cups of milk, three spoons of baking powder, a pint of salt; **rub** the salt and baking powder dry with the flour; melt the butter in one cup of the milk; add the other cold; break in the eggs without beating; stir all together hard, and bake twenty or **thirty** minutes in a hot **oven.**

## SALLY LUNN.

### Miss Annie Yocum, Cairo, Ills.

Three teacups of light dough from hop yeast, three teaspoons melted butter, one cup of sugar, three well beaten eggs, one-half teaspoon of soda dissolved and strained, a pinch of salt, and flour to make the dough stiff enough to knead well; set away to rise, and when light, make out by rolling in cakes **to fit** your pans, one-half inch thick; place **one** in **the** pan, cover well with soft butter and lay another on top; when light bake and serve at once. If properly buttered the layers will separate when baked. This bread we prize very highly for tea, **warm,** and any that may be left is good cold for breakfast.

## SQUASH CAKES.

### Miss C. Harris.

One cup squash, one pint sour milk, one egg, a **little salt, half** a teaspoon soda, flour for a batter thick enough to fry.

## CREAM CAKES.

Six eggs, beaten separately, **a** half pint of sour cream, a pint of sweet milk, one and one-half teaspoonful of baking powder, flour enough to make a thin batter; bake in cups.

## BREAKFAST CAKES.

### Mrs. Rice.

One cup milk, one pint flour, three eggs, piece butter size **of an egg, two** teaspoons cream tartar, **on teaspoonful soda, one** tablespoon butter.

## TEA CAKES.

### Mrs. E. S. Chesbrough.

One quart sifted flour, one pint sweet milk, butter size of egg, two eggs, two teaspoons sugar, one of soda, two of cream tartar; bake in small patty-pans.

## WHEAT GEMS.

### Mrs. W. H. Ovington.

One pint milk, two eggs, flour enough to make a batter not very stiff, two large spoons melted butter, yeast to raise them, a little soda and salt. Bake in gem irons.

*"Richards' Queen Baking Powder;" it makes Biscuit very light.*

## GRAHAM GEMS.

### Mrs. Henry Stevens, Winona, Minn.

One pint sweet milk, two eggs, one-half cup sugar, two heaping teaspoons baking powder, one tablespoon melted butter, Graham flour enough to make a stiff batter; drop in hot gem pans.

## GRAHAM GEMS.

### Mrs. E. Wood.

One quart Graham flour, one-half cup of wheat flour, one-half cup of butter, one teaspoon of cream tartar, one-half teaspoon soda, very little sugar, put in cast iron gem pans to bake.

## GEMS.

### Mrs. H. P. Stowell.

A heaping tea saucer of Graham flour, one-half teacups of white flour, mix with sweet milk or water until somewhat thicker than griddle-cake batter. In the meantime, have your gem-irons a little greased, heating on top of the stove. Bake in a hot oven and in twenty-five minutes you have a dish for your breakfast that is rightly named. Have tried them with and without salt, and we think the latter very preferable.

## GRAHAM GEMS.

### Mrs. E. R. Harmon.

One quart of sweet milk, one cup syrup, one teaspoon soda, two teaspoon cream tartar, little salt; mix cream tartar in Graham flour, soda in the milk, and make it as stiff with the flour as will make it drop easily from the spoon into muffin rings.

## POP OVERS.

### Mrs. Andrews.

One cup milk, one cup flour, one egg, beaten separately. Bake in cups, a tablespoonful to each cup.

*The excellence of the above receipts can only be realized by*

## POP OVERS.

### S. S. Peirce.

One cup flour, one cup milk, one egg, piece butter size of a walnut, a little salt; to be baked in scallops in a very quick oven. This rule makes twelve.

## CORN POP OVERS.

### Mrs. A. T. Hall.

One pint sweet milk scalded; stir into the hot milk a coffee cup of corn meal, a piece of butter half the size of an egg, a little salt, three eggs well beaten and stirred in the last thing. No soda.

## POP OVERS.

### Mrs. King.

Three cups milk, three cups flour, three eggs, a little salt, one tablespoon melted butter put in the last thing; two tablespoons to a puff.

## ROSETTES.

### Mrs. A. S. Ewing.

Mix a quart of milk into a pint of flour, beat the whites and yolks of three eggs separately, one tablespoonful of butter cut fine into the mixture, half teaspoonful salt; add the stiffly beaten whites of eggs last of all. Bake in well warmed and greased rosettes or muffin pans.

## PUFFS.

### Mrs. Wren.

Two eggs beaten separately, two cups of milk, two cups of flour, butter the size of a walnut; drop into hot irons and bake quickly.

## YPSILANTI COCOANUT PUFFS.

One grated cocoanut, a little over one-half pound pulverized sugar stirred in the whites of three eggs, beaten light; drop in small cakes on a dripping pan. Bake in a very quick oven.

*Using "Richards' Queen;" it makes Biscuit delicate and light.*

## PUFFS.

Four cups of milk, four cups of flour, four eggs, butter the size of two eggs; put in cups half full, and bake for tea or breakfast.

## GRAHAM PUFFS.

### Mrs. O. S. Wheelock.

One pint of Graham flour, one egg, teaspoon salt, one tablespoon baking powder; wet with milk or water.

## FRITTERS.

### Mrs. Brown.

One pint sweet milk, four eggs, one quart flour and three teaspoons baking powder sifted together. Serve warm with maple syrup.

## FRITTERS OR PUFFS.

### M.

One pint milk in sauce-pan; when it boils, stir in flour until very thick; when cold, mix with six well beaten eggs, one tablespoon sugar, one-half nutmeg, grated peel of small lemon, one tablespoon brandy. Beat well for fifteen minutes. It should be thicker than pancake batter. Drop into hot lard. Sprinkle with powdered sugar or spiced sugar.

## FRITTERS.

### Mrs. E. R. Harmon.

Four eggs, one quart of milk, a little salt; stir a little stiffer than pancakes, and fry in hot lard.

## FRITTERS.

### M.

One pint boiling water, one tablespoon butter, one pint flour, stirred into water while boiling; let it cool a little, and add four eggs, one at a time. Fry in hot lard when the steam rises.

*You can only realize the excellence of the above receipts by*

## FRENCH FRITTERS.

Beat the yolks of four eggs very light, add to them one pint of milk, cut some slices of baker's bread about an inch thick, cutting off all the crust and lay them in the milk about fifteen minutes. Have your griddle hot, and fry the slices a nice brown, using fresh lard for the purpose. Beat the whites of the eggs very light, and stir into them one cup of powdered sugar, and flavor with lemon; to be used as sauce with the fritters. Some prefer liquid pudding sauce.

## PARSNIP FRITTERS.

### M.

One-half cup milk and a tablespoon of butter; boil five or six medium sized parsnips till tender, mash very fine, add two eggs, three tablespoons flour and a little salt; fry a delicate brown in hot drippings. Serve on a hot dish, or napkin.

## GREEN CORN FRITTERS.

### Mrs. Andrews.

Twelve ears of corn grated, four eggs, tablespoon of butter, salt, very little flour; drop a spoonful of the batter into boiling lard.

## APPLE FRITTERS.

### M.

One tea cup of sweet milk, one tablespoon of sweet light dough dissolved in milk, three eggs beaten separately, one teaspoon of salt, one and one-half teacups of flour, one tablespoon of sugar, the grated peel of a lemon, peeled apples sliced without the core; drop into hot lard with a piece of apple in each one; sprinkled with powdered sugar or spiced sugar. Let them stand after making and they will be lighter. Good.

---

*Using Richards' Queen Baking Powder and Extracts of Fruit.*

## SPICED SUGAR FOR FRITTERS.

### M.

One tablespoon of finely powdered and mixed spices, (sifted,) three tablespoons of powdered sugar well mixed with spices, (two-thirds cinnamon and one-third nutmeg and cloves.)

## GREEN CORN CAKES.

### A. M. G.

Twelve ears of sweet corn grated, one teaspoon of salt, one egg and a little more than a good tablespoon of flour. If the corn is not young and milky, very little or no flour need be used. Drop the cakes from the spoon into hot lard or butter.

Oyster plant fritters may be made in the same way—first boiling and mashing the oyster plant; six plants would be sufficient for one egg.

## GRAHAM MUFFINS.

### S. L. S.

One coffee cup of sour milk, one tablespoon of sugar or molasses, one egg, one scant teaspoon of soda, one-half of salt, enough Graham flour to make a stiff batter; sweet milk and two teaspoons of baking powder can be used instead of sour milk and soda. Bake in muffin pans twenty minutes.

## MUFFINS.

### Mrs. Wm. H. Low.

One tablespoon of butter, two tablespoonful sugar, two eggs —stir all together; add one cup of sweet milk, three teaspoons of baking powder, flour to make a stiff batter. Bake twenty minutes in a quick oven.

## MUFFINS.

### From a Southern Lady.

Beat four eggs into a full tablespoon of lard, mix into them one and one-half pints sour milk, effervescing with a teaspoon-

*No Biscuit so delicate as that made with "Richards' Queen.*

ful of soda; add enough flour to make the consistency of pound cake. Bake in heated rings.

## MUFFINS.
### Mrs. Rice.

Three cups flour, one-half cup sugar, two cups milk, large spoonful of butter rubbed to a cream with the sugar, two eggs, one-half teaspoon soda, one teaspoon cream tartar, one teaspoon salt. Bake one-half hour.

## MUFFINS.
### Mrs. Bartlett.

One pint sweet milk, one-half cup yeast, one-half cup butter, one-half cup sugar, one teaspoon salt; stir a little thicker than fritters; set over night.

## MUFFINS.
### M.

One half-half cup sugar, one-half cup milk, two eggs, two tablespoons butter, two heaping teaspoons baking powder, flour enough to make like cake.

## MUFFINS.
### Mrs. C. M., Winnetka.

Butter size of an egg, three tablespoonsful of sugar, three eggs—yolks beaten to a cream, one-half cup sweet milk, flour to make a stiff batter; add whites of eggs well beaten. Bake in muffin pans in a hot oven.

## MUFFINS.
### Mrs. Hoge.

Five eggs, one quart flour, two small cups of milk, two tablespoons melted butter, four tablespoons sugar, three tablespoons baking powder and a little salt.

We advise the use of "Richards' Queen" for making light biscuit.

## CINNAMON MUFFINS.

### Mrs N. C. Gridley, Evanston.

One teacup sour milk, one cup not quite half full sugar, one teaspoon soda, one tablespoon cinnamon, one egg; stir thick with flour and bake in gem irons.

## MUFFINS.

### Mrs. P. B. Ayer.

No. 1.—One cup milk, three teaspoons baking powder, two tablespoons cream, one egg, flour enough to make a stiff batter; bake in rings.

No. 2.—Melt one-half teacup of butter in a pint and a half of milk, one gill of yeast, four eggs well beaten, and flour enough to make a stiff batter. When light, bake in rings.

## GRAHAM MUFFINS.

### Lake Forest.

One and a half pints of Graham flour, one-half pint wheat flour. Take a pint cup three-fourths full of sour milk; add sour cream until full, soda to sweeten, and little molasses and little salt. Bake in gem irons and have the irons hot before turning in the mixture.

## GRAHAM MUFFINS.

### Mrs. L. Cornell.

One egg, butter half size of an egg, three cups Graham flour, three teaspoonful baking powder, a pinch of salt, one-half pint milk or milk and water; to be of thickness of ordinary cake batter. Corn cake may be made same way, only use two cups flour and one of meal, instead of the Graham flour, as above. Excellent.

## GRAHAM MUFFINS.

### Mrs. L. J. Tilton.

One egg, half a cup of sugar, piece of butter the size of an egg, one cup milk, three teaspoons baking powder, Graham meal to make a batter thick enough to drop in rings without spreading; thoroughly mix the baking powder with the meal; melt the butter and mix well with the sugar and egg; add the milk and gradually stir in the meal.

## GRAHAM MUFFINS.

### Mrs. J. H. Brown.

One egg, one and a half cups of sour milk, one teaspoon saleratus, a little salt, two tablespoons of melted lard or butter, two tablespoons molasses; make as stiff as corn meal. Bake fifteen minutes.

## RYE MUFFINS.

### Mrs. Bartlett.

Two cups of rye, one of flour, one of sugar, one egg, one tea spoon of soda, and a little salt; mix quite stiff with sour milk.

## INDIAN MEAL MUFFINS.

Two cups of Indian meal scalded with as little water as possible, one coffee cup of flour, one tea cup of sweet milk, one tablespoon of shortening, one-half cup of brown sugar, a small cup of yeast; mixed over night.

## CORN MEAL MUFFINS.

### Mrs. A. M. Gibbs.

Soak a pint of meal over night in sweet milk, just enough to wet it; in the morning dissolve half a teaspoon of soda in a teaspoon of hot water; then fill the cup with buttermilk or sour milk; add this with the yolks of two eggs and a tablespoon of thick cream or melted butter to the meal, also half a teaspoon of salt. Have your rings or muffin-frames hot, and bake twenty minutes. If preferred, a shallow pan can be used.

*When in haste you wish to make delicate light and white bread.*

## CORN MEAL MUFFINS.

### Mrs. Spruance.

Two cups flour, three-fourths of white corn meal, three-fourths of butter, one-half of sugar, two eggs, one cup of milk, three teaspoons baking powder.

## WAFFLES.

### Mrs. C. M. Dickerman, Rockford, Ill.

One cup sour cream, two cups butter milk, two eggs, a little salt, one teaspoon soda. Bake in waffle irons.

## WAFFLES.

### M.

One pint sour milk, three tablespoons melted butter, three eggs, beaten separately, one tea-spoon soda, salt, flour enough to make a thick batter.

## RICE CROQUETTES.

### C. T. C., Evanston, Ill.

Boil one cup of rice in one quart of milk or water till tender; while warm, add a piece of butter the size of an egg, two eggs; make into rolls, dip them in cracker crumbs and fry them in lard or butter.

## RICE CROQUETTES.

### Mrs. N. C. Gridley, Evanston.

To about one quart of boiled rice, add the yolks of three eggs and a little salt; make it up into balls, roll them in flour and fry them in hot lard, as you would doughnuts.

## RICE CROQUETTES.

One teacup rice, one pint milk, one pint water, a little salt; butter a tin, put in the mixture and swell on the stove, where it will not quite simmer. When dry, add two eggs, beaten light, with with two tablespoons of sugar and one of **butter.** **Have** ready cracker crumbs spread on a board thickly. Make a roll of the rice in the crumbs; **drop in hot lard and** brown.

## RICE CROQUETTES.
### Mrs. Anna Marble.

Rice boiled in milk and flavored with lemon **or orange flower water;** add sugar and eggs; when cold, cut in small pieces; roll them in flour dipped in egg, then roll again in bread crumbs, **fry in hot** fat, **as** you would doughnuts.

## CORN MEAL PONES.
### Mrs. A. M. Gibbs.

Scald a quart of milk; stir into **one pint of** meal six eggs beaten separately, a little salt, one table spoon flour, two teaspoons baking powder; bake in white cups **or** small bowls and send to the table in the cups, so they may **be hot** to be turned out on to the plate **and eaten with butter or syrup.** For tea or breakfast.

## GOOD BREAKFAST CAKES.
### Mrs. J. H. Brown.

Three eggs well beaten, two and a half teacups of flour, one pint of sweet milk, **a** little salt; make a batter of these, bake in **cups or** rings and bake in a quick oven.

## BANNOCKS.
### M.

One pint corn meal, pour on it boiling water to thoroughly wet it; let it stand a few minutes; add salt and one egg and a little sweet cream, or a tablespoon melted butter. Make into balls and fry in hot lard.

*"Richards' Queen"* in making *Biscuits, Cakes, Bread or Rolls.*

## INDIAN BANNOCKS.

### R. A. Sibley.

One quart Indian meal, with a little salt, wet it quite soft with boiling water or milk, must be boiling; wet your hands; pat them out in small flat cakes; fry in hot lard, not enough to cover them. Cook one side first, then turn. Cheap and good for breakfast.

## STELLA'S CORN CAKE.

### Mrs. F. M. Cragin.

No. 1.—One pint milk, one pint meal, two eggs, a piece of butter size of an egg, one and a half teaspoons cream tartar, three-fourths teaspoon soda, one-half teaspoon salt, a little sugar.

No. 2.—One pint sour milk, two eggs, one pint meal, one tablespoon melted butter, one teaspoon saleratus.

No. 3.—One pint sour milk, one-half pint water, one quart meal, three tablespoons melted lard, one teaspoon saleratus, one teaspoon salt.

## CORN CAKES.

### Mrs. A. M.

One pint of grated sweet corn, three tablespoons milk, one teacup of drawn butter, one teaspoon salt, one-half teaspoon black pepper, one egg. Drop by the tablespoon in hot butter. Fry from ten to twenty minutes.

## CORN CAKES.

### Mrs. B. F. Adams.

Three cups Indian meal, one cup flour, two cups sweet milk, one cup sour milk, one egg, teaspoon salt, teaspoon soda. Bake half an hour. This, with half a cup molasses and one cup suet, makes a nice pudding. Steam four hours.

*The excellence of the above receipts can only be realized by*

# CORN CAKES.

### Mrs. Pulnip.

One pint of milk, one-half pint of corn meal, two tablespoons of flour, two eggs, one tablespoon of lard or butter, three tablespoons of sugar, one-half teaspoon baking powder. Beat well.

# CORN CAKES.

### S. S. Peirce.

One pint meal, one pint flour, one cup white sugar, two eggs, piece of butter size small egg; melt the butter; teaspoon soda, two teaspoons cream-tartar, salt, sweet milk; make as thick as griddle cakes.

# GOOD CORN CAKES.

### Mrs. Wm. C. Harris.

Scald about a pint of corn meal at night, adding a little salt; in the morning stir in one egg, and milk enough to make it thin enough to drop from a spoon on a tin.

# CORN CAKES.

### E. E. Macey.

One and one-half cups of Indian meal, one-half cup fine flour, one-half of molasses, one of milk, one-half teaspoon soda, a little salt. For weak stomachs, it is an improvement to add a little ginger.

# GRIDDLE CAKES.

### Mrs. Orson Smith.

Two quarts warm water, one teaspoon salt, one cup flour, one cup corn meal, one-half teacup yeast, two eggs well beaten and added the last; raise over night.

# GREEN CORN GRIDDLE CAKES.

### Mrs. C. M. Dickerman, Rockford, Ill.

Twelve ears corn grated, four eggs, one cup sweet milk, (cream is better,) one cup flour, three tablespoons butter, if you use milk, none if you use cream; a little salt. Bake on a griddle.

*Using "Richards' Queen;" it makes Biscuit delicate and light.*

## RICE CAKES.

### Mrs. Lunt, Evanston.

One cup soft boiled rice, add one-half cup milk, the yolks of three eggs, two tablespoons flour, a little salt; then beat the whites to a stiff froth and mix with the rest. Fry on a buttered griddle as soon as possible after adding the whites of the eggs. Nice for invalids.

## SQUASH GRIDDLE CAKES.

### Mrs. Rice.

One cup squash, two eggs, one and a half pints milk, salt to flavor, flour to make it of a consistency for frying; add a little soda dissolved in milk.

## QUICK BUCKWHEAT CAKES.

One quart of buckwheat flour, one-half a tea cup of corn meal or wheat flour, a little salt, and two tablespoons of syrup. Wet these with cold or warm water to a thin batter, and add lastly four good tablespoons of baking powder.

## BUCKWHEAT CAKES.

### Lake Forest.

One quart buckwheat flour, four tablespoons yeast, one teaspoon salt, one handful Indian meal, two tablespoons molasses, not syrup. Warm water enough to make a thin batter; beat very well and set in a warm place. If the batter is the least sour in the morning, add a little soda.

## CORN MEAL GRIDDLE CAKES.

### Lake Forest.

Soak three-fourths of a pint of meal over night in three cups of sour milk and one of sour cream; in the morning add one pint of flour, a little salt and two eggs; soda to sweeten the mixture.

*All of our leading Hotels of Chicago are now using*

## CORN MEAL GRIDDLE CAKES.

### M.

One pint of corn meal, two tablespoons melted butter, one teaspoon salt, two eggs, one tablespoon sugar, sour milk enough to make batter; saleratus, (if you should get in a little too much, it is easily remedied by adding a few drops of vinegar.)

## OAT MEAL GRIDDLE CAKES.

#### Mrs. J. M. Wetherell, Englewood, Ill.

One cup oat meal, one cup flour, one teaspoon sugar, one teaspoon baking powder, one-half teaspoon salt; sift the baking powder in with the flour; add cold water to make a batter of the consistency of buckwheat cakes; beat very well together and bake immediately. This recipe is sufficient for a family of three.

## MUSH.

Indian or oat meal mush, is best made in the following manner: Put fresh water in a kettle over the fire to boil, and put in some salt; when the water boils, stir in handful by handful corn or oat meal, until thick enough for use. In order to have excellent mush, the meal should be allowed to cook well, and long as possible while thin, and before the final handful is added. When desired to be fried for breakfast, turn into an earthen dish a ndset away to cool. Then cut in slices when you wish to fry; dip each piece in beaten eggs and fry on a hot griddle.

## OAT MEAL GRUEL.

Take two tablespoons of oat meal, pour on it a pint of cold water; let it stand half a day, then pour it through a sieve and boil well one-quarter of an hour, stirring all of the time; season according to taste. The coarse meal to be rejected. Good for invalids or children.

*"Richards' Queen Baking Powder;" it makes Biscuit very light.*

# WEIGHTS AND MEASURES.

Ten eggs are equal to one pound.

One pound of brown sugar, one pound of white sugar powdered or loaf sugar broken, is equal to one quart.

One pound of butter, when soft, is equal to one quart.

One pound and two ounces Indian meal is equal to one quart.

One pound and two ounces of wheat flour is equal to one quart.

Four large tablespoons are equal to one-half gill.

Eight large tablespoons are equal to one gill.

Sixteen large tablespoons are equal to one-half pint.

A common sized wine glass holds half a gill.

A common sized tumbler holds half a pint.

Four ordinary teacups of liquid are equal to one quart.

ed, turn it over the whites, beating all together rapidly until of the right consistency to spread over the cake. Flavor with lemon if preferred. This is sufficient for two loaves.

## FROSTING.

### Mrs. F. D. Gray.

To two-thirds teacup sugar add two small tablespoons water and let the water boil out. Then turn the syrup slowly on the beaten white of one egg.

## FROSTING FOR CAKE.

### Ella Guild.

One cup frosting sugar, two tablespoons of water boiled together; take it off the stove and stir in the white of one egg beaten to a stiff froth; stir all together well; then frost your cake with it; and you will never want for a nicer frosting than this.

## ICE CREAM ICING FOR WHITE CAKE.

### Mrs. P. B. Ayer.

Two cups of pulverized sugar boiled to a thick syrup; add three teaspoons vanilla; when cool, add the whites of two eggs well beaten, and flavored with two teaspoons of citric acid.

## ICING.

### Mrs. H. P. Stowell.

One pound pulverized sugar, pour over one tablespoon cold water, beat whites of three eggs a little, not to a stiff froth; add to the sugar and water; put in a deep bowl; place in a vessel of boiling water and heat. It will become thin and clear. Afterward begin to thicken. When it becomes quite thick remove from the fire and stir while it becomes cool till thick enough to spread with a knife. This will frost several ordinarily sized cakes.

*Tartar and Soda, Sour Milk and Soda, or other Baking Powder.*

## CHOCOLATE FROSTING.
### Mrs. H. L. Bristol.

Six tablespoons of baker's grated chocolate scalded with enough milk to make a paste that will spread easily; sweeten to taste and flavor with vanilla. This is about enough for one rule of cake.

## CHOCOLATE FROSTING.
### Mrs. E. H. Wheeler.

Whites of two eggs, one and one-half cups of fine sugar, six great spoons of grated chocolate, two teaspoons of vanilla; spread rather thickly between layers and on the top of cake; best when freshly made. It should be made like any frosting.

## CHOCOLATE ICING.
### Mrs. P. B. Ayer.

One cup grated chocolate, one cup sugar, one-half cup milk. Boil until thick and flavor with vanilla while cooling.

## BLACK FRUIT CAKE.
### Mrs. C. H. Wheeler.

Three-fourths pound butter, one pound sugar, (brown,) one pound flour, two pounds currants, three pounds raisins, (seeded,) one-half pound citron, one-fourth pound almonds, eight eggs, one nutmeg, cloves and cinnamon, one wine-glass of brandy; the raisins are better to be soaked-in brandy over night.

## BLACK CAKE.
### Mrs. G. F. DeForest.

Two pounds of flour, two pounds sugar, two pounds butter, eight pounds raisins, four pounds currants, one pint brandy, two pounds citron, twenty-four eggs. two ounces nutmeg, two teaspoons of cloves; add a little molasses to make it more moist and black. This makes two very large loaves, baked in tin-pans or hoops. For weddings. Splendid.

---

# BEST BLACK CAKE.

### Mrs. W. H. Ovington.

One pound of flour, one pound butter, one pound sugar, ten eggs, half a pint of brandy, four pounds currants, four pounds raisins, one pound citron, two tablespoons molasses, two tablespoons cinnamon, one tablespoon cloves, two nutmegs; flour the fruit; bake three hours.

## MOTHER DORCHESTER'S BLACK CAKE.

### Mrs. Kate Johnson.

One pound sugar, one pound butter, one pound flour, ten eggs, three pounds raisins, three pounds currants, one-half pound citron, two teaspoons cinnamon, one teaspoon cloves, two teaspoons nutmeg, one wine glass of brandy or alcohol. Stone the raisins and pour the liquor over them, and cover tight over night. Brown the flour to darken the cake. Bake from two to four hours. Will keep good two or three years.

## FRUIT CAKE.

### Mrs. N. C. Gridley, Evanston.

One pound flour, one pound sugar, three-quarters of a pound of butter, three pounds seeded raisins, one pound currants, one pound citron, one-quarter pound almonds, blanched and powdered in rose water; one nutmeg, one wine glass brandy, ten eggs. Stir butter and sugar to a cream, then add whites and eight yolks of eggs, beaten separately. Stir in the flour, then spices and add the fruit just before it is put in the pans. Bake slowly. This cake will keep two years.

## FRUIT CAKE.

### Mrs. Earle, Peoria, Ill.

One pound flour, three-quarters of pound of sugar, one-half pound butter, one-half pint of cream, four eggs, one pound raisins, one of currants, one-half of citron, two glasses brandy, spices to the taste, small lump soda.

## CHEAP FRUIT CAKE.

### Mrs. Earle, Peoria, Ill.

Three teacups flour, one coffee cup of sugar, three-quarters of a teacup butter, three-quarters of a teacup of milk, three eggs, raisins, and currants.

## NICE FRUIT CAKE.

### Mrs. C. E. Brown, Evanston.

One pound butter, two pounds sugar, three pounds flour, four eggs; put together in the usual manner with plenty of fruit, raisins, currants and citron; four teaspoons baking powder; and sufficient flour to make the batter quite stiff. Spices to your taste. To improve the color of the cake, brown the flour before using. It is not too rich.

## FRUIT CAKE.

### Mrs. W. Guthrie.

Twelve eggs, one pound flour, one pound sugar, one pound butter, two pounds raisins, two pounds currants, one ponnd citron, two tablespoons cinnamon, four nutmegs, one cup sweet milk, one cup molasses, one teaspoon cream-tartar, one teaspoon soda, one gill brandy. Bake two hours or more.

## FRUIT CAKE.

### Mrs. A. P. Wightman, Evanston.

Twelve eggs, one pound flour, fourteen ounces butter, two pounds raisins, two pounds currants, one pound citron, one pound brown sugar, one nutmeg, one teaspoon ground cloves, one teaspoon extract rose, one-half teaspoon soda. Beat the eggs to a froth, and the butter and sugar to a cream; add the eggs and the flour, dissolve the soda in a tablespoon of boiling water; add fruit and bake in a moderate oven. This cake will keep for months.

*When you have Company, and wish elegant Cake, use*

# FRUIT CAKE.

### Louisa Churchill.

One pound of sugar, one pound butter, one pound flour, four pounds raisins, two pounds currants, one and one-half pounds citron, one gill brandy, one cup cream, one nutmeg, one teaspoon soda.

# FRUIT CAKE.

### Mrs. W. H. Ovington.

One pound of flour, one pound sugar, one pound butter, two pound raisins, two pounds currants, one-half pound citron, ten eggs, four large nutmegs, one-fourth ounce mace, one-fourth ounce cloves, one-half ounce cinnamon, one gill brandy, one gill wine.

# FRUIT CAKE.

### Mrs. Creote.

One pound of flour, one pound sugar, one pound butter, three pounds raisins, three pounds currants, one pound citron, two grated lemons, ten eggs, three nutmegs, three ounces cinnamon, one gill brandy, one gill wine.  Bake two and one-half hours in a ten quart pan.

# FARMER'S FRUIT CAKE.

### Lucy Settle.

Three cups of sour dried apples, soak over night in warm water.  In the morning drain off the water, chop them the size of raisins, (not too fine,) then simmer in two cups of molasses two hours or until the apples absorb all the molasses; one and one-half cups butter and one cup of sugar well beaten, one cup sweet milk, four eggs, one teaspoon cloves, one teaspoon cinnamon, one of nutmeg, one and one-half teaspoons soda, one wine-glass wine, four and one-half teacups flour, one teacup currants or raisins rolled in flour.  Bake in a well heated oven.

---

*"Richards' Queen," as it makes Cake very Delicate and Light.*

## FARMER'S FRUIT CAKE.
### Mrs. W. P. Cragin.

Take three cups of dried apples, wash them and soak them over night in water. In the morning drain off the water and chop them; add two cups of molasses, and let them simmer two hours, or until the molasses is all absorbed. Let them cool before adding them to the other ingredients, then take one cup of brown sugar, three-fourths cup butter, two eggs, one cup milk, one small teaspoon soda, one and one-half teaspoon cream-tartar, one large tablespoon cloves, one of allspice, two of cinnamon, one nutmeg, the grated rind of two lemons and the juice of one, one-fourth pound of citron, one cup of raisins, flour enough to make it the consistency of cup cake. Bake in a moderate oven.

## DRIED APPLE CAKE.
### Mrs. G. W. Gage.

One cup of dried apples soaked over night, then steamed till soft; put them into a cup of molasses and simmer slowly till well cooked; when cool, add one egg, one-half cup of sugar, one-half cup of butter, one-half cup of milk, two and a half cups of flour, one teaspoon soda, two of cream tartar and spice to taste.

## DRIED APPLE CAKE.
### Mrs. G. F. De Forest, Freeport, Ill.

Two cups dried apples covered with boiling water and soaked over night; in the morning pour off the water; chop rather fine, put in a sauce-pan, with one and a half cups of sugar and one cup molasses, and a little of the water; simmer until the syrup is nearly absorbed; add two-thirds of a cup of butter, the yolks of two eggs and white of one, one cup of currants, two and a half cups of flour, spice as for other fruit cakes. Take the other white of egg, and frost the cake. This makes two loaves. Cannot be told from rich fruit cake.

*The excellence of the above receipts can only be realized by*

## PORK FRUIT CAKE.

One pound pickled pork chopped fine, one pint boiling water poured upon the chopped pork, one cup sugar, two cups molasses, one pound raisins chopped, one-fourth pound candied citron, two tablespoons ground cloves, three tablespoons cinnamon, one nutmeg, one teaspoon ginger, one tablespoon soda.

## DRIED APPLE CAKE.

### Mrs. J. B. Adams.

Soak six cups good dried apples over night. In the morning chop them and simmer gently two hours in two cups of molasses; when cool, add one-half pound raisins, (chopped,) one cup butter, one cup sugar, one cup sweet milk, two eggs, one and one-half teaspoons soda, nutmeg, cloves, cinnamon and allspice. Make rather stiff.

## RAISED CAKE.

### C. T. Stevens.

Two cups bread dough, two cups sugar, two eggs, one and one-half cups butter, one teaspoon soda dissolved in milk; raisins, cloves and cinnamon to your taste.

## BREAD CAKES.

### Mrs. H. B. Hurd.

Three cups dough, three cups sugar, one cup butter, three eggs, three teaspoons soda, raisins and nutmeg; rub butter and sugar together; add the eggs and spice, mix well with the dough; the cake will be lighter if it stand a short time before putting in oven.

## NEW ENGLAND THANKSGIVING CAKE.

### Miss Nancy Cotton, Long Meadow, Mass.

Five pounds flour, two and one-half pounds shortening, (butter and lard,) three and three-fourths pounds sugar, three pounds

*Using "Richards' Queen," as it makes Cake truly elegant.*

stoned **raisins**, three eggs, three small teaspoons soda, **extract of cinnamon**, five nutmegs, one-half spoon mace, **one large spoon of lemon to the** loaf, one glass of **wine**, one glass of brandy, and **citron.** This makes seven loaves. Make **over night with one large cup of yeast, with half the shortening and sugar. Be sure not to** keep **too warm** or to let **get cold.** In the morning have the shortening warmed, but not hot; add spices and fruit, letting all rise again before putting in pans; rub flour in the chopped raisins, and reserve the citron and one-half the raisins; stir into the top of the pans just before baking; let stand an hour in tins before baking. In first mixing, use warm milk enough for a stiff batter, keeping a handful of flour for the fruit.

### NEW ENGLAND ELECTION CAKE.

Mrs. Jno. King, Jr.

Take three pounds sifted **flour, leaving out a pint** to put in with fruit, and mix in warm milk till it is a stiff batter; weigh **one** and a **half pounds** of sugar, one pound butter; **mix** them to a cream, then mix one-half this with **the batter of** milk and flour, and one-half pint of good **home-made yeast;** beat **very thoroughly together;** when light, which will take several hours in winter, (better to mix at night and stand in a warm place till morning;) add the remainder of butter and sugar with six eggs, and one pound raisins, **one glass brandy,** cinnamon, **mace** or nutmeg, as the taste, **and a little soda;** if in season of scarcity of eggs, it is very **good** without any; **should** rise **the second** time before **putting in pans** for baking. **The more** such cake is beaten the finer and lighter it will be.

### A PLAIN FRUIT CAKE.

Mrs. Ada Sturtevant, Delavan, Wis.

One cup of butter, three of brown sugar, three of sour milk, **six of flour,** two eggs, nutmeg, cinnamon and cloves; two cups **of raisins and** currants improve it. Add the fruit the last thing. Bake in **two tins.**

*Why should the patience of ladies be tried when a child can*

## FRUIT CAKE.

### Mrs. E. H. Dennison.

One-half cup of butter, one-half cup of brown sugar, one-half cup of molasses, one-half cup of sour milk, the yolks of four eggs, one-half teaspoon of soda, one teaspoon of cream tartar, one and one-half cups of flour, one cup of raisins chopped fine, one cup of currants, one teaspoon each of cloves, cinnamon and nutmeg.

## DOUGH CAKE.

### Mrs. W. P. Nixon.

One pint bowl of dough as it is ready to mould into loaves, four eggs beaten separately, one cup of butter, two cups of white sugar, one tablespoon of cinnamon, one nutmeg, one-half teaspoon of soda, one pint bowl of stoned raisins; mix by hand; put the dough in a large bowl; first work in the butter well, then the sugar and spice, next the yolks, then the whites of the eggs, then the soda, first dissolved in a little warm water; lastly, the raisins. Bake about as long as you would bread. This quantity makes two loaves.

## BREAD CAKE.

### Mrs. W. H. Ovington.

Three teacups of light dough, three-fourths cup butter, two cups sugar, three eggs, small teaspoon soda dissolved in a little warm water, nutmeg or cinnamon for spice, a coffeecup of raisins or currants; mix all well together and let it raise in the pan fifteen or twenty minutes before setting in the oven.

## RAISED LOAF CAKE.

### Mrs. F. D. Gray.

Three cups of milk, two cups sugar, one cup yeast, flour to make a thick batter. Stand till light; then add two cups sugar, two cups butter, two eggs, raisins and spices. Stand from one to three hours in the tins.

*Always make delicate and light cake with "Richards' Queen?"*

## DOUGH CAKE.

### Mrs. F. D. Gray.

Four cups dough, one and one-half cups butter, two and one-half cups sugar, two eggs, salt, cinnamon, nutmeg, brandy and a small spoon of soda. Rise from one to three hours. For two loaves.

## BREAD CAKE.

### Mrs. Dickinson.

One cup of sponge, one-half cup butter, one and one-half cups sugar, one-half teaspoon soda, two eggs, one cup raisins, one cup currants, one teaspoon cloves, one of cinnamon, and nutmeg.

## LOAF CAKE.

### Mrs. John King, Jr.

Four pounds light dough, two pounds sugar, one pound butter, four eggs, one pound stoned and chopped raisins, (sliced citron, if you like,) one wine-glass brandy or wine, small teaspoon soda, mace or nutmeg; mix sugar and butter with the eggs, well beaten; then with the hands mix the dough to the ingredients, beating very thoroughly; add spices and fruit, and allow to rise before baking, after putting in the pans.

PLAINER LOAF CAKE.—Six cups light dough, three cups sugar, one and one-half cups butter, three eggs, small teaspoon of saleratus, spice and fruit as you please; mix as the fruit. Dough for cake should always be light, either bread or biscuit; if biscuit dough is used, a little less shortening is needed, and to insure light cake, the bread should be made from good home made yeast.

## FRENCH LOAF.

### Mrs. H. M. Buell.

Ten cups of flour, six cups sugar, three cups butter, six eggs, three nutmegs, two cups milk, one pound raisins, a little citron, glass of wine or brandy, one teaspoon soda, two teaspoons cream-tartar. Makes four loaves.

## LOAF CAKE.
### Mrs. G. F. De Forest, Freeport.

Four pounds flour, two pounds sugar, two and a half pounds butter, (or one and a quarter pounds butter and three-quarters of a pound lard,) three and a half pounds raisins, a little citron; add wine, brandy, four eggs, one teaspoon soda, and spice as you please; rub the butter and sugar well together, then take half and work into the flour; add half a pint of domestic yeast; make the dough not quite as stiff as biscuit. When it has well risen, work in the other half of the butter and sugar, with the spices and brandy. When thoroughly light, add the eggs, beaten separately, and the fruit. Let it rise an hour in the tins; bake one and a quarter hours. It will keep all winter, if frosted. This rule makes eight loaves.

## LOAF CAKE.
### Mrs. C. H. Wheeler.

Two cups light dough, one cup sugar, one cup chopped raisins, small one-half cup of soft butter, one egg, half a nutmeg, teaspoon of cinnamon; one-half a wine glass of wine can be added if desired; dissolve one-half teaspoon of soda in two tablespoons of milk; mix the butter and sugar well into the dough with the hand, before adding the rest of the ingredients; flour the raisins; a little flour may be added if the brandy is used and the cake seems too thin. Mix or stir very thoroughly, and raise about an hour or until it looks light.

## QUICK LOAF CAKE.
### Mrs. H. M. Buell.

One cup of sugar, one-half of butter, one of milk, one egg, two and one-half cups of flour, one-half teaspoon of soda, one teaspoon of cream tartar.

*In the above receipts, if you wish to realize their excellence.*

## POUND CAKE.

### Mrs. W. H. Ovington.

One pound of flour, one of sugar, ten eggs; beat the yolks and sugar together; add one pound of butter, putting in the whites beaten to a froth, and the flour last. Very nice baked in small patty pans and frosted.

## WHITE POUND CAKE.

### Mrs. G. S. Whitaker.

One pound sugar, one of flour, fourteen ounces butter, one cup sour milk, or sweet milk with soda or cream tartar mixed in milk, whites of twelve eggs; flavoring, and citron.

## MOUNTAIN POUND CAKE.

### Mrs. C. M. Dickerman, Rockford, Ill.

One pound sugar, one of flour, one-half of butter, six eggs, (the whites and yolks beaten separately,) three-fourth cup sweet milk, one teaspoon soda, two of cream tartar; sift the soda and cream tartar together into the flour, after sifting the flour; then rub butter and sugar to a cream, and add a part of the whites and the yolks of the eggs, also a part of the flour, and then the milk.

## IMPERIAL CAKE.

### Mrs. H. E. Sargent.

One pound flour, one of sugar, three-fourths of butter, nine eggs, one and a quarter pounds almonds, before being cracked, one-half pound citron, one and a half pounds raisins, one nutmeg, the rind and juice of one lemon. Blanch the almonds, and chop fine.

## IMPERIAL CAKE.

### M. A. T.

One pound sugar, one of flour, one of butter, ten eggs, one pound almonds, three-quarters of citron cut fine, one glass of brandy and mace; put the fruit in the flour, and bake in thick loaves.

## IMPERIAL CAKE.
### Mrs. De Forest.

One pound sugar, one of flour, three-fourths of butter, one of almonds, blanched and cut fine, one-half of citron, one-half of raisins, rind and juice of one lemon, one nutmeg, ten eggs. This is very delicious and will keep for months. Elegant.

## WHITE CAKE.
### Elmina Meeker, Cortland, Ill.

Two cups of white sugar, one of cream, (sweet), two of flour, one tablespoon of butter, the whites of five eggs, one teaspoon of cream tartar, one-half of soda. Flavor with lemon.

## WHITE CAKE.
### Marian Ely, Cortland, Ill.

One cup of sugar, one-half of butter, one-half of sweet milk, whites of two eggs, one teaspoon of cream tartar, one-half of soda, two and one-half cups of flour.

## WHITE CAKE.
### Mrs. C. H. Wheeler.

Two cups of sugar, one-half of butter, the whites of four eggs, one cup sweet milk, three of flour, three small teaspoons of baking powder sifted with the flour. Beat the sugar and butter to a cream, then stir in the milk and flour, a little at a time; add the whites last. All cake should be well stirred before the whites of the eggs are added. Never fails.

## WHITE CAKE.
### L. Sherwood.

The whites of ten eggs, one and one-half cups of sugar, one of flour, one teaspoon of cream tartar, one-half of lemon.

*Tartar and Soda, Sour Milk and Soda, or other Baking Powder.*

## WHITE CAKE.

### Mrs. Brown.

One-half cup of butter, one and one-half sugar, one-half of sweet milk, the whites of four eggs; add last two cups of flour and one and one-half teaspoons of baking powder sifted together. Flavor to taste.

## PRIZE WHITE CUP CAKE.

### Mrs. Kate W. Hoge.

One cup of butter, four cups sifted flour or three of unsifted, two cups of white sugar, one of sour milk with one-half teaspoon soda, five eggs, beaten separately. Beat the yellow of the eggs until light, then add the sugar, and beat it well together, then add the whites of the eggs (beaten well beforehand) alternating with the flour (after being sifted.) Mix the white of the eggs and flour very slowly and bake in a moderately heated oven at first, then finish with a hotter oven. Try it with a straw or knife; when the dough don't stick, it is done. Use flavoring to taste. This will make one large or two small cakes.

## WHITE OR BRIDE'S CAKE.

### Mrs. M. A. Taylor.

The whites of twenty-two eggs beaten to a stiff froth, two pounds of flour, one and one-half pounds of butter, (the butter and flour creamed together,) and two pounds of white sugar. Bake quickly.

## SNOW CAKE.

### Mrs. Lamkin.

Three-fourths cup of butter, two cups sugar, one cup milk, one cup corn starch, two cups flour, one and one-half teaspoons baking powder. Mix corn starch, flour and baking powder together; add to the butter and sugar alternately with the milk; lastly, add the whites of seven eggs. Flavor to taste. Never fails to be good.

## SNOW CAKE.

### Mrs. Kent.

Whites of ten eggs beaten to a stiff froth, one and one-half tumblers powdered sugar, one tumbler of flour, one very full teaspoon of cream-tartar.

## SNOW CAKE.

Beat one cup of butter to a cream, then add one and one-half cups flour, and stir very thoroughly together; next one cup of corn starch, and one cup of sweet milk in which you have dissolved three teaspoons baking powder; last of all, add the whites of eight eggs, and two cups sugar well beaten together; flavor to taste; bake in one large loaf, or in sheets, and put together with icing.

## DELICATE CAKE.

### Mrs. Anson Gorton.

One coffee cup butter, two coffee cups sugar, four coffee cups flour, one-half coffee cup milk. The whites of eight eggs, two tablespoons cream tartar, even teaspoon soda. Flavor to the taste.

## DELICATE CAKE.

### Marian Ely.

The whites of four eggs well beaten, one cup white sugar, one-half cup butter, one-half cup sweet milk, two cups flour, one teaspoon cream tartar, one-half teaspoon soda.

## DELICATE CAKE.

### Louisa Churchill.

One cup corn starch, one of butter, two of sugar, one of sweet milk, two of flour, the whites of seven eggs. Rub butter and sugar to a cream, mix one spoon cream tartar with the flour and starch, one-half spoon soda with the sweet milk; add the milk and soda to the sugar and butter, then add flour, then the whites of eggs and one spoon of lemon flavor.

---

*Baking Powder, as articles made with this are very delicate.*

## DELICATE CAKE.

### Mrs. J. A. Ellis.

One and a half cups powdered sugar, one-half of butter, one and a half of flour, one-half of corn starch, sifted with the flour, one-half of milk, the whites of six eggs beaten to a froth, one small teaspoon cream tartar, one-half teaspoon soda; flavor with almond or vanilla.   Bake in a moderate oven.

## DELICATE CAKE.

### Mrs. A. T. Hall.

One cup butter, two of sugar, one of sweet milk, eight eggs, three cups flour, one teaspoon of cream tartar, one-half teaspoon soda.

## DELICATE CAKE.

### Mrs. Furlong's.

Two cups pulverized sugar, one of butter, two of flour, two-thirds of milk, two teaspoons baking powder; mix well with flour, whites of six eggs, beaten to a stiff froth; flavor to taste.

## DELICATE CAKE.

### Mrs. E. A. Forsyth.

The whites of four eggs, two cups of white sugar well beaten together, four tablespoons melted butter, one cup sweet milk, three cups sifted flour, two teaspoons Dr. Price's baking powder mixed with the flour.   This cake, if baked in a slow oven, will be very nice.

## DELICATE CAKE.

### H. M. Brewer.

One-half cup of butter, one of powdered sugar, one of sweet milk, two teaspoons of cream tartar, one of soda, both stirred into the milk, the whites of six eggs beaten to a froth, two cups of flour; lastly, two-thirds cup of corn starch.   Flavor with bitter almond.

*When you have Company, and wish elegant Cake, use*

## DELICATE CAKE.

### Mrs. M. L., Evanston.

One cup of butter, two of sugar, one of sweet milk, two of flour, one of corn starch, the whites of seven eggs, one teaspoon teaspoon of cream tartar, one of soda.

## DELICATE CAKE.

### Mrs. J. B. Adams.

One and a half cups sugar, two-thirds of butter, two-thirds of sweet milk, three of flour, one and a half teaspoons cream tartar, one-half of soda, whites five eggs. For jelly cake, whites of six eggs.

## DELICATE CAKE.

### Alice M. Adams.

One-half cup butter, two of sugar, nearly three of flour, three-fourths of sweet milk, three teaspoons baking powder, whites of six eggs; use chocolate and white frosting.

## DELICATE CAKE.

### Mrs. C. E. Browne, Evanston.

Two eggs, a trifle over half a cup of butter, one cup sweet milk, one and a half of sugar, and three teaspoons baking powder. Put together in the usual manner, and flavor with extract of almonds or lemon. Made with the whites of four eggs, it is admirable for cocoanut cake; or with yolks, for chocolate. Use your judgemnt in adding flour. This recipe I have had in use for fifteen years, and while inexpensive, it is nice enough for most any occasion.

## DELICATE CAKE.

### Mrs. M. J. Woodworth.

One pound of flour, one pound sugar, three-fourths pound butter, the whites of sixteen eggs beaten to a stiff froth; flavor with bitter almond. Elegant.

---

*"Richards' Queen," as it makes Cake very Delicate and Light.*

## FEATHER CAKE.

### Mrs. A. L. Hutchinson.

One cup of sugar, one egg, butter the size of an egg, two-thirds cup milk, two cups flour, one teaspoon cream-tartar, half of soda, a little nutmeg.

## FEATHER CAKE.

### Mrs. A. P. Wightman.

One cup sugar, one cup flour, one egg, one tablespoon melted butter, one-half cup sweet milk, one teaspoon baking powder, pinch of salt, flavor to taste; put in the baking powder and run through a seive.

## FEATHER CAKE.

### Mrs. W. H. Ovington.

One cup sugar, three eggs beaten well together, butter the size of an egg, one cup flour, one teaspoon cream-tartar mixed with flour, one-half teaspoon soda dissolved in eight teaspoons of water. Season to taste.

## CREAM CAKE.

### Mrs. M. J. Woodworth.

Three eggs, one and one-half cups flour, one cup sugar, two teaspoons baking powder, three tablespoons water, bake in jelly cake pans, making four cakes; cream, one pint milk, one egg, one and one-half tablespoons corn starch, two tablespoons sugar; flavor when cool. Very nice.

## CREAM CAKE.

### Mrs. James Wadsworth, Hyde Park.

Beat five eggs thoroughly, add two cups sugar, two tablespoons cream, two cups flour in which has been mixed one and one-half teaspoons baking powder, a little salt, bake in five jelly tins, leaving about one-sixth of the batter, to this add one cup of

*The excellence of the above receipts can only be realized by*

milk, also lemon or vanilla; boil **till it** thickens, stirring constantly; then spread it over **the cakes as they are** laid together.

## CORN STARCH CAKE.

Mrs. Dickinson.

**One cup** of butter, two cups **sugar,** one cup sweet milk, **two-thirds** cup corn starch and fill **it up with** flour, two **cups flour, two** teaspoons baking powder, whites of **seven eggs.**

## CORN STARCH CAKE.

M. W. Lazear.

One cup butter, **two of sugar, one of** sweet milk, whites seven eggs, one cup corn starch, two cups flour, yolk of one egg, one teaspoon soda, two of cream tartar, (or three teaspoons baking powder) Mix flour, starch and cream tartar together; flavor with almond.

## CORN STARCH CAKE.

**Mrs. H. E. Sargent.**

One and **a half** cups sugar, **one** and a half of flour, one-half of butter, one-half of corn starch, one-half of sweet milk, **one tea-**spoon cream tartar, **one-half teaspoon** soda, one teaspoon almond flavoring, **whites of six eggs.**

## CORN STARCH CAKE.

Mrs. P.

One and a half cups of sugar, one-half **of** butter, one-half of sour milk, one-half teaspoon of soda, one teaspoon cream tartar, one-half cup corn starch; the whites of six eggs put in the last thing.

## CORN STARCH CAKE.

Mrs. Hobbs.

Whites of seven eggs, **one** cup corn starch, two of flour, one of butter, **one** of sweet milk, two of sugar, two teaspoons cream tartar, one teaspoon soda.

*Using "Richards' Queen," as it makes Cake truly elegant.*
13

## CORN STARCH CAKE.

### Lucy D. Fake.

One cup white sugar and one-half cup butter beaten together, one-half cup corn starch, the whites of three eggs beaten to a stiff froth, one cup milk, one cup flour, one teaspoon cream tartar, one-half of soda.   Flavor with lemon.

## LADY CAKE.

### Mrs. Ewing.

One pound sugar, one-half pound butter, one pound flour, whites of sixteen eggs, one and one-half teaspoons soda, one and one-half teaspoons cream-tartar.   Rub butter and sugar together, then stir the whites of eggs into it.   Sift the flour three times with cream-tartar and soda in it, and add lastly.

## LADY CAKE.

### H. M. H.

One and one-half pounds sugar, one pound flour, nine ounces butter, two lemons, grate rinds and squeeze the juice, whites of twenty-one eggs.

## LADY CAKE.

One cup boiled milk, one-half cup butter, two cups powdered sugar, three cups flour, one even teaspoon cream-tartar, one-half teaspoon soda, whites of two eggs; flavor with bitter almond.

## LEMON CAKE.

### Mrs. H. M. Buell.

Four cups of flour, three cups sugar, one-half cup butter, one teaspoon cream-tartar, rubbed into the flour, one-half teaspoon soda dissolved in one cup of milk, four eggs, one teaspoon of essence of lemon.

*Why should the patience of ladies be tried when a child can*

## LEMON CAKE.
Lake Forest, Ill.

Three **cups of** sugar, **one cup** butter, **one** cup milk, five eggs, four cups flour. Stir **the** butter and sugar to a cream, beat the eggs separately, the whites to a stiff froth, and dissolve a little **soda** in the milk. Mix all together; sift the flour and **put in by degrees, and** add the juice and **grated rind of a fresh** lemon. This **cake is delicious.**

## LEMON CAKE.
Mrs. H. B. Hurd.

Five cups flour, one cup butter, **three cups** sugar, **one** cup cream, five eggs, one teaspoon saleratus and the peel **and** juice of two lemons.

## LEMON CAKE.
Mrs. Elmendorf.

Three cups sugar, one cup butter, one cup sweet milk, four cups flour, five eggs, (whites beaten separately,) and add **last, one** teaspoon cream-tartar, one teaspoon **soda, the grated peel and** juice of one lemon.

## LEMON CAKE.
Mrs. J. O. Knapp.

One cup of butter, **three of** sugar, rub them to a cream; stir into this the yolks of five eggs well beaten, one cup of milk, **one** teaspoon of saleratus, juice and grated peel of one lemon, and the whites of five eggs; sift in lightly four cups of flour, bake in **shallow** pans one-half hour.

## LEMON CAKE.
Mrs. Lamkin.

One cup of butter and three cups of powdered sugar, rubbed **to a** cream; add five well beaten eggs, one small or even teaspoon of soda, in **one cup of** sweet milk, the juice and grated yellow of **one** lemon; **stir in as** light as possible four cups of **flour. Bake in two tin sheets.** Is improved by icing.

*Always make delicate and light cake with "Richards' Queen!"*

## SPICE CAKE.
### Mrs. A. T. Hall.

Two cups of sugar, two cups butter, six cups flour, one cup molasses, one cup milk, six eggs, one glass brandy, two teaspoons cream-tartar, one teaspoon soda, two teaspoons cloves, one nutmeg, two pounds raisins.

## CLOVE CAKE.
### Mrs. H. P. Merriman.

Four and one-half coffee cups of sifted flour, three full cups sugar, one and one-half cups butter, one teacup cream or milk, one teaspoon saleratus, four eggs, one tablespoon cloves, one tablespoon cinnamon, one tablespoon nutmeg, one pound fruit and citron.

## SPICE CAKE.
### Mrs. J. C. Mooar.

One and one-half cups sugar, two-thirds cup butter, one cup raisins, two-thirds cup sweet milk, three cups flour, two eggs, one teaspoon cream-tartar, one-half teaspoon soda, cinnamon, nutmegs and cloves to suit taste.

## CURRANT CAKE.
### Fanny L., Evanston.

One and one-half pounds flour, one pound sugar, three-fourths pound butter, seven eggs, one gill milk, one-half teaspoon saleratus, one pound currants.

## BERRY CAKE.
### Fanny L.

Two cups sugar, three-fourths cups butter, two eggs, one cup molasses, two cups milk, two teaspoons cinnamon, one teaspoon saleratus, a little salt, stiffen with flour, one quart berries.

## POOR MAN'S CAKE.
### Fanny L.

Two cups raised dough, one egg, one-half cup molasses, one cup sugar, butter size of an egg, one teaspoon soda; one cup raisins, flour to stiffen.

## COFFEE CAKE.
### Mrs. W. H. Brown.

One cup butter, two cups sugar, one cup molasses, one cup liquid coffee, five and one-half cups flour, five eggs, one pound raisins, one pound currants, one spoonful each of cloves, cinnamon and nutmeg, three teaspoons baking powder or one of soda.

## COFFEE CAKE.
### Mrs. E. S. Chesbrough.

One cup butter, one of sugar, one of molasses, one of strong coffee, five of flour, one pound of raisins, one teaspoon of soda, one of cinnamon, one of allspice, one-half a nutmeg, three eggs, (it can be made with one or two.) Sift the soda in molasses. Excellent.

## COFFEE CAKE.
### Mrs. W. Guthrie.

One and one-half cups of liquid coffee, one and one-half of molasses, one and one-half of sugar, one of butter, two teaspoons of soda, flour to thicken; cinnamon, cloves and nutmeg; fruit, if desired.

## PUFF CAKE.
### Mrs. A. M. Lewis.

One cup brown sugar, one half of butter, two eggs, one-half cup sweet milk, two of Graham flour, (sifted), one-half teaspoon soda, one of cream tartar, or two teaspoons of baking powder, one cup of raisins.

*In the above receipts, if you wish to realize their excellence.*

## CHOCOLATE CAKE.

### C. A. Tinkham.

One cup butter, two of sugar, five eggs, (leaving out the whites of two,) one cup sweet milk, one teaspoon cream tartar, one-half of soda, both dissolved in the milk, three and one-half cups of flour, scant measure. For frosting : Take the whites of the two eggs, one and one-half cups of powdered sugar, six large tablespoons grated chocolate; frost while the cake is hot.

## MARBLE CAKE.

### Mrs. J. Gilbert, Evanston.

WHITE PART.—One cup white pulverized sugar, one-half cup butter, one-half cup sweet milk, whites of four eggs, two and one-half cups flour, two heaping teaspoons baking powder, or one teaspoon cream-tartar and one-half teaspoon soda; stir butter and sugar together to a cream, and beat whites of eggs to a stiff froth, which are to be added the last of all of the ingredients, with the half cup of flour, which must contain the baking powder well mixed in the flour; season to taste. This is a very good recipe for delicate cake, also.

DARK PART.—One cup brown sugar, one-half cup molasses, one-half cup sour milk, two and one-half cups flour, one level teaspoon soda dissolved in the milk and in the molasses, yolks of four eggs and one-half cup butter, to be rubbed well together with the sugar; add one-half teaspoon of cinnamon, allspice and cloves.

Either of these make good cake used separately, or well mixed to represent marble.

## COCHINEAL MARBLE CAKE.

### Miss Anne Yocum, Cairo, Ill.

One cup butter, three cups pulverized sugar, five cups flour, one cup water, ten eggs, (whites only,) three teaspoons yeast powder sifted with flour; cream the butter and sugar by stirring

---

*Use "Richards' Queen Baking Powder" in the place of Cream*

together; beat the whites of the eggs to a froth, and gradually add all together. Before beginning the cake, put a small teaspoon of cochineal to soak in two tablespoons of hot water; bruise it with a spoon, and strain through a piece of swiss muslin into three-fourths teacup of the cake batter, and as you pour the batter into the cake tin, marble with the red dough. A little practice will produce very satisfactory results.

## MARBLE CAKE.

### Mrs. Frances M. Thatcher.

One-half cup of sour cream, one-half cup butter, one cup white sugar, the whites of five eggs, two-thirds teaspoon soda; prepare another mixture, except substituting dark sugar for white, and the yolks instead of the whites; fill a tin with alternate layers of each and bake.

## LEOPARD CAKE.

### Mrs. P.

For DARK PART.—One cup brown sugar, one-half of molasses, one-half of strong coffee, three-fourths of butter, three tablespoons sweet milk, one-fourth of soda, one-half of cream tartar, one of cloves, one of cinnamon, one nutmeg, two tablespoons of brandy.

For LIGHT PART.—Two-thirds of a cup butter, one of white sugar, three tablespoons sweet milk, one of lemon essence, one-fourth of soda, one-half of cream tartar, the whites of four eggs.

## ALMOND CAKE.

### Mrs. W. Hunt.

One cup milk, two of sugar, one of butter, three of flour, four eggs, one and one-half teaspoons yeast powder, one and one-half teacups sour cream beaten with one coffee cup sugar, one pound almonds chopped fine.

*Tartar and Soda, Sour Milk and Soda, or other Baking Powder.*

## COCOANUT CAKE.
### Mrs. Wicker.

One and one-half cups sugar, one and one-half of butter, two of flour, three and one-fourths of sweet milk, the whites of four eggs, three teaspoons baking powder; bake in jelly tins. Grate one cocoanut, beat the whites of two eggs to a froth, adding a little sugar, and two-thirds of the cocoanut put between the layers; frost the top, and carefully throw on the remainder of the cocoanut.

## HICKORY-NUT CAKE.
### Mrs. Hobbs.

One cup meats, (broken,) one and one-half of sugar, one-half of butter, two of flour, three-fourths of sweet milk, two teaspoons baking powder, the whites of four eggs well beaten; add the meats last.

## HICKORY-NUT CAKE.
### Ella J. Roe.

One and one-half cups of sugar, one of butter, one of chopped hickory-nuts, three-fourths of sweet milk; add last, two cups of flour and three teaspoons of baking powder sifted together.

## HICKORY-NUT CAKE.
### Mrs. C. C. Stratton, Evanston.

Two cups pulverized sugar, one cup butter, one cup new milk, four cups sifted flour, (winter wheat flour,) white of eight eggs, one and one-half cups hickory-nut meats, one tablespoon vanilla, three heaping teaspoons baking powder; put the baking powder into the flour, and stir well before using, beat and add the eggs the last; bake slowly one hour.

## HICKORY-NUT CAKE.
### Nellie Gould.

Not quite a cup of butter, one and one-half cups sugar, three-fourths cup sweet milk, three cups flour, three teaspoons baking powder, white of four eggs, one cup hickory-nuts.

## NUT CAKE.

Mrs. Taylor, Fort Wayne.

Two and a half cups sugar, one of butter, three and a half of flour; one of sweet milk, five eggs, one pound stoned raisins, one-half pound of citron, one-half of a lemon peel, one-half of an orange peel, one pint hickory-nut meats, one nutmeg, two teaspoons baking powder.

## WHITE CUP CAKE.

Mrs. A. S. Ewing.

Two cups sugar, one of butter, four of flour, one of sweet cream, one teaspoon soda dissolved in the cream, two teaspoons cream tartar mixed through the flour, whites of eight eggs.

## COMPOSITION CAKE.

Southern Lady's Recipe.

Two cups butter, three of sugar, one of sour milk, five cups flour, eight eggs, one teaspoon soda, one-half nutmeg; fruit.

## COMPOSITION CAKE.

Mrs. H. F. Waite.

Five eggs, our cups sifted flour, two and one-half of sugar, one of butter, one of milk, two teaspoons cream tartar, one of soda. Beat sugar, butter and yolks of eggs a long time, then add milk and part of the flour; with the rest of flour add the whites, beaten very light; raisins or citrons, if desired.

## VANILLA CAKE.

A. E. W.

One-half cup of butter stirred into one cup of sugar till it is like cream, three eggs, one and one-half cups flour, two teaspoons vanilla; bake on tins, dropping.

*Baking Powder, as articles made with this are very delicate.*

## REBECCA'S PLAIN CAKE.
### Mrs. G. H. L.

One cup **sugar**, two of flour, **one-half of butter, one-half of** sour milk, one egg, one teaspoon saleratus.   **One loaf.**

## PLAIN CAKE.
### Harriet N. Jenks.

**One cup of Indian** meal sifted, **one** of flour, one of sugar, one teaspoon soda, about a pint of sour milk, teaspoon full of salt, **one egg,** piece of butter size of a common egg.   Wholesome for **children.**

## EXCELLENT CAKE.
### Harriet N. Jenks.

**One** pound of sugar, two **pounds of flour, three-quarters of a** pound of butter, one-half cup ginger, eight eggs.   **Rub a little** melted butter over the **cake when hot, and sift sugar over it.**

## ONE-EGG CAKE.
### Mrs. P. B. Ayer.

One and a half cups sugar and one-half of butter beaten together, one egg, **one** cup milk, two and a half of flour, two and a half teaspoons of baking powder.   This cake should **have** icing of some kind between, chocolate for example.

## DELICIOUS CAKE.
### Jennie Simons.

Three cups flour, **two cups** white sugar, one **cup butter, one** cup milk, three eggs, **one-half** teaspoon soda, **one** teaspoon cream-tartar; stir butter and sugar together, add the yolks of the eggs, then the flour, soda and cream-tartar together, and the whites of the eggs well beaten, the last thing.

*When you have Company, and wish elegant Cake, use*

## TEA CAKE.

### Mrs. C. S. Horsman, Rockford, Ill.

One cup of butter, two of sugar, three of flour, one cup of milk, the whites of five eggs, three teaspoons of baking powder.

## TIPSY CAKE.

### Mrs. Gen. N. J. T. Dana.

**Take** sponge cake and stick it full **of** almonds which **have** been blanched; turn over it as much white wine as it **will absorb**; put **it** in a deep dish or glass bowl, and let it stand **one** hour, then pour over it as much soft custard as the dish will **hold.** **Let it** stand two or three hours. Very simple and very **nice.**

## TEMPERANCE CAKE.

### Mattie Winslow, Aurora, Ill.

Two and a half cups flour, one of sugar, one of sweet milk, one egg, one tablespoon melted **butter, one** teaspoon cream **tartar,** one-half teaspoon soda. Bake **quickly.**

## CHARITY CAKE.

### Marian Ely.

**One** cup sugar, one egg, butter size of an egg, stir to a cream; **one cup** sweet milk, two cups flour, two teaspoons cream tartar, **one of soda.**

## RUNAWAY CAKE.

### Mattie Winslow, Aurora, Ill.

One egg, one teaspoon sugar, two tablespoons butter, one cup milk, two teaspoons cream-tartar, one teaspoon soda, flour to make a little thicker than griddle cakes. This is very nice eaten hot with butter for breakfast and tea.

---

*"Richards' Queen,"* as it makes Cake very Delicate and Light.

## SURPRISE CAKE.

### Mrs. M. G. Hubbell, Shabbona Station, Ill.

One egg, one cup sugar, one-half cup butter, one cup sweet milk, one teaspoon soda, two teaspoons cream-tartar mixed in two cups of flour.

## TUMBLER CAKE.

### Mrs. Lamkin.

Four eggs, one tumbler sugar, one tumbler butter, one-half tumbler molasses, one-third tumbler milk, one teaspoon saleratus; spices to taste; one-half pound raisins, one-fourth pound currants.   Bake one and one-fourth hours in a slow oven.

## ADAMS' CAKE.

### Mrs. H. P. Stowell.

One cup sugar, two-thirds cup butter, four eggs, one and one-eighth cups flour, very little soda.   Very nice.

## CLAY CAKE.

### Mrs. Ada Sturtevant.

One cup butter, two and one-half cups sugar, one cup sweet milk, four cups flour, the yolks of five eggs and the whites of seven, two spoons cream-tartar, one spoon soda, one spoon of the extract of lemon; stir the butter and sugar till it looks like cream; beat the yolks separately and well, the whites to a stiff froth, adding the whites and flour last, and beat all very thoroughly.   This will make two cakes.   If you lack time, and wish variety, by changing the flavoring and adding fruit to one, you will have two cakes entirely unlike, and very good.

## HARRISON CAKE.

### Mrs. B. F. Adams.

One and one-half cups butter, one cup sugar, one cup molasses, one cup sour milk, four eggs, one teaspoon soda, flour to make as thick as pound cake; fruit and spice.

*The excellence of the above receipts can only be realized by*

## HARRISON CAKE.

### Mrs. T. W. Anderson.

Five cups flour, two and and-half cups molasses, one and one-half cups butter, two pounds raisins, eight eggs, one cup wine or milk, one and one-half teaspoons saleratus, several kinds spices; bake in deep pans three hours.

## LINCOLN CAKE.

### Mrs. E. H. Dennison, Highland Park.

Two cups sugar, three-fourths cup butter, two eggs well beaten, one cup sweet milk, two teaspoons cream-tartar, one teaspoon soda, three cups flour.

## CORK CAKE.

### Mrs. James Wadsworth.

Four eggs, three cups sugar, two cups butter, one cup milk, five cups flour, one teaspoon soda.

## WILMINGTON CAKE.

### Mrs. J. H. Browne.

One cup butter, one of cream, three of sugar, four of flour, five eggs, one teaspoon cream tartar, one-half teaspoon of soda.

## EVANSTON CAKE.

### Mrs. J. H. Browne.

One pound sugar, one of flour, six eggs, (whites beaten separately,) one cup butter, one cup milk, two teaspoons of baking powder; put in the flour and essence to the taste.

## PARADISE CAKE.

### H. S. Lewis.

Three eggs, two and one-half cups sugar, one of butter, one and one-half sweet milk, small teaspoon soda, four cups flour, one pound raisins.

*Using "Richards' Queen" as it makes Cake truly elegant.*

## KENTUCKY CAKE.
### Mrs. C. T. Tupper.

Two eggs, one cup of sugar, one-half of butter, two teaspoons cream tartar, one of soda, one cup sweet milk, two and a half of flour.

## BORDENTOWN CUP CAKE.
### Mrs. M. L.

Four cups flour, two and one-half cups sugar, one cup butter, one cup milk, three eggs, one-half teaspoon tartaric acid, one-half teaspoon soda; beat together butter and sugar, add a portion of flour, next the eggs, well beaten, then more flour, next the milk and remainder of flour, the powders dissolved separately in a little water; stir in well and bake immediately.

## IDLE WILD.
### Fannie L., Evanston.

Two cups flour, one cup Indian meal, one teaspoon cream-tartar, one-half teaspoon saleratus, one cup sugar, piece butter size of an egg, one coffeecup milk or water, one or two eggs; make stiff as cake.

## RIVER FOREST CAKE.
### Mrs. D. W. Thatcher.

One and one-half cups sugar, one-half cup butter, one-half cup sweet milk, two cups flour, two eggs, two spoons baking powder; if wanted white, use the whites of four eggs beaten to a froth.

## NEWPORT TEA-CAKE.
### Mrs. L. J. Tilton.

One pint flour, three eggs, piece of butter the size of an egg, one teaspoon cream-tartar, one-half teaspoon soda, a small cup milk, and the same of sugar. Dissolve the cream-tartar in the

**milk,** melt the butter and beat **it** thoroughly with the eggs and sugar; mix this with part of **the flour, an**d half the milk; lastly, dissolve the soda **in the** half cup **of milk,** and while effervescing stir in quickly with **the** remaining flour. Bake **in** a bread pan twenty minutes or half an hour. The oven should be decided-**ly hot to begin with,** and gradually **cooled** off.

## SODA CAKE.

### Mrs. J. C. Knapp.

**One** pound flour, six ounces butter, rubbed **well** into the flour, one-half **pound** currants, and **six** ounces sugar, all mixed well together; **three** eggs beaten **with** one cup of milk, mix **it well** with the eggs and milk, then add one teaspoon **of soda; beat** that well in with a spoon, put **it** in your pan and bake two hours **in** a bread oven.

## GOLD CAKE.

### Mrs. Russell.

One and one-half **cups** sugar, **one-half** cup butter, one cup sweet milk, one teaspoon cream-tartar, one-half teaspoon soda, nutmeg, flour, yolks of six eggs.

## SILVER CAKE.

### Mrs. Russell.

**One and one-half cups** sugar, one-half cup butter, **one** cup **sweet milk,** one-half teaspoon soda, one teaspoon cream-tartar, **w**hites of six eggs beaten to a froth, and flour.

## GOLD CAKE.

### Mrs. L. Bradley.

Take yolks of twelve eggs, **five** cups sifted flour, three cups white powdered sugar, one cup butter, one and a half cups of cream or sweet milk, one teaspoon cream tartar and half a tea-spoon of soda.

**Baking** Powder, as articles made with this are very delicate.

## SILVER CAKE.
### Mrs. L. Bradley.

Take whites of one dozen eggs, five cups flour, three cups powdered sugar, one cup butter, one cup cream or sweet milk, one teaspoon cream tartar, half a teaspoon soda.

## GOLDEN CAKE.
### Mrs. A. T. Hall.

One coffee cup of sugar, one-half of butter, two-thirds of sweet milk, two of flour, one teaspoon cream tartar, one-half of soda.

## SILVER CAKE.
### Mrs. Monroe Heath.

Half pound sugar, half pound flour, one-fourth to one-eighth pound of butter, whites of seven eggs; beat the butter and sugar to a cream; add the eggs, beaten to a stiff froth; rub a teaspoon of baking powder into the flour and stir it into the mixture; flavor with vanilla or almond water. Bake in flat pans, and ice.

## FRENCH SPONGE CAKE.
### Mrs. James Wadsworth, Hyde Park.

Two eggs, two cups of sugar, one of milk, three of flour, two tablespoons butter, two teaspoons baking powder.

## CREAM SPONGE CAKE.
### Mrs. W. G. Morgan.

Break two large eggs into a teacup and fill it with sweet cream; add one cup white sugar, a little salt, and put in a pan; add two cups of sifted flour, two teaspoons baking powder, one of lemon essence; put in a square baking tin and bake fifteen minutes.

*"Richards' Queen" makes Cake very Delicate and Light.*

## WHITE SPONGE CAKE.
### Mrs. L. H. Smith.

One tumbler sifted flour, one and one-half of powdered sugar, one heaping teaspoon cream tartar, and a little salt; sift altogether into a dish; beat the whites of ten fresh eggs, and stir (not beat) very carefully into the flour and sugar until well mixed. Bake with great care in a moderate oven, in one good-sized round tin, with an opening in the centre: Flavor with extract lemon, and put it in with the whites of the eggs. This is an excellent cake.

## WHITE SPONGE CAKE.
### Mrs. Dr. Evarts.

Whites of ten eggs, a tumbler and a half pulverized sugar, one of flour, one heaping teaspoon cream tartar, a pinch of salt; put all in a sieve and sift twice; then stir in lightly the eggs beaten to a stiff froth. Flavor with vanilla or rose.

## WHITE SPONGE CAKE.
### Miss Leonore Tryon and Mrs. D. W. Thatcher.

The whites of ten eggs beaten to a stiff froth, one and one-half tumblers of sugar, one tumbler of flour, one teaspoon cream tartar rubbed in the flour; flavor with lemon; stir as lightly as possible.

## MRS. DREW'S SPONGE CAKE.
### From Toledo Home Cook Book.

Two cups sugar, one cup of flour, four eggs, one and one-half teaspoons of baking powder, pinch of salt, rind and juice of one lemon.

## CREAM SPONGE CAKE.
### Mrs. R. M. Patrick, Marengo, Ill.

One cup of flour, one cup of sugar, one half a cup of cream, two eggs, one-half a teaspoon of cream of tartar, one-fourth of soda.

14

## WHITE SPONGE CAKE.

### Mrs. Sanford.

The whites of ten eggs, one-half pound powdered sugar, three ounces flour, two teaspoons essence of lemon, salt, one teaspoon cream-tartar; mix the flour, sugar and cream-tartar together, and add to the beaten whites. This makes one large loaf.

## WHITE SPONGE CAKE.

### M. Wheeler.

Whites of ten eggs, one tumbler of flour, one teaspoon pulverized sugar, one teaspoon cream-tartar in the flour and sift it; a very little salt.

## DELICATE SPONGE CAKE.

### Mrs. J. W. Preston.

One and one-half cups sugar, one cup flour, whites of ten eggs, one teaspoon cream-tartar, one teaspoon salt. Sift the cream-tartar and salt with the sugar. Then add the eggs, and lastly the flour, stirring very lightly.

ICING FOR THE ABOVE.—White of one egg, two-thirds teacup powdered sugar, one teaspoon vanilla, three tablespoons grated chocolate spread smoothly upon the surface of the cake. No soda to be used.

## TELEGRAPH SPONGE CAKE.

### Mrs. F. E. Stearns.

Four eggs, two cups sugar, two cups flour, one teaspoon baking powder, and two-thirds cup water.

## BERWICH SPONGE CAKE.

### Fannie L.

Beat six eggs two minutes, (yolks and whites together); add three cups sugar and beat five minutes; two cups flour and one teaspoon cream-tartar and beat two minutes; add one cup cold

water with one-half teaspoon of saleratus dissolved in it, and beat
one minute; add the grated rind and half the juice of a lemon,
a little salt and two more cups of flour, and beat another minute,
observing the time exactly. Bake in rather deep cake pans. Extract of lemon will answer.

## SPONGE CAKE.

### Mrs. E. D. G.

Two cups sugar, two cups flour, four eggs, one-half cup cold
water, two teaspoons baking powder, and a little salt.

## SPONGE CAKE.

### Mrs. L. J. Tilton.

Weight of twelve eggs in sugar, and of seven eggs in flour,
beat yolks and sugar together, and the whites separately very
light, gradually add beaten whites to the yolks and sugar; stir in
the flour quickly and smoothly, and bake immediately.

## SPONGE CAKE.

### Mrs. Sarah I. Parrish.

Thirteen eggs, one pound and one-half of sugar, one pound
flour, essence of lemon; stir the yolks of the eggs with the sugar, until very light; then add the whites of the eggs after they
are beaten to a stiff froth; stir lightly together, and add the flour
just before it is to be put into the oven.

## NELLY'S SPONGE CAKE.

### Mrs. Henry Stevens.

Two cups sugar, two cups flour, nine eggs; beat the yolks and
sugar fifteen minutes, then add whites already beaten, beat ten
minutes; stir in flour lightly; put in oven (pretty hot) as soon as
possible.

---

*Exposition in Paris, in 1867, for "Perfection of Preparation."*

## SODA SPONGE CAKE.

### C. T. Stevens.

Two cups white sugar, one cup butter, three cups flour, four eggs, one teaspoon soda dissolved in half a cup of sweet milk, two teaspoons cream-tartar in flour. This is very nice for jelly cake, if not preferred in a

## SPONGE CAKE.

### Mrs. Banks.

Take four eggs, two cups sugar; beat the eggs and sugar well together; two coffeecups flour, two heaping teaspoons baking powder; two-thirds cup of boiling water; lemon to flavor; add the water last. Pour into a pan, place in a well heated oven. This will seem very thin, but will come from the oven a most delightful cake.

## SPONGE CAKE.

### H. M. Brewer.

Twelve eggs, the weights of the eggs in powdered sugar, and the weight of six eggs in flour; separate the yolks from the whites, beating yolks and sugar, and adding the grated rind and juice of one lemon; then beat the whites to a stiff froth and add to the beaten yolks and sugar; lastly, put one small teaspoon of cream tartar into the weighed flour, and stir in thoroughly with the other ingredients. Bake quickly.

## SPONGE CAKE.

### Mrs. J. B. Stubbs.

Two cups sugar, two cups flour, six eggs, one teaspoon salt, one tablespoon vinegar or lemon juice, four tablespoons water.

## MRS. WILDER'S SPONGE GINGER BREAD.

In two cups molasses, sift two teaspoons soda and a dessert spoon ginger. Stir to a cream, then add four well beaten eggs,

one cup butter melted, one cup sour milk in which is dissolved
one teaspoon soda; mix all together, then add flour to the consistency of pound cake. Two loaves.

## SOFT GINGER BREAD.

### Mrs. D.

One quart flour, one-half cup butter, one tablespoon ginger,
one teaspoon saleratus put into the dry flour with one cup boiling water; beat one egg and stir in. If not soft enough, add a
little more water. It is very nice.

## SOFT GINGER BREAD.

### Mss. Blaikie.

One cup of butter, one of sugar, one of milk, two of molasses,
four of flour, five eggs, one tablespoon of strong ground cinnamon, one-half teaspoon of ground cloves, sufficiently strong ginger to suit the taste, three teaspoons baking powder mixed with
the flour. Be careful that the oven is not so hot as to burn before baking through.

## GINGER BREAD.

### Mrs. Annie Marble.

One and a half cups sour milk, two cups molasses, one cup
melted butter, one and a half teaspoon soda, five teaspoons ginger; flour enough to thicken.

## SOFT GINGER BREAD.

### Mrs. N. C. Houghton.

One-half cup butter, one cup molasses, one cup milk, one egg,
one teaspoon ginger, one teaspoon soda.

## GINGER BREAD.

### Mrs. H. M. Kidder, Evanston.

One cup sugar, one cup butter, one cup molasses, one
sour milk, five cups flour, three eggs, half teaspoon ginger, h

Durkee's Improved Corn St          the best.

teaspoon cinnamon, one teaspoon soda; mix butter and sugar to a cream; add molasses, eggs and spices, flour, and some milk; last, soda dissolved in warm water.

## THIN GINGER BREAD.

### Mrs. J. A. Ellis.

Two cups sugar, one cup butter, one cup milk, six cups flour, one teaspoon soda, one tablespoon ginger; roll out on tin sheets very thin, mark with a crimped roller and bake; then cut into strips.

## HARD GINGER BREAD.

### Mrs. J. A. Ellis.

One pound lard, one-half pound butter, beaten to a cream, one and one-half pounds brown sugar, three pints of West India molasses, ginger, cinnamon, allspice and cloves, enough flour to make a stiff dough; roll out very thin, and cut with a cutter.

## MRS. HAMILTON'S GINGER BREAD.

### Mattie M. Winslow, Aurora, Ill.

Two eggs, one cup molasses, one cup sour cream, two table-spoons ginger, one teaspoon soda. Stir quite thin.

# LAYER CAKES.

## GENTLEMAN'S FAVORITE.

### Miss Anna M. Whitman, Indianapolis, Ind.

Seven eggs beaten separately, one-half cup butter, two cups white sugar, two cups flour, two tablespoons baking powder, two tablespoons water, one-half teaspoon salt; bake in jelly cake pans in a quick oven. The jelly for the cake—One egg, a cup of sugar, three grated apples and one lemon; stir till it boils and becomes thick, let it cool before putting between the layers.

## IMPROMPTU JELLY CAKE.
### Mrs. P. B. Brown.

One cup butter, two cups sugar, three cups flour, four eggs; stir the sugar and butter to a cream, then add the yolks of the eggs, and lastly the beaten whites and flour. Have ready the jelly, made as follows: One grated apple, the grated rind and juice of one lemon, one cup sugar and one egg; boil until it jellies, stirring constantly; cool before using. Bake your cake in jelly cake pans, or in thin layers, putting the jelly between each layer, as in ordinary jelly cake.

## JELLY CAKE.
### Mrs. John Edwards.

One and one-half cups of sugar, one-half of butter, one-half of sweet milk, two and one-half of flour, three eggs, whites and yolks beaten separately, and add two teaspoons baking powder.

THE JELLY.—One cup of sugar, one egg, grate the rind and use the juice of one lemon, one tablespoon of water, one teaspoon of flour; put your dish in a kettle of boiling water, and let it come to a boil; have your cake ready and put it together.

## LEMON JELLY CAKE.
### Miss Bell Gassette.

Six tablespoons melted butter, two cups sugar, two and a half cups flour, one-half cup sweet milk, six eggs, two teaspoons baking powder.

JELLY.—The grated rind and juice of three lemons, one pound sugar, one-third cup of butter. Beat all together and scald till thick as boiled custard. This jelly is sufficient for two cakes.

## LEMON JELLY CAKE.

### Mrs. D. McPherson.

One teaspoon of butter, one cup of sugar, two eggs, one-half cup sweet milk, three cups flour, two teaspoons baking powder.

THE JELLY.—Grated rind and juice of one lemon, one cup of sugar, yolks of three eggs.

## APPLE JELLY CAKE.

### Mrs. W. G. Morgan.

Prepare and grate three large apples, (Greenings preferred), the juice and rind of a lemon, half a cup of sugar, one egg well beaten; put the ingredients together in a tin basin; simmer until cooked, with constant stirring; set to cool until the cake is ready. Take three eggs, stir whites and yolks separately. To a cup and a half of white sugar, add half a cup sweet milk and a piece of butter the size of an egg; mix butter and sugar together, four cups of flour and three teaspoons of baking powder; divide in four equal parts, and put in baking tins or jelly pans; use the jelly as in other cases, while the cake is hot.

## APPLE JELLY CAKE.

### Mrs. Monroe Frank.

One egg, one cup sugar, one cup sweet milk, butter the size of an egg, two cups flour, three teaspoons baking powder.

THE JELLY.—Two large apples grated, one cup sugar, one egg, one grated rind of lemon and juice. Boil three minutes.

## CHOCOLATE CAKE.

### Mrs. Monroe Frank.

One cup of butter, two cups sugar, four cups flour, four eggs, three teaspoons of Royal Baking Powder, one cup sweet milk.

FOR FROSTING.—One-half cake Baker's chocolate, one-half cup sugar, (pulverized;) enough hot water to cover; set in a pan of boiling water over the fire three minutes. When cold, add one-half teaspoon vanilla. Spread the same as for jelly cake.

## CHOCOLATE CAKE.

### Julia French, Evanston.

Two cups sugar, three-fourths cup butter, six eggs, one-half cup milk, three cups flour, two teaspoons baking powder.

CUSTARD.—Whites of five eggs beaten stiff, two cups sugar, two teaspoons vanilla, one-eighth cake of chocolate.

## CHOCOLATE CAKE.

### Julia French.

Six eggs, four cups sugar, one cup butter, two cups milk, six cups flour, five teaspoons baking powder.

CUSTARD.—One tablespoon of corn starch; wet and stir into a teacup of boiling milk; a large cup of brown sugar, one-fourth cake chocolate, piece of butter the size of an egg, two teaspoons vanilla, pinch of salt; boil altogether three or four minutes. This makes two loaves of four layers each.

## WHITE MOUNTAIN CAKE.

### Mrs. John Edwards, Rockford.

Two cups sugar, two-thirds cup butter, whites of seven eggs well beaten, two-thirds cup sweet milk, two cups flour, one cup corn starch, two teaspoons baking powder; bake in jelly cake tins.

FROSTING.—Whites of three eggs and some sugar beaten together—not quite as stiff as for frosting; spread over the cake, add some grated cocanut, then put your cakes together; put cocoanut or frosting for the top.

## WHITE MOUNTAIN CAKE.

### Mrs. C. E. Cheney.

Six eggs, six cups flour, three cups sugar, two cups butter, one cup butter, one cup milk, two teaspoons baking powder; flavor with lemon. Frost thickly with chocolate, cocoanut, or plain white icing. Bake in three loaves.

## WHITE MOUNTAIN CAKE.

### Mrs. McDowell.

Two cups sugar, two of butter, three of flour, three-fourths of milk, whites of eight eggs, one teaspoon soda, two teaspoons of cream tartar.

## YELLOW MOUNTAIN CAKE.

### Nellie Spencer.

Yolks of ten eggs, one cup butter, two of sugar, one of milk, three of flour, one teaspoon soda, two of cream tartar.

## WHITE MOUNTAIN CAKE.

### Mrs. Earle, Peoria.

Two cups sugar, one-half of butter, three-fourths of milk, three cups flour, whites of eight eggs, three teaspoons baking powder.

Icing.—Whites of four eggs, one pound sugar; put sugar dissolved in three-fourths cup water upon the stove, and boil till ready to turn, then pour on egg and flour with two teaspoons vanilla and one of lemon syrup.

## WHITE MOUNTAIN OR COCOANUT CAKE.

### Mrs. Hill.

Two and two-thirds cups of sugar, one cup butter, one cup of sweet milk, four cups flour, whites of six eggs, one teaspoon of soda dissolved in milk, two teaspoons cream tartar in flour. Bake in thin cakes, spread frosting between like jelly cake; the whites of five eggs will ice it all. Use one grated cocoanut in the frosting for cocoanut cake.

## COCOANUT MOUNTAIN CAKE.

### Mrs. J. P. Hoit.

One cup butter three cups sugar, one cup milk, three and a half cups flour, whites of ten eggs, one teaspoon cream tartar, one-half teaspoon soda, essence of almond; bake in sheets. Make an icing of the whites of three eggs and one pound sugar; ice each sheet, and sprinkle one grated cocoanut lightly over all.

## COCOANUT MOUNTAIN CAKE.

### Mrs. C. H. Wheeler.

One cup flour, one of sweet milk, two of sugar, three of flour, four eggs, two heaping teaspoons baking powder, bake in three or four layers. Grate one cocoanut; take the juice of two lemons, (or less, if they are large and juicy), one cup fine sugar, the white of one egg, well beaten; set all on the fire in an earthen dish, and heat until the sugar is well dissolved, then spread on the cake; enough of the cocoanut should be reserved to spread thickly over the top layer. Excellent, if nicely made.

## COCOANUT CAKE.

### Mrs. M. G. Hubbell, Shabbona, Ill.

Two eggs, one cup sugar, two-thirds cup of milk, one-half cup butter, two cups flour, two heaping teaspoons baking powder.

FROSTING.—Whites of two eggs, eight teaspoons sugar, flavor to suit. Bake the same as jelly cake; spread a thin layer of frosting, sprinkled with prepared cocoanut, and frost the top and thickly sprinkle with the cocoanut.

## COCOANUT CAKE.

### Mrs. Harry Pearsons, Evanston.

One cup sugar, one-half cup butter, whites of four eggs, two cups flour, flavor to taste, one teaspoon baking powder, one-half cup sweet milk; yolks the same, making two layers of the whites, and two of the yolks. Prepare the cocoanut as for the other cakes.

*Finish, and is the easiest to use.*

## ALMOND CAKE.

### Mrs. Henry Stevens.

Two cups sugar, one-half cup butter, one cup sweet milk, two and one-half cups flour, whites of eight eggs, one teaspoon of cream-tartar, one-half teaspoon soda; mix butter and sugar to a cream; mix other ingredients alternately, putting in soda last; bake in layers like jelly cake; spread each layer with soft frosting and add blanched split almonds about an inch apart on each layer.

## ALMOND CAKE.

Two cups of sugar, six tablespoons melted butter, six eggs, beaten separately, half cup milk, three cups flour, two tablespoons baking powder.

CUSTARD FOR THE CAKE.—Three-fourths pint of milk, scald, sweeten, and stir in three beaten eggs; then let cool; blanch a pound of almonds and chop or pound; then stir into the cold custard, and spread between the layers just before eating; flavor the custard with vanilla for custard cake.

## ALMOND CREAM CAKE.

### Mrs. H. W. Loomis, Rockford, Ill.

One pound of butter, sugar and flour, the whites of twelve eggs and yolks of seven.

CREAM.—One pint of sweet cream, one pound soft almonds, whites of four eggs; beat to a froth with four tablespoons of sugar, the yolks of four eggs beaten separately with the same quantity of sugar; chop the almonds and add the flavoring almonds the last thing.

## ALMOND CAKE.

### Mrs. Booth.

One cup milk, two cups sugar, three cups flour, four eggs, one-half cup butter, one teaspoon cream tartar, one-half of soda.

FROSTING.—One teacup sour cream well beaten, one coffee cup sugar, one cup blanched almonds. Bake the cake in jelly pans, make it in layers, and put the above frosting between each layer when baked.

## BOSTON CREAM CAKE.
### Mrs. E. S. Chesbrough.

One pint of water, one-half pound butter, three-fourths pound flour, ten eggs; boil the butter and water together; stir in the flour when boiling; when cool, add the eggs, and soda the size of a pea; drop by the spoonful on a buttered baking pan, leaving space so that the cakes will not touch when risen. Bake in a very quick oven about ten minutes. When cold, make an incision at the side and fill with the following cream: Six gills of milk, one and one-half cups flour, three cups sugar, six eggs; beat the flour, sugar and eggs together and stir into the milk while boiling. Flavor with the rind of a lemon.

## CUSTARD CAKE.
### Mrs. James P. Clarke.

Two cups sugar, six tablespoons melted butter, six eggs beaten separately, two and one-half cups flour, one-half cup milk, one teaspoon soda, two teaspoons cream-tartar.

CUSTARD FOR THE SAME.—One-half pint milk, two eggs, sweeten to taste, flavor with vanilla; bake on pie plates, and put custard between as jelly cake.

## CUSTARD CAKE.
### Mrs. Downs.

Six eggs less one white, two cups sugar, six tablespoons melted butter, two and one-half cups flour, one-half cup sweet milk, one teaspoon cream-tartar, one-half teaspoon soda, two teaspoons vanilla.

CUSTARD.—One pint milk, three eggs, three large tablespoons sugar, three teaspoons vanilla. Very nice.

*Excellent for Food"—London Exposition, 1862.*

# ORANGE CAKE.

### Mrs. H. W. Loomis, Rockford.

Two teaspoons baking powder, three cups flour, one and one-half cups sugar, four eggs, one-half cup butter, one-half cup sweet milk.

Use for Frosting—The whites of three eggs and sugar, the juice of one orange, also the peel grated.

## ORANGE CAKE.

### Mrs. A. N. Arnold.

Yolks of five eggs, whites of four beaten separately, two cups of sugar, two of flour, one-half cup of cold water, the juice and grated rind of one large orange, and the usual quantity of baking powder, beat the white of the remaining egg to a stiff froth, with the juice and rind of another orange, and one cup of powdered sugar. Put this between the layers, and put it on the top.

## ORANGE CAKE.

### Mrs. D. S. Covert.

Two cups sugar, two of flour, one-half of cold water, yolks of five eggs, whites of three eggs, three teaspoons of baking powder, grated rind and juice of one orange; bake in jelly tins.

Dressing.—Whites of two eggs beaten stiff, grated rind and juice of one orange, made stiff with pulverized sugar, and spread between as jelly cake.

## ORANGE CAKE.

### Mrs. H. E. Sargent.

One tumbler sugar, two tumblers flour, one-half tumbler milk, two eggs, two spoons baking powder, five tumblers melted butter.

Frosting.—Whites three eggs, and juice and grated rind of one orange, with sufficient powdered sugar to make it like any frosting. Bake the cake in jelly cake tins, and put the frosting between the layers.

---

*Duryeas' Starch, the Prize Medal Starch of the world.*

## ORANGE CAKE.

### Mrs. J. D. L. Harvey.

Two cups flour, two cups pulverized sugar, one-half cup cold water, yolks five eggs and whites of two, juice and rind of one orange, one teaspoon cream-tartar, one-half teaspoon soda. Bake in four long tins.

FROSTING.—Beat the whites of two eggs stiff; add the juice and rind of one orange; then add sugar to the thickness of jelly; put this between the loaves, and frost the top with the same frosting.

## ORANGE CAKE.

### Mrs. S. W. Cheever, Ottawa, Ill.

Beat the whites of three and the yolks of five eggs separately, stir to a cream; two cups sugar, one-half cup butter; add one-half cup cold water, two and one-half cups flour with two teaspoons baking powder, grated rind of one orange and all the juice (except about one tablespoon) stirred into the cake. Bake in two square tins.

FROSTING.—Whites of two eggs, two small cups sugar, with a tablespoon of the orange juice served from the cake. When the cake is cold, join them with this frosting and frost the tops.

## ORANGE CAKE.

### Mrs. A. M. Gibbs.

Two cups flour, one of corn starch, one tablespoon baking powder, one teaspoon of extract of lemon, one teaspoon of vanilla mixed with the flour and put all through the sieve together; one cup of butter, two cups of sugar stirred to a cream; add one tea cup of milk and one-half of above ingredients; stir well, and add the whites of seven eggs well beaten, and then the rest of the flour mixture. Bake in jelly tins.

THE JELLY.—Whites of two eggs, one cup of pulverized sugar, juice and grated pulp of two oranges; meringue top adds to its appearance when piled on quite high.

---

*Duryeas' Improved* Corn Starch is made from the choicest corn.

## LEMON HONEY CAKE.

### Home Messenger, Detroit.

Two cups of sugar, two-thirds of a cup of butter, one cup of milk, one cup of corn starch, three cups of flour, three teaspoons baking powder; rub the butter and sugar to a cream, then add the milk; lastly, the whites of eight eggs beaten to a stiff froth, then the corn starch and flour, to which has been added the baking powder. Bake in jelly tins.

LEMON HONEY FOR THE CAKE.—One pound loaf sugar, the yolks of eight eggs with two whole ones, the juice of six lemons and grated rind of two, one-fourth pound butter. Put the sugar, lemon and butter into a sauce pan, melt over a gentle fire; when all is dissolved, stir in the eggs which have been well beaten; stir rapidly until it is as thick as honey. Spread this between the layers of cake; set aside the remainder in a closely covered vessel for future use.

## SMALL CAKES AND COOKIES.

## CHESS CAKES.

### Mrs. Lamkin.

Peel and grate one cocoanut, take one pound sugar, one-half pint water, and boil fifteen minutes; stir in the grated cocoanut, boil fifteen minutes longer, while warm stir in one-fourth pound butter, then add the yolks of seven well beaten eggs. Bake in patty pans lined with a rich paste; will keep some time, and mixes prettily in a basket of cake. The small oval patty tins are prettier than scallops.

# FINGER CAKES.

### Mrs. Lamkin.

Two eggs beaten very light, to which add a cup of granulated sugar, (excepting a tablespoonful;) sift in a very small teaspoon cream-tartar, half as much soda, a little salt; stir in flour enough for a stiff dough; roll very thin, and sprinkle with a tablespoon of sugar from the cupful, giving it a light roll; cut the dough in strips a finger width; do not let them touch in the pan. Bake in quick oven, watching them, as they readily scorch. Add a good size teaspoon of vanilla.

# WINE CAKES.

### Mrs. A. M. Chetlain.

One pint of sweet milk, three eggs, well beaten, flour to make a thick batter, have hot lard and fry as you would fried cakes; take a spoon of batter, and let your hand shake as you drop it into the lard; serve warm with wine and sugar, or sweet cream.

# DOUGHNUTS.

### Maggie Trainer.

One egg, one cup sugar, ten cups sour milk, one large spoon cream, one teaspoon soda, a little salt, nutmeg, flour enough to roll.

## DOUGHNUTS.

### Mrs. Beyer.

One cup sugar, two eggs, one cup sour milk, in which dissolve one teaspoon soda, six tablespoons melted butter, a pinch of salt, and nutmeg; after cooking, let them cool, and then roll in pulverized sugar.

## FRIED CAKES.

### Mrs. Dr. Evarts.

Two cups sweet milk, two cups sugar, three-fourths cup butter, four eggs, two teaspoons cream-tartar, one teaspoon soda.

## OLD-FASHIONED YANKEE DOUGHNUTS.
### Mrs. H. M. Riddle, Evanston.

One pint milk, one teacup yeast; put yeast in milk, stir in flour and let it rise over night; in the morning add two teacups sugar, one teacup lard, two eggs, one teaspoon soda; work in flour, and let it rise very light; add nutmeg or cinnamon to suit taste.

## DOUGHNUTS.
### Mrs. Benham.

Two cups milk, one cup sugar, one-half cup butter, one-half cup lard, one cup sponge yeast, two eggs; add flour to make a stiff dough; let it rise; when light, roll it out, and after they are cut out, let them stand on the moulding board until light. Fry in hot lard, and when hot dip them in pulverized sugar.

## DOUGHNUTS.
### Mrs. H. W. Loomis, Rockford, Ill.

One quart new milk, four eggs, one cup of yeast, one cup of butter, two cups of sugar, one large nutmeg; at night, take one quart of scalding milk, and stir in your flour until very thick; beat the eggs with one cup of sugar, and add the butter as soon as it can be done without scalding the eggs; then add the cup of yeast and let it rise until morning. In the morning add the butter and sugar that has previously been stirred; then the nutmeg, with flour enough to make it as stiff as soft biscuit; let it rise again. When very light, roll out three-fourths of an inch thick, and cut with a small cake cutter; let them stand two hours before frying. Roll in sugar when nearly cold.

## DOUGHNUTS.
### Mrs. L. H. Clement.

One cup of sugar, one and one-half of sour milk, one-half of butter, two eggs, and one teaspoon of soda; flavor with nutmeg.

# FRIED CAKES.

## Mrs. B. J. Seward.

One cup of sugar, four tablespoons of fat, three eggs, one cup sweet milk, one teaspoon soda, two of cream tartar, or three teaspoons baking powder; **roll half an inch thick** after mixing **soft, and fry in** hot lard.

# FRIED CAKES.

## Mrs. A. Kesler, Evanston.

Two quarts **unsifted flour, two** teaspoons soda, four **of cream** tartar, two **of salt, two** eggs, one-half **cup** shortening, **two of** sugar, milk to mix.

## CRULLERS.

### Ella Waggoner, Toledo.

Eight heaping tablespoonfuls sugar, **four** eggs, **four table-** spoonfuls melted **butter, two** tablespoons milk and two **of wine,** (or four of milk,) and **a pinch of soda dissolved** in water. **Fry** in hot lard; sprinkle sugar over **when hot.**

## CRULLERS.

### Mrs. Arnold.

Three eggs, two cups sugar, one-half cup butter, one cup of **sweet** milk, three teaspoons baking powder; **spice to** taste.

## RUSK COOKIES.

### Mrs. E. A. Forsyth.

One cup melted butter, one and **a** half cups sugar, **one** cup **of** tepid water, two teaspoons **Dr. Price's** baking powder mixed well with sifted flour; **roll out very thin,** and cut with **a** round cake cutter, baking **in a quick oven.**

---

*Exposition in Paris, in 1867, for "Perfection of Preparation."*

## WATER COOKIES.

### Mrs. F. D. Gray.

One cup sugar, one-half of butter, one-half of water, caraway seed, wet hard and roll very thin, indeed; sprinkle with sugar after putting them in the tins.

## LEMON COOKIES.

### Ella J. Roe.

One pint sugar, one cup butter, one teaspoon soda, juice and grated rind of one lemon. Roll soft and thin, and bake quickly.

## VANILLA COOKIES.

### Mrs. C. S. Bartlett.

One cup of butter and two cups of sugar, beaten well; one cup of cold water, one teaspoon of soda, two teaspoons of vanilla, flour to make a very stiff dough. Roll very thin, and bake brown.

## BOILED COOKIES.

### Mrs. F.

Boil one cup of milk, two of sugar, three of flour; cool it off; then add one teaspoon of soda, the yolks of three eggs; cut in rounds and bake in a quick oven.

## EVERLASTING COOKIES.

### Mrs. John Edwards, Rockford.

Two cups sugar, one of butter, three-fourths of sweet milk, two teaspoons baking powder; season to taste; rub butter and sugar together; then add two eggs, milk and flour to make a soft dough; roll thin, sprinkle a little sugar over the top, and bake in quick oven.

## COOKIES.

### Mrs. Russell.

One cup butter, two of sugar, one of sour cream, one teaspoon soda, two of cream tartar, three eggs, three tablespoons caraway seed, a little nutmeg, flour enough to form a soft dough ; roll out thin and bake in a quick oven.

## COOKIES.

### Mrs. Solomon Thatcher, Sr.

Two cups of sugar, one of butter, one of sour cream, three eggs, beat separately, one teaspoon of soda; beat cream and yolks well together, then mix soft and roll not very thick; bake in a quick oven.

### COOKIES.

#### Mrs. W. S. Bogue.

Six cups of flour, two cups of sugar, one cup of butter, one cup of sour milk, one egg, one teaspoon of saleratus; first mix well together the flour, sugar and butter; then put the saleratus in the milk, beat the egg and mix all together very light.

### COOKIES.

#### Virginia West, Evanston.

Two eggs, two teacups sugar, one teacup butter, one teacup milk, one nutmeg, one teaspoon cream-tartar, one-half teaspoon soda; flour to roll.

## MOLASSES COOKIES.

### Amelia Gravis.

One cup of butter, one cup of sugar, one cup of molasses, one cup of sweet milk, one tablespoon of saleratus, one tablespoon ginger.

### WHIG JUMBLES.

#### Mrs. W. H. Ovington.

One teacup and a half of butter; three teacups of sugar, one cup of sour cream, four eggs, one teaspoon of soda dissolved in it, six cups of flour, nutmeg; drop in heaping teaspoons on buttered paper in pans.

## JUMBLES.

### Mrs. W. H. Ovington.

One pound of butter, one pound of sugar, six eggs, grated peel of a fresh lemon, flour sufficient to make a soft dough; put in teaspoons in papered pans; on top of each cake put a blanched almond, and some coarse lumps of crushed sugar before baking.

## RICH JUMBLES.

### Mrs. Kate Johnson.

One-half pound butter, one-half pound sugar, two eggs well beaten, three-quarters pound flour; have plenty of rolled sugar on the board, and work little lumps of the dough (which is very soft) in it; make into little rings, and turn them over into buttered pans and bake with care; they will keep for two or three months.

## EXCELLENT JUMBLES.

### Mrs. J. H. Brown.

One cup butter, two cups sugar, one cup cream, one teaspoon soda, one egg, a little bit of nutmeg, flour enough to stiffen it so as to bake in rings; bake quickly.

## COCOANUT JUMBLES.

### Mrs. F.

Two cups of sugar, one of butter, two eggs, small teaspoon of soda, mixed with the flour, two cups of cocoanut.

## JACKSON JUMBLES.

### Mrs. C. A. Rogers.

One cup of butter, one cup cream, three cups of sugar, five eggs, five cups of flour.

## SAND TARTS.

Mrs. W. H. Ovington.

One pound sugar, three-fourths pound of butter, two eggs, flour enough to make very stiff; roll them out and wet the tops with whites of eggs, then put two almonds on each one; sprinkle over them cinnamon and sugar.

## SUGAR DROPS.

Mrs. H. M. Buell.

One pound flour, three-fourths pound of sugar, one-half of butter, four eggs; a gill of rose water. To be baked on paper. This will make sixty drops.

## COCOANUT DROPS.

Mrs. H. M. Buell.

The meat of one cocoanut, pared and grated, weight of the same in sugar, one-half cup of flour, white.

## NO MATTERS.

M. A. Bingham.

Three cups sour milk, three tablespoons of cream or butter; one cup of sugar; roll about the size of a plate, fry in hot lard, cover each with nicely seasoned apple sauce; lay over each other.

## COOKIES.

M. A. Bingham.

Two cups of butter, three cups of sugar, four eggs, one table-spoon of vinegar, one teaspoon of saleratus; roll thin, bake in a hot oven.

## CINNAMON WAFERS.

Mrs. Beyer.

Two and a half cups of sugar, one-half cup butter, three eggs, one tablespoon cinnamon, one-half teaspoon soda; put in enough flour to roll out.

## GINGER SNAPS.

Sarah Waldo.

One pint of molasses, one teacup of sugar, one of butter, one of lard, one-half of sour milk, two teaspoons soda, two tablespoons of ginger.

## GINGER CAKE.

Mrs. Mann, Freeport.

One half cup butter, one of molasses, one of sugar, one of cold water, one heaping teaspoon soda, one quart of flour. Ginger and salt to taste; drop on the tins and bake in a quick oven.

## GINGER COOKIES.

Mrs. J. O. Knapp.

One cup of sugar, one of butter, one of molasses, two tablespoons ginger, and two teaspoons saleratus dissolved in three tablespoons of hot water. Bake quickly.

## GINGER SNAPS.

Miss Gilbert, Evanston.

One cup molasses, one-half of sugar, two-thirds of butter, one-half of water, one tablespoon ginger, one-half teaspoon of alum dissolved in hot water, two teaspoons saleratus, dissolved in the molasses; mix the whole, with flour enough to roll out nicely.

## GINGER SNAPS.

Mrs. John Edwards, Rockford.

One cup of molases; let it come to a boil, then add two teaspoons of soda, when cool; mix one cup of butter, three-fourths of sugar, and two eggs well together; then add your molasses and two tablespoons of water, two tablespoons ginger, some cinnamon, and some cloves, and allspice; add flour and roll very thin; bake in a quick oven.

*Duryeas' Improved Corn Starch, the "Perfection of*

# CONFECTIONERY.

"Sweets to the Sweet."
—SHAKSPEARE.

## CANDY.

One pound sugar, one and a half cup water, three tablespoons rose water; boil twenty minutes; then pull.

## CANDY.

### Carrie A.

One-half pound sugar, one-half cup syrup, butter the size of a walnut; add little water to the syrup, and have the sugar thoroughly dissolved; to try it, drop a spoonful in a glass of ice water; if brittle, it is done.

### CANDY CARAMELS.

#### Mary H.

One pint cream, one pound sugar, one cup butter, one-fourth cup chocolate, one cup of molasses.

### CHOCOLATE CARAMELS.

#### Etta C. Springer.

Two pounds sugar, two ounces butter, one cup of cream, boil over a good fire until the syrup is brittle; try in water as you do taffy; then pour it in pans, and when it is most cold cut it in squares.

## CHOCOLATE CARAMELS.

One cup of fine granulated sugar, one cup of New Orleans molasses, one-fourth cup of milk, a piece of butter the size of an egg, one cup of chocolate after it is cut up, if made single quantity; if doubled, it is as well not to put the chocolate in till about done, and then the same quantity of this recipe will suffice, as it retains the flavor if not cooked as much. Boil till it will stiffen in water; pour into flat buttered pans to the thickness of half an inch. Use Baker's chocolate.

## CHOCOLATE CARAMELS.
### Mrs. P. B. Ayer.

Two cups of brown sugar, one cup molasses, one cup chocolate grated fine, one cup boiled milk, one tablespoon of flour; butter the size of a large English walnut; let it boil slowly and pour on flat tins to cool; mark off while warm.

## COCOANUT DROPS.
### Mrs. P. B. Ayers.

To one grated cocoanut, add half its weight of sugar and the white of one egg, cut to a stiff froth; mix thoroughly and drop on buttered white paper or tin sheets. Bake fifteen minutes.

## CREAM CANDY.

One pound white sugar, one wineglass vinegar, one tumbler water, vanilla; boil one-half hour, and pull, if you choose.

## KISSES.
### E. S. P.

One egg, one cup sugar, one-half cup of butter, one-half cup milk, one teaspoon cream tartar, one-half of soda, flour enough to make a stiff dough; **drop on tins and sprinkle** over with powdered sugar. Bake **in a quick oven.**

## MOLASSES CANDY.

### Mrs. Benham.

One cup molasses, **two** cups sugar, one tablespoon vinegar, **a little butter** and vanilla; **boil ten** minutes, then **cool enough to pull.**

## MOLASSES CANDY.

### Julia French.

One cup molasses, **one cup sugar, one** tablespoon **vinegar,** piece of butter size of an egg; boil (but do not stir) until it hardens when dropped in cold water; then stir in a teaspoon of soda, and pour on buttered tins; when cool, pull and cut in sticks.

**Or, two** cups sugar, two tablespoons vinegar, boil, when done add a teaspoon soda, cool and pull, or cut in squares without pull**ing: do** not stir while it **is boiling.**

## BUTTER SCOTCH CANDY.

Four cups brown sugar, **two of butter, vinegar to taste,** two tablespoons water, and **a little soda; boil half an hour;** drop a little in hot water, and if crisp, **it is done.**

## BUTTER SCOTCH.

### Fannie Waggoner, Toledo.

Three tablespoons of molasses, two of sugar, **two of water, one** of butter; add a pinch of soda before taking up.

*Finish, and is the easiest to use.*

# FRUITS.

Bring me berries or such cooling fruit
As the kind, hospitable woods provide.
—COWPER.

Fruits for preserving should be carefully selected, removing all that are imperfect; they are in the best condition when not fully ripe, and as soon as possible after they are picked. Small fruits should not be allowed to stand over night after they are picked, when they are to be preserved. Use only the finest sugar for preserving. When fruit is sealed in glass cans, wrap paper of two or three thicknesses around the cans. The chemical action of light will affect the quality of the preserves when perfectly air-tight. With this precaution, glass cans are preferable to any other for preserving fruit. One-half a pound of sugar to a pound of fruit is a good rule for canned fruit, although many housekeepers use but one-quarter of a pound of sugar to a pound of fruit.

An excellent rule for canning the larger fruits, as peaches, pears, &c., is to place them in a steamer over a kettle of boiling water, laying first a cloth in the bottom of the steamer; fill this with the fruit and cover tightly. Let them steam for fifteen minutes, or until they can be easily pierced with a fork, (some fruits will require a longer time.) Make a syrup of sugar of the right consistency. As the fruit is steamed, drop each for a moment in the syrup, then place in the cans, having each one-half full of fruit, and then fill up with the hot syrup, then cover and seal.

## ORANGES FOR DESSERT.

### Mrs. J. Young Scammon.

Slices of orange dipped in spiced wine, is a famous dessert in Jaffa.

## AMBROSIA.

### Mrs. S. W. Cheever, Ottawa, Ill.

Take one dozen sweet oranges, peel off the skins and cut them in slices; take a large sized fresh cocoanut, grate it on a coarse grater, then put alternate layers of the orange and grated cocoanut in a glass dish, and sprinkle pulverized sugar over each layer of the cocoanut. This makes a beautiful and palatable dish.

## MOCK STRAWBERRIES AND CREAM.

### Mrs. Bartlett.

Take any quantity of sound ripe peaches, and well flavored eating apples, say in proportion of three peaches to one apple, peel the fruit nicely, cut a layer of peaches and then of apples, alternately, they should be cut, (not sliced) about the size of a large strawberry. When finished, cover the top with a layer of crushed sugar, then pour over all two or three spoons of cold water. Let the whole stand about two hours; then mix the peaches and apples indiscriminately; let stand one hour longer, serve with, or without cream. The flavor of strawberry is more perfect without cream.

## BAKED APPLES.

Pare as many apples as you wish of some nice variety, neither sweet nor sour; core them by using an apple corer or a steel fork; set them in biscuit tins, and fill the cavities with sugar, a little butter and some ground cinnamon, if you like; set them in the oven and bake until done.

*Excellent for Food"—London Exposition,* 1862.

## BAKED PEARS.

### Mrs. J. B. Stubbs.

Place in a stone jar, first a layer of pears, (without paring,) then a layer of sugar, then pears, and so on until the jar is full. Then put in as much water as it will hold. Bake in oven three hours. Very nice.

## BAKED QUINCES.

One dozen nice quinces, cored and well rubbed. Put in baking pans, and fill the centre with pulverized sugar. Bake and serve cold, with or without cream.

## JELLIED GRAPES.

### Mrs. A. M. Lewis.

A very delicate dish, is made of one-third of a cup of rice, two cups of grapes, half a cup of water, and two spoons of sugar. Sprinkle the rice and sugar among the grapes, while placing them in a deep dish; pour on the water, cover close and simmer two hours slowly in the oven. Serve cream as sauce, or cold as pudding. If served warm as pudding, increase slightly the proportion of rice and sugar.

## CITRON PRESERVES.

### Carter.

Cut the citron in thin slices, boil in water with a small piece of alum until clear and tender; then rinse in cold water. Make a syrup of three-fourths pound of sugar to the pound of citron; boil a piece of ginger in the syrup; then pour the citron in and let it boil a few minutes. Put in one lemon to five of the fruit.

## PRESERVED QUINCES.

### Mrs. Anna Marble.

As you peel and core the quinces, throw them in cold water; strain them out of the water and make a syrup. To a pint of water, put a pound of sugar, to every pound of fruit. When the syrup boils, put in fruit, and boil until soft. Boil the syrup down as usual with other preserves.

## PRESERVED ORANGE PEEL.
### Mrs. A. N. Arnold.

Peel the oranges, and cut the rinds into narrow shreds, boil till tender; change the water three times; squeeze the juice of the orange over the sugar put pound to pound of sugar and peel; boil twenty minutes all together.

## SPICED PEACHES OR PEARS.
### Mrs. Henry M. Knickerbocker.

To ten pounds good mellow peaches, use five pounds sugar, one pint of good vinegar, and some whole cloves or cinnamon. Take the sugar, vinegar and cloves, and let them come to a boil, and turn over the fruit. This do three days in succession, and the last day put the fruit into the syrup, a few at a time, and let them just boil up.

## CANNED PINE APPLE.
### Mrs. F. L. Bristol.

For six pounds fruit when cut and ready to can, make syrup with two and a half pounds sugar and nearly three pints of water; boil syrup five minutes and skim or strain if necessary; then add the fruit, and let it boil up; have cans hot, fill and shut up as soon as possible. Use the best white sugar. As the cans cool, keep tightening them up.

## CANNED STRAWBERRIES.
### Miss Blaikie.

After the berries are pulled, let as many as can be put carefully in the preserve kettle at once, be placed on a platter. To each pound of fruit add three-fourths of a pound of sugar; let them stand two or three hours, till the juice is drawn from them; pour it in the kettle and let it come to a boil, and remove the scum which rises; then put in the berries very carefully. As soon as they come thoroughly to a boil, put them in warm jars, and seal while boiling hot. Be sure the cans are air tight.

## GOOSEBERRY SAUCE.
### Mrs. R. Harris.

Four pounds brown sugar, eight pounds gooseberries, one pint vinegar, two ounces cloves (ground,) two ounces cinnamon, boil four hours.

## GOOSEBERRY SOY.
### M. A. Bingham, Elgin, Ill.

Take six pounds gooseberries that are nearly ripe, and three pounds sugar, one pint best vinegar, and boil altogether until quite thick. To be eaten with meats; will keep good a long time; season to suit your taste with ground cloves and cinnamon.

## CHERRY OR CURRANT SAUCE.
### M. A. Bingham, Elgin, Ill.

Four pounds of cherries or currants, two pounds sugar, one cup vinegar, one-half ounce cinnamon; cook slowly about one hour.

## CANNED CURRANTS.
### Mrs. Wicker.

Put sufficient sugar to prepare them for the table, then boil ten minutes and seal hot as possible.

## TO CAN TOMATOES.
### Mrs. Edward Ely.

Wash your tomatoes, and cut out any places that are green or imperfect, then cut them up, and put over to cook with a little salt; boil them till perfectly soft; then strain them through a

colander; turn them back **to cook,** and when they **have come to**
to a boiling heat, pour them into stone jugs, (one or two gallon
jugs as you prefer;) they will keep a **day or two in** winter, **if** all
are not used at a time; put the cork in, and have some canning
cement hot, and pour over **the cork.** The jug must, of course,
be hot when the tomatoes **are poured** in.

## CRANBERRY SAUCE.

Mrs. Bartlett.

**One quart cranberries,** one quart **water, one quart** sugar; **stew**
slowly.

## PIC NIC LEMON BUTTER.

Etta C. Springer.

Grate the rind, add juice of three lemons, **one** pound sugar,
two ounces butter, three eggs; **mix** together, let come to boil;
stir all the time.

## LEMON BUTTER.

Mrs. D. S. Munger.

Beat six eggs, one-fourth pound butter, one pound sugar, the
rind and juice of three lemons; mix together and **set it** in a pan
**of** hot water to cook. Very nice for tarts, **or** to eat with bread.

## PEACH BUTTER.

Mrs. M. L.

Take pound for pound of peaches and sugar; cook peaches
alone until they become soft, then put in one-half the sugar, and
stir for one-half an hour; then the remainder of sugar, and **stir**
an hour and a half. Season with cloves **and** cinnamon.

## TOMATO BUTTER.

Mrs. Johnson.

Nine pounds peeled tomatoes, three pounds sugar, one pint
vinegar, three tablespoons cinnamon, one tablespoon cloves, one

16

and one-half tablespoons allspice; boil three or four hours until quite thick, and stir often, that it may not burn.

## CURRANT CATSUP.

### Mrs. C. M. Dickerman, Rockford, Ill.

To five pounds currants add three pounds brown sugar, two tablespoons cinnamon, two tablespoons cloves and one pint of good cider, or white wine vinegar, and boil two hours.

## APPLE JELLY.

### Mrs. J. H. Brown.

Take nice green apples that will cook nicely; quarter the apples without paring, put them in a pan or kettle and cover over with water, and keep them covered; let them boil slowly until entirely done; then put in a bag and drain (not squeeze) them. Put a pound of white sugar to a pint of juice. This is very easily made in the winter; is best made the day before using.

## APPLE JELLY FOR CAKE.

### Mrs. P. B. Ayer.

Grate one large or two small apples, the rind and juice of one lemon, one cup of sugar; boil three minutes.

## APPLE JELLY.

### Mrs. N. P. Iglehart.

Take juicy apples, (Rambos, if possible;) take the stem and top off, and wash them nicely, then cut up in quarters and put cold water on them, just enough to cover them; boil them soft, afterward strain them through a jelly bag; then take two pints at a time with two pounds of crushed sugar; boil twenty minutes, then do the same with the other juice left; to be economical, pare and core the apples; don't strain so close, but that you can, by adding a little more water, use the apples for sauce or pies.

---

## CRAB APPLE JELLY AND JAM.
### Mrs. Ludlam, Evanston.

Remove stems and blossoms from the apples; let them scald and pour off the first water; next **put** them in plenty of water and let them cook slowly; as they begin to soften, dip off the juice for jelly, straining it through flannel. One pound of juice **to a** pound of sugar, for jelly. Next add more water; let apples **stew very** soft, strain through a sieve, which takes out cores and **seeds**; to this pulp add brown sugar, pound for pound; **it needs careful** cooking and stirring.

## GRAPE JELLY.

Allow fourteen ounces of sugar to a pint of juice. Boil fifteen minutes alone; add sugar and boil five minutes.

## LEMON JELLY.
### M. A. P.

Grate the outside, and squeeze the juice of two lemons; add one cup of sugar, one-half of butter, yolks of three eggs; place the ingredients on the fire, stirring all the time until it forms a jelly, which will be in about ten minutes.

## LEMON JELLY.
### Mrs. P. B. Ayer.

Grate the outsides of two lemons, and **squeeze** the juice; add one cup of sugar, one-half of butter, yolks of three eggs; beat the three last ingredients thoroughly, **then** add the juice **and** grated rind, and put it over your fire, stirring until thick; mould to fancy.

## ORANGE JELLY.
### Mrs. J. P. Hoit.

Soak one package of gelatine in one-half pint cold water for one hour; add juice of three lemons, two pounds sugar, and one

---

quart of boiling water; when all are dissolved, add one pint of orange juice; strain carefully and set on ice till ready for use; eight oranges usually make it, but a pint of wine may be used instead of oranges.

### CURRANT JELLY.
#### Mrs. J. P. Hoit.

Jam and strain the currants, to each pint of juice, add one pound sugar; boil the juice fifteen minutes without sugar, and the same time after it is in. Strain into glasses.

When pouring hot fruit or jelly in cans or glasses, wring a towel out of cold water, lay it on a table, and set the cold cans upon it, pouring the boiling fruit into them. Care should be taken not to set two cans on the same spot without first wetting the towel.

### CURRANT JELLY.
#### Mrs. C. Wheeler.

Use the currants when they first ripen; pick them from the stems and put them on the stove in a stone jar, bruising them with a wooden spoon; then when warm, squeeze through a coarse cloth or flannel, and put the juice on in a new tin pan or porcelain kettle; one quart of juice requires two pounds of sugar, or a pound to a pint; boil fifteen minutes; to be a nice color, the currants should not come in contact with iron spoons or tin dishes, unless new and bright; should be made quickly. It never fails to jelly good if the currants are not to ripe. The same method for jam, only do not strain the currants, but mash them well. Currants should not be dead ripe for jelly or jam.

### GOOSEBERRY JELLY.
#### E. M. Walker.

Boil six pounds of green unripe gooseberries in six pints of water, (they must be well boiled, but not burst too much); pour them into a basin, and let them stand covered with a cloth for twenty-four hours, then strain through a jelly bag, and to every pint of juice add one pound of sugar. Boil it for an hour, then skim it, and boil for one-half hour longer with a sprig of vanilla.

## CIDER JELLY.

Soak a package of gelatine in a pint of cider until the cider is absorbed; then add a pound and a half of sugar, and the juice of three large lemons, (or one pound of sugar and no lemons, if desired). Stir in quickly and thoroughly a quart and a half of boiling water; wet moulds in cold water, and pour in the mixture; let it stand from eight to twenty-four hours before using.

## CIDER JELLY.
### Mrs. George Frost, Detroit.

One package of gelatine (one and one-half ounces,) the grated rind of one lemon and the juice of three; add one pint of cold water, and let it stand one hour; then add two and one-half pounds of loaf sugar, three pints of boiling water, and one pint of cider, put into moulds and set in a cool place.

## CHAMPAGNE JELLY.
### Mrs. H. E. Sargent.

One package Cox's gelatine, pour upon it a pint of cold water and let it soak for half an hour, adding the juice of one lemon and half the rind, one quart of sugar, one quart of champagne; mix all thoroughly together and add a scant quart of boiling water, stirring well all the time; strain through a flannel bag, and pour into moulds to cool.

## WINE JELLY.
### Kitty King.

Dissolve one ounce package of Cox's Sparkling Gelatine, in a pint of cold water for half an hour; then pour over it a quart of boiling water; add the grated rind of one and the juice of three lemons, half a pint of sherry wine, a pinch of ground cinna-

... sweeten to taste, and strain into moulds. Set in a cool place for twelve hours.

## WINE JELLY.

Mrs. E. P. Thomas, Rockford, Ill.

One box gelatine, one pint cold water; let it soak one hour, then add one pint boiling water, one pound white sugar, the juice and grated rind of two lemons, one pint sherry wine; let it all just come to a boil, then strain and turn it into moulds.

## WINE JELLY.

Mrs. Dr. T. N. Moss.

One box Cox's gelatine, or eight sheets, one pint cold water, juice of three lemons, two pounds sugar, one pint wine or cider, one quart boiling water.

## WINE JELLY.

Mrs. Oren Smith.

One box Cox's gelatine soaked in one pint cold water for half an hour, two pounds white sugar, one pint wine, juice of three lemons and rind of one. When these are well mixed, add three pints of boiling water. Half this recipe is enough for an occasion.

## CORN STARCH JELLY.

One pint boiling water, wet five tablespoons corn starch, one teacup sugar, a pinch of salt, with cold water, and one teaspoon lemon or vanilla extract for flavoring; stir the mixture into the boiling water, boil five minutes, stir all the while; pour into cups previously dipped in cold water. This quantity will fill six or seven cups. If wished richer, milk may be used instead of water. Good for invalids.

## TAPIOCA JELLY.

Mrs. G. F. Gray.

One cup tapioca, three cups cold water, juice of a lemon, and a pinch of the grated peel; sweeten to taste; soak the tapioca in

water four hours; set within a sauce pan of boiling water; pour
more lukewarm water over the tapioca, if it has absorbed too
much of the liquid and heat, stirring frequently. If too thick
after it begins to clear, put in very little boiling water. When
quite clear, put in the sugar and lemon. Pour into moulds.
Eat cold with cream, flavoring with rose water and sweetened.

## GELATINE JELLY.

### Mrs. S. E. Brown.

One package of gelatine, three lemons, one and one-half pounds
white sugar and a pint of any kind of wine or cider.   Let the
gelatine soak one hour in one pint of cold water, grate the rind
of one and the juice of the three lemons into the gelatine whilst
while it is still in the cold water; then pour three pints of boiling water and the sugar and cider or wine all into the other;
stir all well together, and let it stand ten minutes, and then strain
it off and set it in a cool place.   It is best to make it the day before using it.

## RHUBARB JAM.

### Mrs. T. W. Anderson.

Cut into pieces about an inch long, put a pound of sugar to
every pound of rhubarb, and leave till morning, pour the syrup
from it and boil till it thickens; then add the rhubarb and
boil gently fifteen minutes; put up as you do currant jelly in tumblers, it will keep good a year.

## GOOSEBERRY JAM

Take what quantity you please of red rough ripe gooseberries,
take half the quantity of lump sugar, break them well, and boil
them together for half an hour, or more, if necessary.   Put into
pots and cover with paper.

## GRAPE JAM.

### Mrs. S. W. Cheever, Ottawa, Ill.

Take your grapes, separate the skin from the pulp, keeping them in separate dishes, put the pulps in your preserving kettle with a teacup of water; when thoroughly heated, run .them through a colander to separate the seeds; then put your skins with them and weigh; to each pound of fruit, put three-fourths of a pound of sugar; add merely water enough to keep from burning; cook slowly three-fourths of an hour. This is a delicious jam, and worth the trouble.

## BLACKBERRY JAM.

### M. A. T.

To each pound of fruit, add three-fourths of a pound of sugar; mash each separately; then put together and boil from one-half to three-fourths of an hour.

## QUINCE JAM.

### Mrs. P. B. Ayer.

Boil your fruit in as little water as possible, until soft enough to break easily; pour off all the water and rub with a spoon until entirely smooth. To one pound of the quince, add ten ounces of brown sugar, and boil twenty minutes, stirring often.

## PINE APPLE JAM.

### Mrs. P. B. Ayer.

Grate your pine apple; to one pound of the apple, add three-fourths of a pound of loaf sugar; boil ten minutes.

## ORANGE MARMALADE.

### Mrs. J. Young Scammon.

One dozen Seville oranges, one dozen common oranges, one dozen lemons; boil the oranges and lemons whole in water for five hours; scoop out the inside, removing the seeds; cut the peel into thin slices with a knife, and add to every pound of pulp and peel, a pint of water, and two pounds of sugar. Boil twenty minutes.

## ORANGE MARMALADE.

### Mrs. Wm. Brackett.

Take seven oranges and five lemons; boil in water two or three hours; throw away the water, and open the oranges and lemons, taking out the seeds and preserving all the pulp and juice possible; cut the rinds in small strips or chop them, but cutting in strips is better; weigh it all, when this is done; then put three pounds of sugar, to two of the pulp and boil slowly till clear.

## SPICED CURRANTS.

### Mrs. B. P. Hutchinson.

Five pounds of currants, three pounds of sugar, one pint of vinegar, one tablespoon cloves, and one of cinnamon.    Boil twenty minutes.

## SPICED CURRANTS.

### Mrs. Meek and Mrs. O. L. Wheeler.

Five pounds currants, four pounds sugar, two tablespoons cloves, two tablespoons cinnamon, one pint vinegar; simmer two hours.

## SPICED GOOSEBERRIES.

### Mrs. F. B. Orr.

Ten pounds fruit, seven pounds sugar, three quarts vinegar, six large spoons cinnamon, one spoon cloves, two spoons allspice; put all together and boil thick.   To be eaten with meats.

## SPICED GOOSEBERRIES.

### Mrs. C. H. Wheeler.

Five pounds fruit, four pounds sugar, one pint vinegar, two teaspoons pulverized cloves, two tablespoons cinnamon, simmer three hours; more spices can be used, if desired.

# PICKLES.

Glittering squares of colored ice,
Sweetened with **syrups,** tinctured with spice ;
Creams and cordials and sugared dates ;
Syrian apples, Othmanee quinces,
Limes and citrons and apricots,
And wines that are **known to** eastern **princes.**

   *     *     *     *     *     *

**And all** that the curious palate **could** wish,
**Pass in and out of the cedarn doors.**
                —T. B. ALDRICH.

" **Who** peppered the highest **was surest to** please."

## SWEET PICKLES.

### PICKLED CHERRIES.

Six quarts cherries, three pounds of sugar, three quarts of best cider vinegar, **one** ounce cloves, one ounce cinnamon; put spice in a muslin **bag,** and boil with the sugar and vinegar; **when** this boils up for **a few** minutes, add the cherries.

## PICKLED PLUMS.

### Mrs. Meek.

To seven pounds plums, **four pounds** sugar, two ounces stick cinnamon, two ounces cloves, one quart vinegar, add **a little mace**; put in the jar first a layer plums, **then a** layer of spices alternately; scald the vinegar **and** sugar together; pour **it over the** plums, repeat three times for plums, (only **once** for cut apples and pears;) the fourth time scald all together; put them into glass jars and they are ready for use.

## PICKLED APPLES.

### Mrs. Watson Thatcher.

For one peck of sweet apples, take three pounds of sugar, **two** quarts of vinegar, one-half ounce of cinnamon, one-half ounce cloves; pare the apples, leaving them whole; boil them in part of the vinegar and sugar, until you can put a fork through them; take them out, beat the remainder of vinegar and sugar, and pour over them. Be careful not to **boil them** too long, or **they** will break.

## PICKLED APPLES.

### Mrs. Henry Stevens.

Ten pounds fruit, four pounds sugar, **one** quart vinegar, cloves and cinnamon. **Pare** and core the apples. Boil apples in syrup until soft. **Eat** with pleasure, **not** with sauce.

## PICKLED PEACHES.

### Mrs. Dr. Evarts.

One quart sugar, one pint vinegar, one gallon fruit; let sugar and vinegar come to a boil; pour over the fruit, next day draw off, and let the liquor come to a boil again; repeat till the ninth **day,** then boil fruit **and** syrup ten minutes. Spice to taste.

*Finish, and is the easiest to use.*

## PICKLED PEACHES.

### Mrs. C. D. Howard.

Take five pounds of brown sugar to one gallon of pure cider vinegar; boil it hard for thirty minutes, skimming off the scum till clear; rub off the peaches in the meantime out of boiling water, (quickly,) with a flannel cloth, sticking four cloves in each peach, and a bag of cinnamon put into the boiling syrup. If the peaches are clingstones, put them into the boiling syrup for fifteen or twenty minutes; if freestones, lay them in the jar in layers, and pour the syrup over them while hot; then put a small plate over to keep them from rising, and cover tightly with cloth or paper. In four days look at them, and if necessary, boil the syrup again, and pour on while hot; keep them in a cool place while the weather is hot to prevent their souring. The White Sugar Cling is nice for pickling, and the Blood Peach is very rich, but dark. Small pears can be pickled in the same manner, if the skin is taken off.

# SOUR PICKLES.

## PREPARED MUSTARD.

### C. D. Adams.

Two tablespoons mustard, one teaspoon sugar, one-half tea-spoon salt, boiling water enough to mix it; when cold, add one tablespoon salad oil, and vinegar enough to thin it. This will keep a week or two.

## TOMATO CATSUP.

### Mrs. Monroe Heath.

Select good ripe tomatoes, scald and strain through a coarse sieve to remove seeds and skins; then add to each gallon when

cold, four tablespoons of salt, three of ground mustard, two of
black pepper, one of ground allspice, one-half of cloves, one-half
of cayenne pepper, and one pint of white wine or cider vinegar;
simmer slowly four hours; bottle and cork tight.

## PICKLED CUCUMBERS.
### Mrs. A. P. Wightman.

Pick those that are small and of quick growth, wash well and
pour boiling water over them with a little salt. Let them stand
twelve hours; put them into cold vinegar. To a gallon of vinegar, put one tablespoon of pulverized alum, and a teacup of
salt; let them remain in this until your vinegar is full of cucumbers, then scald them in it, and put them into new vinegar.
Red peppers improve them.

## OUDE SAUCE.
### C. Kennicott.

One pint green tomatoes, six peppers, (not large), four onions,
chop together; add one cup salt, and let it stand over night; in
the morning, drain off the water; add one cup sugar, one cup
horse radish, one tablespoon ground cloves, one tablespoon cinnamon, cover with vinegar, and stew gently all day.

## MY MOTHER'S FAVORITE PICKLES.
### Mrs. Savage.

One quart raw cabbage chopped fine; one quart boiled beets
chopped fine; two cups of sugar, tablespoon of salt, one teaspoon
black pepper, one-fourth teaspoon red pepper, one tea cup of
grated horse radish; cover with cold vinegar, and keep from the
air.

## FRENCH PICKLES.
### H. N. Jenks.

One peck of tomatoes sliced, six large onions, some cauliflower, (much or little as you prefer), a pint of salt thrown over them

at night, the liquor drained off in the morning; **then boil the to-matoes, onions, &c.,** in two quarts of water, **and one quart of vin-egar,** fifteen **or twenty** minutes. After **boiling, put it in a** colander and **drain it off; add seven pints of vinegar, two pounds brown sugar, one-half of white** mustard seed, two tablespoons of **ground allspice, two of cloves, two of ginger,** two of cinnamon, **two of** ground **mustard, one-half a tablespoon of cayenne;** put **all in a kettle** and boil fifteen **or twenty minutes, stir and be very careful not to burn.**

## MIXED PICKLES.

### Mrs. F. M. Cragin.

Three hundred **small cucumbers,** four green peppers sliced fine, two large or three small heads cauliflower, **three heads of** white cabbage shaved fine, **nine large** onions **sliced, one large** root horse-radish, **one quart of green beans** cut one **inch long, one quart green tomatoes sliced; put this mixture in a pretty** strong brine **twenty-four hours; drain** three hours, **then** sprinkle in one-fourth pound of black and one-fourth **pound of** white mus-**stard seed, also** one tablespoon black ground **pepper; let** it come to a good **boil in just** vinegar **enough to cover it,** adding a little alum. Drain **again, and when cold, mix** in one-half pint of ground mustard : **cover the whole with** good cider vinegar ; **add** tumeric enough **to color, if you like.**

## PICKLED CABBAGE.

### Mrs. A. N. Arnold.

Select solid heads, slice very fine, put in **a jar, then cover with** boiling water ; when cold, **drain** off the **water and season with** grated horse-radish, salt, equal parts **of black and** red pepper, cinnamon, and cloves whole ; cover with **strong vinegar.** This is convenient and always good.

## WEST INDIA PICKLE.

Mrs. Edward Ely.

One white crisp cabbage, **two** heads cauliflower, three heads celery, **one** quart each of **small** green plums, peaches, grapes, **radish** pods, masturtion **seeds,** artichokes, tomatoes, and string **beans.** The green part of **a** watermelon next to the rind; one **quart** small onions parboiled in milk; one hundred small cucumbers about an inch or so long, a few green peppers, and three **limes or green** lemons. Cut fine the cabbage, cauliflower, celery, pepper and limes, and green ginger; mix well with the rest, **then** pour a strong hot brine over them, and let them **stand three** hours, then take out and let them drain over night. Mix one ounce tumeric powder, with a little cold vinegar, **add** one bottle French mustard, ground cinnamon, allspice, two nutmegs, black pepper, four pounds white sugar, and one gallon vinegar, pour boiling hot over the pickle; if not sufficiently liquid to moisten nicely, add more **vinegar.**

## PICKLED ONIONS.

Mrs. Anna Marble.

Peel your onions, and let them **lie in a** weak brine made of salt and water **(over** night); then put them **in** a jar, cover them with boiling white wine and vinegar. Cover close, and tie down when **cold.**

## PICKLED MELONS.

Mrs. Wicker.

Take ripe melons, wash, pare and take out the seeds, **cut** them in slices; put them in a stone jar, cover with vinegar, and let them stand twenty-four hours. Take out, and to each quart of fresh vinegar, add three pounds brown sugar; for twelve melons take three ounces cinnamon, two of cloves, two of allspice; boil the sugar and spices in the vinegar; skim it well, then put in the melons, and boil for twenty minutes; let the syrup boil a few minutes after taking them out, then pour it over them.

## PICKLED CAULIFLOWER.

After cutting off all the green leaves, put the cauliflower into boiling water, with a good supply of salt, and boil from three to five minutes; take them out of the salt and water, dip them in clear cold water one minute, to send the heat to the heart of the cauliflower, cut them in pieces convenient to put in jars, then make a mixture of one tablespoon of mace, one of cloves, one allspice, one of ginger, two of white mustard seed and a red pepper pod, with each gallon of vinegar. Let the mixture boil, and pour it upon the cauliflower, cover them closely, and let them stand one week, then pour off the vinegar, scald it and return it again hot to the cauliflower; then put them in jars ready for use. The best cider vinegar should be used, and if it is not perfectly clear, it will dissolve the cauliflower.

## BRINE FOR CUCUMBERS.

### Mrs. J. B. Adams.

Three pails water, two quarts coarse salt, (rock is good,) one pound alum, one pound black pepper, tied in a bag; dissolve the alum in a little hot water; put all into a jar or keg; wash the cucumbers with great care, and have none that are bruised; throw them in and place a weight to keep them under. When wanted for pickling, soak a short time, changing the water as often as necessary.

## CONGRESS PICKLES.

### S. S. Peirce.

Wash the cucumbers; take one pint of fine salt to one hundred medium sized cucumbers, and sprinkle it over them; pour on boiling hot water enough to cover them; let them stand forty-eight hours; take them out of the brine, wipe them, put them

in the jars, and pour over them scalding hot vinegar **with any**
spices you **like.** If the vinegar becomes tasteless, put them into
fresh vinegar before using them. *Keep **them covered tight.**

## RECIPE FOR 600 PICKLES.
### Mrs. F. D. Gray.

**Make a** brine of cold water and salt strong enough to bare an
egg; heat boiling hot and pour over the cucumbers; let them stand
twenty-four hours, then take out and **wipe dry;** scald vinegar and
pour over them and let them stand twenty-four hours; then pour
off, and to fresh vinegar add one quart brown sugar, two large
green peppers, one-half pint white mustard, **six cents' worth of**
ginger root, the same of cinnamon, allspice and **cloves; one ta-**
blespoon celery seed, alum the **size** of a butternut; scald **these**
together and pour boiling hot on the cucumbers.

## PICKLED CUCUMBERS.
### Mrs. Packard.

Wash **with care your cucumbers, and place in jars.    Make a**
**weak** brine (a **handful of salt to a gallon and a** half of water.)
.When scalding hot, **turn over the** cucumbers and cover; repeat
this process three **mornings in** succession, taking care to skim
thoroughly.    On **the fourth** day have **ready** a porcelain kettle of
vinegar, in which **has been added** a piece **of** alum the size of a
walnut.    When scalding hot, put in as many cucumbers as may
be covered with the vinegar; do not let them boil, but skim out
**as** soon as scalded **through, and** replace with others, adding each
time a small piece **of alum.**    When **this process** is through,
throw out the vinegar, and replace with good cider or white **wine**
vinegar; add spices, mustard seed and red peppers.    Sort the
pickles and **place in** stone or glass jars, turn over the hot spiced'
vinegar; seal and put away the jars not needed for immediate
use.    Pickles thus prepared, are fine and crisp at the expiration
**of** a year.    Those that are kept in open mouth jars may be covered with a cloth, which **will need** to be taken off and rinsed oc-

casionally. I prefer green peppers, and prepare them with the cucumbers in brine. They are not as apt to become soft.

## GREEN TOMATO PICKLES.

### Mrs. J. L. Harris, Keokuk, Iowa.

Chop one-half peck tomatoes, three onions, a gill of horse-radish, three green peppers; put them in a sieve and drain dry, salt in layers and let them stand one night; drain the next day, scald vinegar and pour over it; let it stand two or three days; drain again, scald a pound of sugar to a quart of vinegar, a ta-blespoon black pepper, the same of allspice, three ounces of ground cloves, three ounces of mustard, a gill of mustard seed. Boil the spices in a little vinegar.

## RIPE TOMATO PICKLES.

### Mrs. C. M. Dickerman, Rockford, Ill.

To seven pounds ripe tomatoes add three pounds sugar, one quart vinegar; boil them together fifteen minutes, skim out the tomatoes, and boil the syrup a few minutes longer. Spice to suit the taste with cloves and cinnamon.

## PICCALILLI.

### Mrs. C. Bradley.

One peck of green tomatoes, slice them thin, add one pint of salt, cover with cold water, and let them stand twenty-four hours; then chop very fine one head of cabbage, six onions, twelve green peppers; then cover it with hot vinegar, drain it through a seive, add one pint of molasses, one tablespoon cloves, allspice, two ounces of white mustard seed and cover with cold vinegar.

## PICCALILLI.

### Mrs. Lamkin.

One peck of green tomatoes; (if the flavor of onions is desired, take eight, but it is very nice without any,) four green peppers; slice all, and put in layers, sprinkle on one cup of salt, and let them remain over night, in the morning press dry through a sieve, put it in a porcelain kettle, and cover with vinegar; add one cup of sugar, a tablespoon of each kind of spice; put into a muslin bag; stew slowly about an hour, or until the tomatoes are as soft as you desire.

## PICCALILLI.

### Mrs. C. Bradley.

One peck of green tomatoes, slice them thin, add one pint of salt, cover with cold water, and let them stand twenty-four hours; then chop very fine one head of cabbage, six onions, twelve green peppers; then cover it with hot vinegar, drain it through a sieve, add one pint of molasses, one tablespoon cloves, allspice, two ounces of white mustard seed and cover with cold vinegar.

## SWEET GREEN TOMATO PICKLES.

### Mrs. P.

One peck of green tomatoes sliced, six large onions sliced; sprinkle through them one teacup of salt, let them stand over night; drain off in the morning; take two quarts of water and one of vinegar, boil the tomatoes and onions five minutes; drain through a colander, take four quarts of vinegar, two pounds of brown sugar, one-half pound of ground mustard, two tablespoons of cloves, two of ginger, two of cinnamon, one-half teaspoon of cayenne pepper, or instead five or six green peppers chopped; boil fifteen minutes. This will keep good a year, if prepared according to the recipe, and is generally liked.

## PICKLED GREEN TOMATOES.

### S. S. Peirce.

One peck tomatoes, two quarts small white onions, one dozen green peppers, one cup salt, one cup sugar, one tablespoon of cloves, allspice, stick of cinnamon; slice your tomatoes over night, and mix in the salt. In the morning drain off the water and throw it away; put all the ingredients together and let it come to a boil. Put away for use.

## CHOW-CHOW.

### Mrs. John Corthell.

Two heads of cabbage, two heads cauliflower, one dozen cucumbers, six roots of celery, six peppers, one quart of small white onions, two quarts of green tomatoes, cut into small pieces, and boil each vegetable separately until tender, then strain them. Two gallons of vinegar, one-fourth pound of mustard, one-fourth pound of mustard seed, one pot of French mustard, one ounce of cloves, two ounces of turmeric; put the vinegar and spices into a kettle and let them come to a boil; mix the vegetables and pour over the dressing.

## CHOW-CHOW.

### Mrs. C. A. Rogers.

One-half bushel green tomatoes, one dozen onions, one dozen green peppers, (chopped fine,) sprinkle with salt, and let stand over night; then drain off the lime, cover it with vinegar, and cook one hour slowly; drain again, and pack closely in a jar; take two pounds sugar, two tablespoons of cinnamon, one pound of allspice, one each of cloves and pepper, one-half cup ground mustard, one pint horse-radish, and vinegar enough to mix them; then, when boiling hot, pour it over the mixture in the jar, and cover tightly.

## CHOW-CHOW.

### Mrs. King.

Take a peck of cucumbers, one peck of onions, half a peck of string beans, three heads of cauliflower, three bunches of celery, a half dozen sweet peppers; soak the whole in strong salt and water over night; in the morning scald them all in weak salt and water, but before scalding cut them into shape so that they will go easily into glass jars; add three-quarters of a pound of mustard, two packages of curry powder, and six quarts of good vinegar ; put the mustard and curry **powder** into the vinegar, and let it come to **a** boil ; put the pickles into the cans, and pour the liquid over them while hot. **Do not cover while scalding.**

## CANTELOPE **PICKLES.**

Mrs. Earle.

Take fine ripe cantelopes, **wash,** pare and cut into small pieces, **taking out the** seeds; cover **them** with **vinegar for twenty-four hours; throw** away one quart **of the vinegar to each quart** re-**maining, allow three pounds sugar to a dozen cantelopes, three** ounces stick **cinnamon, two ounces** cloves, **two** ounces **of** all-spice, (spices whole,) boil **them with** the vinegar, when well skimmed put in the fruit, **boil fifteen minutes,** then take out, boil and skim **syrup,** and pour **boiling hot over** the fruit.

# DRINKS.

The bubbling and loud hissing **urn**
**Throws** up a steaming column ; and **the cups**
That cheer, but not inebriate, **wait** on each ;
**So let us** welcome peaceful evening **in.**
—COWPER.

## TEA.

**When the water** in the tea-kettle begins to **boil,** have ready a tin tea-steeper ; pour into the tea-steeper just a very little of the boiling water, and then put in tea, allowing one teaspoonful of tea to each person. Pour over this boiling water until the steep-**er is a** little more **than** half full ; **cover** tightly and **let** it stand where it will keep hot, but not to boil. Let the tea infuse for ten or fifteen minutes and then pour into the tea urn, adding more boiling water, in the proportion of one cup of water for every teaspoon of dry tea which has been infused. Have boiling water in a water pot, and weaken each cup of tea, as desired. Do not use water for tea that has boiled long. Spring water is best for tea, and filtered water next best.

## COFFEE.

Cleanse the coffee, dry and roast the berries evenly but quickly, until they are browned to the centre, and are of a dark chestnut color. Grind as you use it, keeping the rest in a closely covered glass can. Allow one heaping tablespoon of ground coffee for every person, and one or two over. Mix with the grounds, a part or whole of an egg, according to the amount of coffee used. Pour boiling water in the coffee-pot before using, and scald it well; then put in the coffee and pour over half as much water as will be used. Let the coffee froth up, stir down the grounds, and let it boil for about five minutes; then stand the coffee pot where it will be hot, (but not to boil the coffee,) for five or ten minutes longer. Mocha, is the richest and most delicate flavored coffee. Old Government Java is an excellent coffee, and more economical than Mocha. An excellent authority in coffee making allows to one pound of Mocha coffee, five quarts of water, made after the above recipe.

## CHOCOLATE.

### M.

Scrape baker's chocolate fine, mix with a little cold water and the yolks of eggs well beaten; add this to equal parts of milk and water, and boil well, being careful that it does not burn. Sweeten to taste and serve hot.

# SODA CREAM.
### M. G. Band.

Two and one-half pounds white sugar, one-eighth pound tartaric acid, both dissolved in one quart of hot water; when cold, add the beaten whites of three eggs, stirring well; bottle for use. Put two large spoons of this syrup in a glass of cold water and stir in it one-fourth of a spoon of bicarbonate of soda. Any flavor can be put in the syrup. An excellent drink for summer.

# EGG-NOG.
### Mrs. A. W. D.

Beat separately the yolks and whites of six eggs; stir the yolks into a quart of rich milk, or thin cream; add one-half pound of sugar; mix in one-half pint of rum or brandy. Flavor with a grated nutmeg.

# SANGAREE.
### Mrs. A. W. D.

One-third of wine, ale or porter; two-thirds of water, warm or cold; stir in sufficient sugar to sweeten it. Flavor with nutmeg. By adding lemon juice you make what is called negus.

# MULLED CIDER.
### Mrs. A. W. D.

Allow five eggs to a quart of cider, put a handful of cloves into the cider and boil it; while it is boiling, beat the eggs in a large pitcher, adding to them as much sugar as will make the cider very sweet; by the time the cider boils the eggs will be sufficiently light. Pour the boiling liquor on the beaten egg, and continue to pour the mixture from one pitcher to another until it foams lightly. Pour it warm into your glasses, and grate nutmeg over each. Port wine may be mulled in the same way.

# RASPBERRY ACID.
### Mrs. G. W. Pitkin.

Dissolve five ounces of tartaric acid in two quarts of water; pour it upon twelve pounds of red raspberries in a large bowl;

let it stand twenty-four hours, strain it without pressing; to a pint of this liquor, add one and one-half pounds of white sugar, stir until dissolves. Bottle but do not cook for several days, when it is ready for use. Two or three tablespoons in a glass of ice water will make delicious beverage.

## RASPBERRY VINEGAR.

### Mrs. W. S. Walker.

To four quarts red raspberries, put enough vinegar to cover, and let them stand twenty-four hours; scald and strain it; add a pound of sugar to one pint of juice, boil it twenty minutes, and bottle; it is then ready for use and will keep years. To one glass of water, add a great spoonful. It is much relished by the sick. Very nice.

## BLACKBERRY SYRUP.

### Mrs. Bausher.

To one pint of juice, put one pound of white sugar, one-half ounce of powdered cinnamon, one-fourth ounce mace, and two teaspoons cloves; boil all together for quarter of an hour, then strain the syrup, and add to each pint a glass of French brandy.

## LEMON SYRUP.

### Mrs. De Forest.

Pare off the yellow rind of the lemon, slice the lemon and put a layer of lemon and a thick layer of sugar in a deep plate; cover close with a saucer, and set in a warm place. This is an excellent remedy for a cold.

## CURRANT WINE.

### Mrs. Caroline L. Warner.

One quart of juice, two quarts of water, three pounds of brown sugar; mix well until the sugar is all dissolved; set your keg or barrel in the cellar, where it can stand undisturbed; fill with the

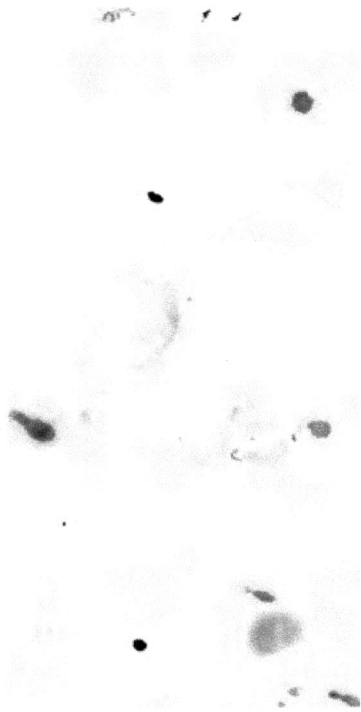

Coffee Cake, Dutes

one cup sugar, one molasses
one cold strong coffee
3 eggs, 5 scant cup flour
1 lb raisins, 1 lb currants
1/2 pound citron, if you like it
cloves cinnamon, nutmeg to taste
3 teaspoonful baking powder
Sprinkle fruit plentifully with
flour

wine made as above; let it stand with the bung out until it has stopped working, **then** put in the **bung** and it will be fit for use in two months.

## CURRANT WINE.

### Mrs. A. W. D.

**Put into a ten** gallon keg, thirty pounds **crushed sugar, ten** quarts of juice, and fill up with water; leave **open the bung, and as it works** fill up with water. When done **working, stop up the keg,**

## RED CURRANT WINE.

### Mrs. N. B. Iglehart.

One gallon **of** juice, ten pounds **of** loaf sugar, two gallóns of water; the currants should be ripe, and fresh picked; **crush** them and let them be well strained; pour it on the sugar **and** add water until all the sugar **is** dissolved; mix well, and put **it in** a strong cask in **a** cool cellar; after **it** is done fermenting, **bot**tle it.

## SPLENDID GINGER BEER.

### Mrs. H. L. Bristol.

Five gallons of water, one-half pounds ginger root boiled, four pounds **of** sugar, one-eight pound cream tartar, **one bottle es**sence of lemon, one ounce of tartaric acid, **one** quart **of yeast.**

## HOP BEER.

### Mrs. Dickinson.

One handful **of hops,** boil an hour, strain, and add one pint of molasses, and enough water to **make** two gallons. When milk warm, add one cup or cake of yeast, let it stand over night, skim and pour it off from the yeast carefully; add one tablespoon of wintergreen, and bottle for use.

---

*Preparation."—Grand Exposition, Paris,* 1867.

# MISCELLANEOUS.

What does COOKERY mean? It means the knowledge of all fruits and herbs and balms and spices, and of all that is healing and sweet in fields and groves, and savory in meats. It means carefulness and inventiveness, and watchfulness and willingness, and readiness of appliance. It means the economy of your great grandmother and the science of modern chemists. It means much tasting and no wasting; it means English thoroughness, and French art, and Arabian hospitality; and it means, in fine, that you are to be perfectly and always ladies—loaf givers; and as you are to see imperatively that everybody has something pretty to put on, so you are to see even yet more imperatively that everybody has something nice to eat.—RUSKIN.

## GENERAL HINTS.

It is a matter of great convenience to have a covered tub or pail for sifted flour ready for use. It will save half the time in an emergency.

Always sift soda, when not dissolved in hot water, through a fine wire sieve.

Sugar for fried cakes should be dissolved in the milk, to prevent the cake from absorbing the lard while frying.

Two kinds of coffee mixed, (Java and Mocha,) are better than one alone; but should be browned separately.

Tea should never be boiled, but be sure the water boils that you use for steeping. From three to five minutes is sufficient time; if it stands longer, **the tea is apt to lose** the aroma, and have the bitter **taste** of the leaf.

An old house **keeper of** fifty years experience thinks the very best way of making coffee is to **use the** National Pot, no egg; nothing to settle is required, simply use a muslin bag, and let the water boil around it ten or fifteen minutes. A very impor-**tant** advantage is, that none of the aroma is lost by standing. **If the** "gude mon" **of** the home is late to breakfast, **his** coffee **is late to** breakfast, his coffee is just as nice and hot as when first made.

**When bread is like a honey** comb all **through, is the time to** make it **up in loaves. When the** loaves **do** not retain **the** dent of the finger, **it** is ready for **the oven.**

When meats **are** put in to roast, have no water in the **pan.** When they begin **to** brown, is time enough for water.

Chicken for salad **is** nicer cut with **a** knife than chopped in a bowl, and the celery should always be cut with **a knife.**

If you would be a **true economist, do not** burn letters, envelopes, &c., but tear them **across once or twice,** and put them in the scrap bag for the rag man.

A silver spoon put into a glass jar, **will** temper it so **that it can at once be** filled with anything **hot, even** to the boiling point.

## LIME WATER.

**Mrs.** E. B. Lynde, Milwaukee.

**One** of the most useful agents of household economy, if rightly understood, is lime water. Its mode of preparation is as follows : Put a stone of fresh unslacked lime about the size of a half-peck measure into a large stone jar or unpainted pail, and pour over it slowly and carefully, (so as not to slacken too rapidly,) a tea-kettle full, (four gallons,) of hot water, and stir thoroughly; let it settle, and then stir again two or three times in twenty-four hours. Then bottle carefully, all that can be poured off in a clear and limpid state.

---

*Finish, and is the easiest to use.*

Uses.—It is often sold by druggists as a remedy for children's summer complaint, a teaspoonful being a dose in a cup of milk, and when the diarrhœa is caused by acidity of the stomach, it is an excellent remedy, and when put into milk gives no unpleasant taste, but rather improves the flavor.

When put into milk that might curdle when heated, it will prevent its so doing, and can then be used for puddings and pies. A little stirred into cream or milk, after a hot day or night, will prevent its turning when used for tea or coffee.

It is unequalled in cleansing bottles or small milk vessels, or babies' nursing bottles, as it sweetens and purifies without leaving an unpleasant odor or flavor.

A cupful, or even more, mixed in the sponge of bread or cakes made over night, will prevent it from souring.

## PRESERVING AUTUMN LEAVES.

### Mrs. C. H. Wheeler.

These may be easily preserved and retain their natural tints, or nearly so, by either of the following methods: As they are gathered they may be laid between the leaves of a magazine until the book is full, and left with a light weight upon them until the moisture of the leaves has been absorbed; two or three thicknesses of paper should intervene between the leaves. If the leaves are large or in clusters, take newspapers, lay them on a shelf and use in the same manner as above.

Another method, is to iron each leaf with a middling hot iron until the moisture is all out of them. Are best with out varnish.

## SKELETON LEAVES.

Boil the leaves in equal parts of rain water and soft soap until you can separate the pulp from the skin; take them out into clear water; lay the leaf to be cleaned on glass, the upper side of the leaf next to the glass; then, with a tooth-brush remove all pulp and skin, turn the leaf and repeat the process; when thoroughly done, put the leaf to bleach in this solution: One

pound sal soda, dissolved in five pints rain water; one-half
pound chloride of lime, in three pints water; allow twenty-four
hours for the latter to dissolve. Strain out the sediment, and
pour the clear solution of lime into the solution of sal soda. The
result will be a thick butter-milk solution, otherwise the lime was
not strong enough. Filter this until it is perfectly **clear.** For
leaves, use one part of solution to one part of water; for ferns,
use the solution full strength. When perfectly white, remove to
clear water; let stand for several hours, changing two or three
times; the last water should be a little blue; float out on paper,
press in book when nearly **dry.** In mounting use mucilage made
of five parts gum arabic, three parts white sugar, two parts of
starch; add a very little water, boil and stir until thick and white.

### FOR CRYSTALIZING GRASS.
#### Mrs. Dudlam, Evanston.

Take one and one half pounds of rock alum, pour on three
pints of boiling water; when quite cool, put into a wide-mouth
vessel, hang in your grasses, a few at **a time. Do** not let them
get two heavy, or the stems will not support them. **You** may
again heat alum and add more grasses. By adding a little coloring, it will give variety.

### COLOGNE.
#### Etta C. Springer.

One ounce **oil** citronella, one ounce oil burgemot, and **one**
ounce oil lemon, cut with equal quantities **of 95 per cent.** alcohol.

### CAMPHOR ICE.
#### Mrs. A. M.

One ounce of lard, one ounce spermaceti, one ounce camphor,
one ounce almond oil, one-half cake **of** white wax; melt and
turn into moulds.

*Excellent for Food."—London Exposition,* 1862.

## CAMPHOR ICE.

### Mrs. Bartlett.

One-half ounce each of camphor gum and white wax, sperma-ceti and sweet oil; melt slowly the hard ingredients and then add the oil.

## COLD CREAM.

### Mrs. Anna Marble.

Four ounces sweet almond oil, two of rose water, two of white wax, two of cocoa butter, two of spermaceti; put a bowl in a pan of boiling water; cut the spermaceti, white wax and cocoa butter in small pieces; put them in the bowl, also the oil and rose water. When melted, stir contents until cold.

## TO BEAUTIFY TEETH.

Dissolve two ounces of borax in three pints of boiling water, and before it is cold, add one teaspoon of spirits of camphor; bottle it for use. A teaspoon of this with an equal quantity of tepid water.

## HAIR TONIC.

### Mrs. A. M.

One-half ounce sugar of lead, one-half of lac sulphur, one quart of rose water, six tablespoons castor oil.

## FOR CLEANING HAIR BRUSHES.

### Mrs. C. H. Wheeler.

Use spirits of ammonia and hot water; wash them well and shake the water out, drying on a coarse towel; they will look white and clean as new, little or no soap is needed.

## TO CLEAN HAIR BRUSHES.

### E. A. Forsyth.

Do not use soap, but put a tablespoon of harts-horn into the water, having it only tepid, and dip up and down until clean;

they dry with the brushes down, and they will be like new ones; if you do not have ammonia, use soda; a teaspoon dissolved in the water will **do very well.**

## JAPANESE CLEANSING CREAM.

One-fourth pound white castile soap, **three** ounces ammonia, **one of** ether, one of spirits of wine, **one of glycerine;** cut the **soap** fine and dissolve in **one** quart **rain water; then** add four quarts rain water and then all **the** ingredients. **For** cleansing silks.

## FOR CLOTHES THAT FADE.

One ounce of lead in a pail of rain water. Soak **over night.**

### TO WASH CALICO.

Mrs. Edward Ely.

Blue calicoes **or** muslins **will retain** their **color,** if one small teaspoon of sugar of lead is **put into a pail** of water, and the articles washed in the water.

### BLACK CALICOES.

Wash black percales or calicoes, **as usual,** rinse in water with a strong solution of salt. **This** will **prevent** black **from** running, and also colors.

## TO WASH WOOLEN BLANKETS.

Mrs. J. A. Packard.

Dissolve soap enough to **make** a good suds in **a** boiling water, add **a** tablespoon of aqua ammonia; when scalding hot, turn over your blankets. If convenient, use a pounder, or any way to work them thoroughly through the suds without rubbing on a board. Rinse well in hot water. There is usually soap enough **from the** first suds, to **make** the second soft; if not, add a little **soap** and ammonia; **and after** being put through the ringer, let two persons, standing opposite, pull them into shape ; dry in the sun. White flannels may be washed in the same way without shrinking.

## TO WASH WOOLEN.
### E. A. Forsyth.

To every pail of water, add one tablespoon of ammonia, and the same of beef gall; wash out quickly, and rinse in warm water, adding a very little beef gall to the water; this will remove spots from carpets, making them look fresh.

## TO WASH CARPETS.
### E. A. Forsyth.

Spread the carpet where you can use a brush; take Irish potatoes and scrape them into a pail or tub of water and let them stand over night, using one peck to clean a large carpet; two pails of water is sufficient to let them stand in, and you can add more when ready to use; add two ounces of beef gall and use with a brush, as to scrub a floor; the particles of potatoe will help cleanse; when dry, brush with a broom or stiff brush.

## WASHING FLUID.
### Mrs. A. P. Iglehart.

Nine tablespoons unslacked lime, two pounds of sal soda, four quarts water; let this simmer half an hour, then bottle up, take a small teacup to a boiler of water.

## WASHING FLUID.
### Mrs. A. W. D.

One pound sal soda, one pound potash, each dissolved in one gallon of water, (separately;) then mixed together and bottle.

## TO MAKE GOOD STARCH.
### Mrs. D.

Mix the starch with cold water, add boiling water until it thickens, then add dessert spoon of sugar, and a small piece of butter. Makes a stiff and glossy finish equal to laundry.

---

*The whitest, strongest and most economical Starch—Duryeas'.*

## AN EXCELLENT HARD SOAP.
### Mrs. Kate Johnson.

Pour twelve quarts soft boiling water on two and one-half pounds of unslacked lime; dissolve five pounds sal soda in twelve quarts soft hot water; then mix and let them remain from twelve to twenty-four hours. Pour off all the clear fluid, being careful not to allow any of the sediment to run off; boil three and one-half pounds of clean grease and three or four ounces of rosin in the above ley till the grease disappears; pour into a box and let it stand a day to stiffen and then cut in bars. It is as well to put the lime in all the water and then add the soda. After pouring off the fluid, add two or three gallons of water and let it the lime and soda dregs a day or two. This makes an excellent washing fluid to boil or soak the clothes in, with one pint in a boiler of water.

## CLEANING SILVER.
### Mrs. O. L. Parker.

Never put a particle of soap about your silver, if you would have it retain its original lustre. When it wants polish, take a piece of soft leather and whiting and rub hard. The proprietor of one of the oldest silver establishments in the City of Philadelphia says that house-keepers ruin their silver in soap suds, as it makes it look like pewter.

## STOVE POLISH.
### Mrs. O. L. Parker.

Stove lustre, when mixed with turpentine and applied in the usual manner, is blacked more glossy and more durably than when mixed with any other liquid. The turpentine prevents rust, and when put on an old rusty stove, will make it look as well as new.

## TO EXTRACT INK.

To extract ink from cotton, silk and woolen goods, saturate the spot with spirits of turpentine and let it remain several hours;

then rub it between the hands. It will crumble away without
injuring either the color or the texture of the article.

## PATENT SOAP.

Five pounds hard soap, one quart ley, one-fourth ounce pearl-
ash; place on the fire and stir well until the soap is dissolved;
add one-half pint spirits turpentine, one gill spirits hartshorn and
stir well. It is then fit for use. The finest muslins may be put
to soak in this suds, and if left for a time will become beautifully
white. A small portion of soap put into a little hot water, and a
flannel cloth will save hard labor and a brush in cleaning paint.

## FOR BLEACHING COTTON CLOTH.
### Mrs. C. H. Wheeler.

One gound of chloride of lime, dissolved and strained; put
in two or three pails water; thoroughly wet the cloth and leave
it in over night; then rinse well in two waters. This will also
take out mildew and is equally good for brown cotton or white
that has become yellow from any cause, and will not injure the
fabric.

## TO REMOVE TAR.

Rub well with clean lard, afterwards wash with soap and warm
water. Apply this to either hands or clothing.

## JAVELLE WATER FOR MILDEW STAINS.

One pound of chloride of lime, two of washing soda, two gallons of soft water; pour one gallon of boiling water to the ingredients to dissolve them, adding the cold water when dissolved.

## COLORING COTTON CARPET RAGS.
### Mrs. S. I. Parker, Channahon, Ill.

BLUE.—For five pounds of cloth, take five ounces of copperas, with two pails of water in a tin or copper boiler; set it
over the fire till the copperas is dissolved and it begins to heat,

then put in the cloth, stirring it frequently till it boils, one-half
or three-fourths of an hour; then remove the cloth where it can
drain; pour away the copperas water and take two ounces of
prussiate of potash in about two pails of water in the same
vessel; when it is well dissolved and hot, put in the cloth from
the copperas water, stirring it thoroughly till it boils one-half an
hour, then remove the cloth; add, (with care and caution, on
account of the spattering which ensues,) one tablespoon of oil
of vitriol, and stir it well in the dye; replace the cloth, stirring
it briskly till it has boiled one-half an hour. Should be well
rinsed and washed in clear water to prevent the dye from
making it tender after coloring.

YELLOW.—For five pounds of cloth, dissolve one-half pound
of sugar of lead in a tub of warm water and twelve ounces of
bi-chromate of potash in another tub of cold water ; soak, rinse,
and wring the cloth in the leak water first, then in the other, and
return from one to the other till the right shade of color is obtained.

ORANGE.—Dip the yellow colored cloth in strong lime water
—if it should not turn, boil it, rinse all well.

GREEN.—Put your blue cloth in the yellow dye in the same
manner as for coloring yellow. Old calico will take a darker
shade of blue or green in the same dye with the white cloth.

## TO BOIL CORN BEEF.
### Mrs. E. A. Forsyth.

Put into boiling water when you put it on to cook, and do
not take it out of the pot when done, until cold. This will leave
the meat juicy, instead of dry, when cold.

## FOR PRESERVING EGGS.
### Mrs. B. F. Adams.

To one pint of unslacked lime and one pint of salt, pour one
pail full of boiling water; when cold, pour over the eggs, having
placed them in a jar or tub, with the small end of the egg down.

*We advise the use of "Richards' Queen" for making light biscuit.*

## CLEANING MARBLE.

### Mrs. Gray.

Dissolve a large lump of Spanish whiting in water which has previously dissolved a teaspoon of washing soda; take only sufficient water to moisten the whiting, and it will become a paste; with a flannel cloth rub the marble well, leaving it on for a while and repeating the process two or three times, if necessary. Wash off with soap and water, then dry the marble well and polish with a soft duster.

## FURNITURE POLISH.

No. 1. Shellac varnish, linseed oil and spirits of wine, equal parts.

No. 2. Linseed oil, alcohol, equal parts.

No. 3. Linseed oil five ounces, turpentine two ounces, oil of vitriol one-half ounce.

## CLEANING WHITE PAINT.

### Mrs. C. H. Wheeler.

Spirits of ammonia, used in sufficient quantity to soften the water, and ordinary hard soap will make the paint look white and clean with half the effort of any other method I have ever tried. Care should be taken not to have too much ammonia, or the paint will be injured.

## HARD SOAP.

### Mrs. Mary A. Odell.

Six pounds of clean grease, six pounds of Sal Soda, three pounds of stone lime; slake the lime and put it into four gallons of soft water; add the sal soda, and when dissolved let it settle. Pour off the water into an iron kettle, and add the grease melted, and boil. If the soap does not come after boiling a few minutes, add more soft water till it is of the consistency of honey. Wet a tub and pour the hot soap into it. When cold, cut it into pieces and lay it away to dry. Always make soap in an iron kettle.

# THE SICK ROOM.

EGG GRUEL.—Boil eggs from one to three hours until hard enough to grate; then boil new milk and thicken with the egg, and add a little salt. Excellent in cases of nausea.—MRS. BARTLETT.

GRUEL FOR INFANTS.—To make a gruel for infants suffering from marasmus, take one pint of goat's milk and the yolks of two eggs boiled sufficiently hard to reduce to an impalpable powder; add a pint of boiling water, a little salt or sugar and administer by a nursing bottle.—Dr. SMALL.

BEEF TEA.—To one pound of lean beef add one and one-half tumblers of cold water; cut the beef in small pieces, cover and let it boil slowly for ten minutes, and add a little salt after it is boiled. Excellent.

PANADA.—Two thick slices of stale bread half an inch in thickness; cut off the crust, toast them a nice brown, cut them into squares of two inches in size, lay them in a bowl, sprinkle a little salt over them and pour on a pint of boiling water.

REMEDY FOR CANCER.—Col. Ussery, of the Parish of De Soto, informs the editor of the Caddo *Gazette*, that he fully tested a remedy recommended by a Spanish woman, native of the country. Take an egg and break it, pour out the white, retaining the yolk in the shell; put in salt, mix with the yolk as long as it will receive it; stir them together until the salve is formed; put this on a piece of sticking plaster and apply it to the cancer twice a day.

A citizen of Philadelphia used a weak solution of carbolic acid, as a wash to neutralize the offensive odor arising from a cancer, discovered that the latter was removed by the application. The solution consisted of one-fourth of an ounce of acid, diluted in a quart of water.—Mrs. R.A.SIBLEY.

*Exposition in Paris, in 1867, for "Perfection of Preparation."*

**FEVER AND AGUE.**—Four ounces galangal root in a quart of gin, steeped in a warm place; take often.—MRS. R. A. SIBLEY.

**SMALL POX REMEDY.**—The following remedy a friend tried in Ohio in case of confluent small pox, when the Doctor had little hope of saving the patient, and it saved the woman's life. The remedy is sure in scarlet fever. "I herewith append a recipe which has been used to my own knowledge in a hundred cases. It will prevent or cure the small pox, even though the pittings are filling. When Jenner discovered cow-pox in England, the world of science hurled an avalanche of fame upon his head, and when the most scientific school of medicine in the world (that of Paris,) published this panacea for the small pox, it passed unheeded. It is unfailing as fate, and conquers in every instance. It is harmless when taken by a well person. It will also cure scarlet fever. Take sulphate of zinc, one grain; fox glove, (*digitalis*,) one grain; half a teaspoon of water. When thoroughly mixed, add four ounces water. Take a spoonful every hour, and either disease will disappear in twelve hours. For a child, smaller doses, according to age.

**FOR HYDROPHOBIA.**—Franklin Dyer, a highly respectable farmer of Galena, Kent County, Md., gives the following as a sure cure for the bite of a mad dog. He has tested it with most gratifying results: Elecampane is a plant well known and found in many gardens. Immediately after being bitten, take one and a half ounces of the root of the plant, the green root is preferable. The dried, to be found in drug stores, will answer; bruise it, put it in a pint of fresh milk, boil down to half a pint, strain, and when cold, drink it, fasting at least six hours afterwards. The next morning repeat the dose, fasting; using two ounces of the root. On the third morning, take another dose prepared as the last, and this will be sufficient. After each dose, nothing to be eaten for at least six hours. I had a son who was bitten by a mad dog, eighteen years ago, and four other children in the neighborhood were also bitten. They took the above, and are now alive and well. I have known many who were cured. It is supposed that the root contains a principle, which, being taken up by the blood in its circulation, conteracts or neutralizes the deadly effect of the virus of hydrophobia. I feel so much confidence in this simple remedy, that I am willing you should give my name in connection with this statement.

**FOR FELON.**—Take common rock salt, as used for salting down pork or beef, dry in an oven, then pound it fine and mix with spirits of turpentine in equal parts; put it in a rag and wrap it around the parts affected;

as it gets dry, put on more, and in twenty-four hours you are cured. The felon will be dead. No harm to try it, as I have with success.

CURE FOR NEURALGIA.—A friend who suffered horrible pains from neuralgia, hearing of a noted physician in Germany who invariably cured the disease, went to him, and was permanently cured after a short sojourn. The Doctor gave him the remedy, which was nothing but a poultice and tea made from our common field thistle. The leaves are macerated and used as a poultice on the parts affected, while a small quantity of the same is boiled down to the proportion of a quart to a pint, and a small wine glass of the decoction drank before each meal. Our friend says he has never known it to fail of giving relief, while in almost every case it has effected a cure. God gave herbs for the healing of the nations.

FOR HOARSENESS.—Squeeze the juice of half a lemon in a pint bowl, add loaf sugar, (two tablespoons,) one full teaspoon of glycerine, and one full tablespoon of whiskey; pour over this boiling hot water to nearly fill the bowl, and drink hot just before going to bed.

FOR SORE THROAT.—Cut slices of salt pork or fat bacon; simmer a few moments in hot vinegar, and apply to throat as hot as possible. When this is taken off, as the throat is relieved, put around a bandage of soft flannel. A gargle of equal parts of borax and alum, dissolved in water, is also excellent to be used frequently.

HEALING LOTION.—One ounce glycerine, one ounce rosewater, ten drops carbolic acid. This preparation prevents and cures chapping of the skin, and at the same time bleaches it. It is also excellent for sore lips and gums. I consider it an indispensible adjunct to the toilet table.—Miss A. Yocum, Cairo, Ill.

TO STOP BLEEDING.—A handful of flour, bound on the cut.—Mrs. A. M.

TO PREVENT CONTAGION FROM ERUPTIVE DISEASES.—Keep constantly in plates or saucers, sliced raw onions in the sick room, as possible. As fast as they become discolored, replace by fresh ones. During any epidemic of skin diseases that are eruptive, onions, except those taken fresh from one earth, are unsafe, as they are peculiarly sensitive to disease.

TO RESTORE FROM STROKE OF LIGHTNING.—Shower with cold water for two hours; if the patient does not show signs of life, put salt in the water, and continue to shower an hour longer.

FOR TOOTH-ACHE.—Of powdered alum and fine salt, equal quantities; apply to the tooth and it will give speedy relief.—Mrs. Bartlett.

_When in haste you wish to make delicate light and white bread._

**FOR HEADACHE.**—Pour a few drops of ether on one-half ounce of gum camphor and pulverize; add to this an equal quantity of carbonate ammonia pulverized; add twenty drops peppermint; mix and put in an open mouthed bottle and cork.—MRS. A. M. GIBBS.

**SALVE FOR CHILBLAINS.**—Fry out nicely a little mutton tallow; into this while melted and after it is nicely strained, put an equal quantity of coil oil; stir well together while it is cooling.

**TO REMOVE DISCOLORATION FROM BRUISES.**—Apply a cloth wrung out very hot water, and renew frequently until the pain ceases. Or, apply raw beef steak.

**CURE FOR WASP STING.**—Apply a poultice of saleratus water and flour, and bind on the sting. Apply slices of raw onion for a bee sting.

**CURE FOR SUMMER COMPLAINT.**—Two ounces tincture rhubarb, one of paregoric, one-half of essence of peppermint, one-half of essence of annis, one-half of prepared chalk. Dose for adult, one teaspoon in a little water; take as often as needed.—MRS. L. BRADLEY.

**THE BEST DEODORIZER.**—Use bromo-chloralum in the proportion of one tablespoon to eight of soft water; dip cloths in this solution and hang in the rooms; it will purify sick rooms of any foul smells. The surface of anything may be purified by washing well and then rubbing over with a weakened solution of bromo-chloralum.

A weak solution is excellent to rinse the mouth with often, when from any cause the breath is offensive. It is also an excellent wash for sores and wounds that have an offensive odor.

**TO DESTROY BED BUGS, MOTHS AND OTHER VERMIN.**—Dissolve alum in hot water, making a very strong solution; apply to furniture or crevices in the walls with paint brush. This is sure destruction to these noxious vermin, and invaluable because easily obtained; is perfectly safe to use, and leaves no unpleasant traces behind. When you suspect moths have lodged in the borders of carpets, wet the edges of the carpets with a strong solution; whenever it reaches them, it is certain death.

# TABLE ETIQUETTE.

" **Man** in society is like a flower
**Blown** in its native land; '**tis there alone**
**His** faculties, expanded in full bloom,
**Shine** out—there only reach their proper **use.**"

## THE BREAKFAST.

How to serve our **food, is no less** important **than how to** cook it. The æsthetics of eating have an effect upon our **lives that** is far-reaching and most powerful in its influences. Food served gracefully **and** without confusion, with the accompaniments of fruits, flowers, dainty table napery and beautiful **forms** in the **service, are** grateful **to the senses;** give zest **to** the most delicate appetite; **and make** the plainest meal a season of enjoyment. **The great purpose of rules** of etiquette, is to inculcate good manners, and thus **render us** mutually agreeable. That they have **a** solid basis in taste and good sense, is apparent to every one who will consider **the** subject; and while many ceremonious observances may seem at first sight frivolous to the sensible and practical **person, those** formalities that are practically useful are of importance, and should be generally adopted. We offer **no** apology for presenting in these **pages a** few hints upon **social** customs and formalities, feeling assured that to many they may prove both interesting and **profitable.**

The decoration and arrangement of the table, is a very essential point to be regarded, and can seldom be wholly left to the care of servants. The breakfast table, in accordance with this unceremonious repast, should be simply dressed. The damask table cloth and napkins; the quaint and fanciful service of China; the shining urn and the glistening vessels of glass, all arranged symetrically, have a freshness very enticing to a morning's repast. The centre of the table should be adorned with fruits and flowers, if they can be obtained. "A table," says a high authority upon these matters, "may be well set as expeditiously and with no more expense, than if every article was out of line with its fellows."

The tea urn and cups and saucers should be placed in front of hostess, and so arranged that they may be used without clatter or confusion. Butter, which is in order at the breakfast table, should be served upon the small individual butter-plates. Bread is most elegantly served at breakfast, placed first on the table in the bread-tray in the loaf, and then cut by a servant at the side-board, as desired. Coffee and tea are stylishly served at the close of the meal, though this is a custom not always favorably regarded among ceremonious people at breakfast.

An authority upon table etiquette says that when the drinker leaves his spoon in the tea or coffee-cup, it is an indication that he has had enough; when it is placed in the saucer, the hostess may understand that another cup is wished. The order of serving viands, as at present observed in some fashionable circles, may be found in our arrangement of bills of fare.

## DINNER.
"Dinner best lubricates business."

In laying the cloth for dinner, the table should be first covered with a white cloth, over which is spread a fine white damask table cloth. This is now rarely removed for dessert, because large damask cloths or napkins are placed under dishes liable to soil the cloth, and are easily removed with the last course, while the adornments of the table are not so easily displaced as formerly. Gracefully shaped epergnes, composed of crystal and silver, are very handsome, and **when** arranged with low plates or branches and shallow dishes to hold bon-bons, fruits, flowers and ferns, artistically mingled, the effect **is** always pleasing to the eye.

At elaborate dinners and suppers, the centre ornament is usu**ally** a candelabrum, a plateau, and epergne or a vase of flowers. **The** mats for the various dishes arranged, the ornamental vases are placed between the bottom and the top dishes or wine cool**ers, with the wines** in the original bottles loosely corked. The spoons for helping the various dishes—asparagus tongs, fish knife and fork, **or slice and carving** forks—are placed in front of the respective dishes to which they belong, and knife-rests and a bill of fare opposite to those who are to carve. Small boquets are often placed upon the napkin of each guest, and many of the dishes may be tastefully decorated with leaves and flowers. **At** stylish dinner parties, an ornamental card tastefully designed is often laid upon each plate, with the name of the guest upon it. Lights at or after dinner, should be subdued, and, **if possi**ble, above the guests, so as to be shed upon the tables without interrupting the view. White kid-gloves are worn at large din**ner** parties, but are taken off before the knives and forks are brought into requisition. Beside the napkin should be placed a small **square** piece of bread, three inches in width and thickness; **or rolls may be** used instead. Butter **is never** in **order for din**ner.

The arrangement of silver and cutlery upon the table varies with the style of the entertainment. Care should be taken that each guest is provided with silver spoons and cutlery **for the** different viands served. At dinner two large knives and forks are needed—knives at the right and forks at the left of the plate; also, a soup spoon, and when dessert is served, a silver knife, fork and spoon are placed upon the dessert plate, with a glass finger-bowl and doily at the left. The guest places the knife and spoon at the right side and the fork at the left of the **doily** with the finger-bowl upon it, and when **the re**-

*"Richards' Queen" in making Biscuits, Cakes, Bread or Rolls.*

past is finished, he dips his fingers into the bowl, and then dries them upon the napkin. In some circles, the fashion prevails of placing finger-glasses just preceding dessert; while in others cut-glass bowls, partially filled with rose or orange flower water, iced in summer and lukewarm in winter, are passed down each side of the table, into which the guest dips the corner of the dinner napkin and just touches the lips and tips of the fingers.

When wines are used, each guest should be provided with three glasses of different styles, one for claret wine, one for madeira or sherry, and one for champagne. When the latter is served, it is handed around upon a waiter or salver, commencing at the right hand side of the table, (from the top and bottom simultaneously,) without distinction as regards ladies and gentlemen; or, instead of being handed upon a salver, the bottle being enveloped in a clean dinner napkin as far as the neck, the servants pour the wine into the glass at the right hand of the guest. Liquors are served when the sweets are on the table. It is not customary now, as formerly, to drink healths. The servant passes the wine and you accept or decline, at pleasure. If you do not drink it, quietly cover the top of your glass with your fingers, saying, "Please excuse me."

Raw oysters or clams upon the shell are usually the first course at dinner; then follows the soup of which every one partakes. At dinners there will often be two kinds of soup, one dark colored and the other white, of which you may take your choice. (Never be helped to soup twice.) Then the fish should be served with sauce, sliced lemons and jelly. The second course consists of roasts—turkey or fowls, game, ham garnished, tongue, or fricandeau, with small dishes for corners, curries, ragouts or vegetables.

For formal occasions, however, the Russian mode or the *diner a la Russe*, has become fashionable. The dishes, when this style is adopted, are not served until cut up, when they are handed in succession to each guest by the waiters. The plates of soup are generally put on the table before the guests are called in, and a bill of fare, as well as the name of each person, to indicate the seat he is to take, printed or written upon a card, is placed upon the napkin.

Dishes served should always be handed to the left of the guest. This custom is the most convenient, and withal, the correct thing.

Salads should be served after the meats and just before the dessert.

## THE DESSERT.

When the party is large and ices are served, the ice-plates are placed around the table, the ices at both ends, and dishes of wafer biscuits at the sides. Some persons have the ice served in glass dishes, which, together with the wafer biscuits, are handed around before the usual dessert. When there is preserved ginger, it follows the ices, as it serves to stimulate the palate, so that the delicious coolness of the wines may be better appreciated. The side and corner dishes usually put on for dessert, consist of compotes in glass dishes; frosted prints served on lace paper in small glass dishes; and biscuits plain and fancy with fresh fruit. Coffee should always be the last thing served, and handed around in cups; should be very strong and taken without cream or sugar. When the dinner is over, the hostess gives the signal by rising from the table and all return to the drawing-room. Here tea and coffee are provided. Unless additional company has been invited for the evening, the guests soon after take their leave. The present style of taking coffee at the close of both breakfast and dinner, is a healthful custom and should be generally adopted on hygienic principles.

## TEAS.

Those Attic nights and those refections of the Gods.

—CURRAN.

After-dinner teas stylishly consist of simple refections of cups of fragrant tea and coffee, served with cream and sugar, accompanied with thinly cut slices of rolled bread or sandwiches, wafer

*Excellent for Food."—London Exposition,* 1862.

biscuits, and sometimes mixed cakes. Hot suppers are ,now seldom served. Late dinners are in order with simple refections later. Russian tea is made in the ordinary way, with the addition of sliced lemon, and is very much in vogue.

## LUNCHES.

It seems he had taken
A light breakfast—bacon,
An egg with a little broiled haddock, at most
A round and a half of some hot buttered toast,
With a slice of cold sirloin from yesterday's roast;.
And then—let me see—!
He had two—perhaps three—
Cups, (with sugar and cream,) of strong gun-powder tea,
With a spoonful in each of some choice *eau de vie.*

—Hood:

Of late years, the Luncheon or *dejeuner a la fourchette* has taken its place in society as a ceremonious repast. At these receptions, tea and *bouillon* in cups, (which is simply beef froth,) chocolate and cakes are served. These repasts, however simple or elaborate, are set before the guests at once. When only one or two partake of the meal, it is served on a tray ; but when there are a number of guests, the table is laid at once.

Refreshments at matinees, wedding receptions and dancing parties, are stylishly served, as at New Year's receptions, where servants in attendance help the guests to refreshments, which are laid in a side room or the dining room.

# BILLS OF FARE.

In the accompanying Bills of Fare, the arrangement of the various courses will be suggested by the form in which they are given:

# MENU.

### BREAKFAST—No. 1.

Fine Hominy.     Buttered Toast.
Beefsteak.
**French Rolls.**     **Potatoes a la Creme.**
Buckwheat Cakes.
Tea.     **Coffee.**     Chocolate.

### BREAKFAST—No. 2.

Boiled Spring Chickens.
**Parker House** Rolls.     Saratoga Potatoes.
Scrambled Eggs.     Fried Oysters.
Rye and Indian Loaf.
**Coffee.**     Tea.     Chocolate.

### BREAKFAST—No. 3.

White Fish.     Potatoes.
Muffins.
Fried **Ham.**     **Egg Omelette.**
Coffee.     **Tea.**     **Chocolate.**

*"Richards' Queen Baking Powder;" it makes Biscuit very light.*

# LUNCHES.

### LUNCH PARTY—No. 1.

Beef Tea, served in small porcelain cups.
Cold Chicken and Oyster and other forms of Croquettes.
Chicken Salad.    Minced Ham Sandwiches.
Escalloped Oysters.
Tutti Frutti.    Chocolate Cream.
Cake Basket of Mixed Cake.
Mulled Chocolate.
Mixed Pickles.    Biscuits, etc.
Ice Creams and Charlottes can either be added or substituted.    For twenty
guests, allow one gallon.

### LUNCH PARTY—No. 2.

Broiled Partridge.
Oyster Pie.    Cold Ham.
Sweet Pickles.    Sandwiches.
Pound and Fruit Cake.    Pyramids of Wine Jelly.
Blanc Mange.    Snow Jelly.
Pineapple Flummery.
Kisses.    Macaroons.    Ice Creams.

# DINNERS.

### DINNER No. 1.

FIRST COURSE.
Oyster Soup, with Celery.
SECOND COURSE.
Roast Turkey.
Croquettes of Rice.    Sweet and Irish Potatoes.
THIRD COURSE.
Quail on Toast.
Vegetables.    Pickles.    Escalloped Tomatoes.
Macaroni.    Jelly.
DESSERT.
Almond Pudding.
Mince Pie.    Lemon Pie.
Cheese.    Fruits.    Nuts.
Coffee.

*The whitest, strongest and most economical Starch—Duryeas'.*

## DINNER—No. 2.

**FIRST** COURSE.

Raw Oysters.
White and **Brown Soup.**

SECOND **COURSE.**

Boiled White Fish, with **Sauce** and Sliced Lemon.

THIRD **COURSE.**

Roast **Beef.**

**FOURTH COURSE.**

Roast Turkey. **Ducks.**
Vegetables in season. Croquettes of Rice or **Hominy.**
Cranberry Sauce. Currant Jelly.

DESSERT.

Cream Custard. **Lemon** Pie.
Fruits. **Nuts.**
**Coffee.**

# TEA COMPANY.

Tea. Coffee. Chocolate.
Biscuits.
Oyster Sandwiches. Chicken Salad.
Cold Tongue.
**Cake** and Preserves.
Ice Cream and Cake later in **the** evening.

## TEA COMPANY No. 2.

**Tea,** Coffee or Chocolate.
Escalloped or Fried Oysters. Muffins.
Sliced Turkey and Ham.
Cold Biscuits.
Sardines and Sliced Lemons.
**Thin slices of Bread, rolled.** Sliced Pressed Meats.
**Cake in variety.**

# SUPPERS.

## SUPPER—No. 1.

Cold Roast Turkey.    Chicken Salad.
Quail on Toast.
Ham Croquettes.    Fricasseed Oysters.
Charlotte Russe.  Vanilla Cream.
Chocolate Cake.    Cocoanut Cake.
Mixed Cakes.
Fruit.
Coffee and Chocolate.

## SUPPER—No. 2.

Cold Roast Partridges or Ducks.
Oyster Patties.    Cold Boiled Ham.    Dressed Celery.
Oyster or Minced Ham Sandwiches.
Raw Oysters.    Chicken Croquettes or Fricasseed Oysters.
Wine Jelly.    Ice Cream.  Biscuit Glace.    Cakes.
Fruits.    Chocolate.    Coffee.
Pickles and Biscuits.

## Allowance of Supplies for an Entertainment.

In inviting guests, it is safe to calculate that out of one hundred and fifty, but two-thirds of the number will be present. If five hundred are invited, not more than three hundred can be counted upon as accepting.

Allow one quart of oysters to every three persons present. Five chickens, (or, what is better, a ten-pound turkey, boiled and minced,) and fifteen heads of celery, are enough for chicken salad for fifty guests; one gallon of ice cream to every twenty guests; one hundred and thirty sandwiches for one hundred guests; and six to ten quarts of wine jelly for each hundred; for a company of twenty, allow three chickens for salad; one hundred pickled oysters; two molds of Charlotte Russe; one gallon of cream, and four dozen biscuits.

## Cold Lunches for Washing Days or Other Days of Extra Labor.

LUNCH No. 1.—Cold corn beef, nicely sliced; baked potatoes; bread, butter and pickles. Dessert—mince pie and cheese.

LUNCH No. 2.—Chicken pie; baked potatoes; rolled bread or biscuit. Dessert—cake and custard.

LUNCH No. 3.—First course; Raw oysters, with lemon and crackers. Second course: Cold veal with jelly and Saratoga potatoes; bread and butter. Dessert—cherry pie with cheese.

LUNCH No. 4.—Casserole of fish, with mushroom catsup; bread with butter. Dessert—pie with cheese.

## Economical Dinners.

SUNDAY.—Roast beef; potatoes and greens. Dessert—pudding or pie; cheese.

MONDAY.—Hashed beef; potatoes and bread pudding.

TUESDAY.—Broiled beef; vegetables; apple pudding.

WEDNESDAY.—Boiled pork; beans; potatoes; greens, and pie or rice pudding.

THURSDAY.—Roast or broiled fowl; cabbage; potatoes; lemon pie; cheese.

FRIDAY.—Fish; potatoe croquettes; escalloped tomatoes; pudding.

SATURDAY.—A la mode beef; potatoes; vegetables; suet pudding and mince pie; cheese.

For such valuable information, Bills of Fare, &c., as have been derived from the following authorities, we would make due acknowledgement, viz: To *The Practical Housekeeper*, by Mrs. ELLET; *The Housekeeper's Encyclopedia*, by Mrs. HASKELL; *The Home Messenger Recipe Book;* and *Harper's Book of Decorum.*

*Finish, and is the easiest to use.*

# INDEX.

## POULTRY AND GAME.

## MEATS.

## SAUCES AND SALADS.

## CUSTARDS, CREAMS, &c.     PAGE.

## BREAD AND YEAST.

## CAKES.

## CONFECTIONERY.

## FRUITS.

## PICKLES.

*Exposition in Paris, in 1867, for "Perfection of Preparation."*

## DRINKS.

### MISCELLANEOUS.

### THE SICK ROOM.

### TABLE ETIQUETTE.

www.ingramcontent.com/pod-product-compliance
Lightning Source LLC
Chambersburg PA
CBHW031358270326
41929CB00010BA/1235